P9-CDT-579

P9-CDT-579

THE TB12 METHOD

HOW TO ACHIEVE
A LIFETIME OF SUSTAINED
PEAK PERFORMANCE

TOM BRADY

Simon & Schuster

New York   London   Toronto   Sydney   New Delhi

Simon & Schuster
1230 Avenue of the Americas
New York, NY 10020

First Simon & Schuster hardcover edition September 2017

SIMON & SCHUSTER and colophon are registered trademarks of Simon & Schuster, Inc.

For information about special discounts for bulk purchases, please contact Simon & Schuster Special Sales at 1-866-506-1949 or business@simonandschuster.com.

The Simon & Schuster Speakers Bureau can bring authors to your live event. For more information or to book an event, contact the Simon & Schuster Speakers Bureau at 1-866-248-3049 or visit our website at www.simonspeakers.com.

Book design: Shubhani Sarkar, sarkardesignstudio.com
Creative direction: Hilario Bango, Martian Arts

Manufactured in the United States of America

10 9 8 7 6 5 4 3 2 1

Library of Congress Cataloging-in-Publication Data is available.

ISBN 978-1-5011-8073-6
ISBN 978-1-5011-8075-0 (ebook)

All photographs are by Kevin O'Brien, with the following exceptions: exercise photos are by Josh Campbell; recipe photos are by Jayna Cowal; photo on page 227 is by Gilad Haas; photos on pages 11, 12, 17, 217, 219, 221, 228, 229, and 262 are courtesy of Getty Images; photos on pages 222 and 239 are courtesy of Shutterstock; photos on pages viii and 8 are courtesy of Under Armour; and photos on pages 3, 4, 5, and 296 are courtesy of the author.

I dedicate this book to all the people who have loved me, supported me, and helped me achieve my dreams—my incredible family; my loving wife and beautiful children; my lifelong friends; my Serra High School, University of Michigan, and New England Patriots teammates; my encouraging coaches; and the loyal mentors who have played a part in who I am and what I believe in. Thank you. I love you all.

CONTENTS

INTRODUCTION   ix

CHAPTER 1
WHAT I USED TO BELIEVE

1

CHAPTER 2
WHAT I NOW BELIEVE

21

CHAPTER 3
12 PRINCIPLES OF TB12

31

CHAPTER 4
PLIABILITY: A DEEPER DIVE

43

CHAPTER 5
TRAINING AND METHODS

75

CHAPTER 6

WORKOUTS

119

CHAPTER 7

HYDRATION

205

CHAPTER 8

NUTRITION

215

CHAPTER 9

BRAIN TRAINING,
REST, AND RECOVERY

269

CHAPTER 10

CONCLUSION

283

TESTIMONIALS   287

FAQ   293

ACKNOWLEDGMENTS   297

INDEX   299

INTRODUCTION

JUST BEFORE THE START OF THE PATRIOTS' 2016 championship season, I went to a field near my house to throw the football with one of my dearest friends, my body coach and the cofounder of the TB12 Method Alex Guerrero, and a former teammate. It was a brisk, late summer afternoon—perfect New England football weather. As I was running through my typical football training regimen, I knew one thing for sure: I'd never thrown the ball as well as I did that day—not when the Patriots won the Super Bowl in 2001, or in 2004, 2005, or 2014—not ever, in fact, in my life. It was one of those days. I was "in the zone." I was throwing the ball better than I ever had, and I remember being really excited about the opportunity to play and to show all the things I'd been working on in the off-season.

I also remember thinking, *My ability to sustain my peak performance over the past ten years is almost unbelievable to me.* But I suppose that's what peak performance really means—continuing to get better year after year—or at least that's what it means to me. In my belief, it would not be possible without an ongoing commitment to the very different holistic wellness and training program that Alex and I began developing over a decade ago. We call it the TB12 Method. At its core, the TB12 Method focuses on developing and maintaining something that many people have probably never heard of: *muscle pliability*. Over the past few years we have designed the principles of the TB12 Method—principles that have created far more sustained peak performance than anything I've ever read, studied, experienced, or trained against, and that have also given me the confidence and the capability

to reach for higher and higher levels of achievement as each year passes. Every year we seek to improve—and I would love for you to do the same.

Nearly eighteen seasons of playing professional football have shown me that sustained peak performance isn't about luck. It's about hard work, dedication, discipline, and the support of my great team. You can't do it alone. I am beyond blessed. I turned forty years old this past August, and not only do I feel as healthy as I ever have but, more to the point, I'm proud to still be playing at the highest level and standard for my game. My ability to sustain my peak performance over the last ten years came from rethinking how to train, and, specifically, *how to train with pliability.* I now realize that this is something that can help not only elite athletes but anyone and everyone who's willing to commit to living a life of wellness and vitality—casual athletes, weekend warriors, yoga practitioners, marathon runners, *anyone.* In this book, I'll be sharing the principles that have allowed me to sustain peak performance and showing you how to apply them to your own daily life. I also believe the TB12 Method can inspire a movement that radically reforms the way we train and helps us live a more natural, holistic, healthy lifestyle while lowering our risk of injury, increasing our vitality, and taking our performance to the next level. As such, I'm writing this book in the hope that my experiences and discoveries can resonate with everyone and allow them to achieve beyond what they can even envision for themselves. As far as pliability is concerned, an ounce of prevention really *is* worth a pound of cure.

What *is* pliability? I'll go into it in more detail later in this book, but for now, and briefly, Alex and I define pliability training as targeted, deep-force muscle work that lengthens and softens muscles at the same time those muscles are rhythmically contracted and relaxed. This happens in sessions that take place both before and after any sport or activity—in my case, football. Regular pliability training, coupled with the right holistic routine to maintain that pliability, conditions our brains and bodies—and therefore our muscles—to maintain this same lengthened, softened, primed state as they carry out whatever activity we're asking them to do, from carrying a baby to lifting luggage to climbing stairs to getting out of a chair to playing pro sports.

But pliability is also bigger than that. To me, and within the TB12 Method, pliability is the missing leg of the traditional strength and conditioning model of aerobic activity and lifting weights. Of course, it goes without saying that we all need strength and conditioning—enough strength to do the job we need to do, including the acts of daily living, and enough endurance to do it over a desired time frame. But by incorporating pliability training into your workout regimen, you'll be able to sustain your own peak performance in ways that minimize the risk of injury. If an injury happens, pliability training will put you on a faster road to recovery. We'll discuss specific methods of practicing pliability in a later chapter.

So why this book, and why now? Well, most people don't realize it, but the typical training and lifestyle

For many years, friends, family members, and teammates asked the same question: Why was I spending so much time practicing alternative methods to conventional training that focused on pliability?

regimens come up short. For so many athletes, it looks like this: *Work out. Compete hard. Get injured. Visit the doctor. Do physical therapy. Possible surgery. Back to rehab. Compete hard again. Get injured again. Back to the doctor. More rehab. Repeat. Repeat. Repeat.* That's the vicious cycle of sports training, which takes place far too often, is talked about all too little, and has been around since before I was in high school. But it doesn't have to be that way. We all need to become *active* participants in our own health. With this book, I want to establish a new model of training for sustaining peak performance and optimal living over the long term. The TB12 Method is both a regimen and a way of life that has allowed me to play football at a high level over the course of my career, and also to live a vital, energetic life off the field.

Over the years, like many athletes, I've read a lot of books about sports, health, wellness, and longevity. Most offer conflicting information, and to my mind, a lot of them come up short. Put simply, they're confusing—even *I* get confused. That's why I want to write a new athlete's bible for anyone committed to a lifetime of peak performance, whether you're a professional, an amateur, or a man or a woman of any age who wants to stay healthy and vital. My hope is that *The TB12 Method* will revolutionize the age-old sports and conditioning model that statistics tell us over and over again is incomplete. With this book, I'm on a mission to inspire coaches, parents, trainers, athletes, and anyone who wants to lead a healthier lifestyle to consider how pliability training, and a commitment to a holistic and disciplined lifestyle, will lead to a more enjoyable life that allows them to achieve any goal they set for themselves.

Nothing would give me more joy than to pass on what I've learned during my life and career—whether it's the importance of pliability training, the exercises you should do to reduce the chance of injury, the best ways to work out, what proper hydration means, what foods you should eat, what supplements you should take, how to recover and rest, or what kinds of brain exercises can ramp up your performance. There's a famous quote: "Youth is wasted on the young." It's true, too. We grow up believing that our physical prime is in our mid-to-late twenties, and our mental peak is somewhere between the ages of thirty and fifty. One of the goals of the TB12 Method is to *combine* our physical peak with our mental peak, while extending both of them for as long as possible. Ultimately, our stated purpose at TB12 is *sustained peak performance*, which is something I want as many people as possible to experience in their own lives.

We're all born with natural pliability, and we have more pliability than strength, at least when we're young—meaning that our muscles are naturally longer and softer than they are dense. Our natural pliability allows us to play hard and recover quickly. (Usually, a good night's rest is all it takes when we're

> Today, I look back and think, Thank God I did it differently. Thank God I had the courage to step outside the conventional wisdom. Thank God I followed what my heart, mind, and body were always telling me—that the things we were working on would allow me to do things that I always wanted to accomplish in my sport.

young.) Many of us begin focusing on strength and conditioning when we're in our teens in order to play sports. We stay on this path for the rest of our lives, not understanding that as time goes on and we continue to work on strength and conditioning alone, our bodies become tighter, stiffer, and unbalanced—both through strength training and the acts of daily living—which leads to compensation, which leads to overload, therefore making us more and more susceptible to injury.

What actually happens when an injury occurs? An injury takes place when one of our muscles, ligaments, tendons, or bones is unable to absorb or disperse the amount of force placed on it. Put simply, when any of these body parts comes up against more force, or stress, than it can handle, an injury happens. Are injuries avoidable? Certainly not all of them, but many of them are. I recently read a comment given by a professional soccer coach after a game in which one of his players got injured. "Injuries happen," he said. "They're part of a player's life, and there's nothing anyone can do about it." I don't completely agree. What if, instead of accepting injury as inevitable and a part of what it means to play sports, trainers and coaches began incorporating pliability training into the traditional strength and conditioning system, educating bodies to absorb and disperse the forces placed upon them? With pliability acting as a form of the body's defense

Exercise, working out, and engaging in physical activity are all parts of a joyful life. The principles of the TB12 Method are ones I've always wanted to share with other athletes who, like myself, may not be "natural" athletes but who have the same drive, desire, and work ethic that I do.

system against external forces, I believe many of those "inevitable" injuries could be avoided.

The principles of the TB12 Method are ones I've always wanted to share with other athletes who, like me, may not be "natural" athletes—many people forget I was a sixth-round draft pick!—but who have the same drive, desire, and work ethic that I do, and who are tired of putting all their energy into methods that are likely to disable them in the end. I've seen this firsthand over the past twenty-five years, watching one athlete after another get hurt and rehab, rehab, rehab. Exercise, working out, and engaging in physical activity are all parts of a joyful life, and I'm positive that if athletes follow the TB12 Method, they will perform significantly better over a much longer period of time. The bottom line is that the conditioning and endurance training that clients practice at TB12 help create the energy and vitality they need to perform the acts of daily living in an optimal way.

I also want to emphasize that the TB12 Method isn't just for athletes who work in elite environments like the NFL, the NHL, the NBA, and MLB, and who stress and break down their bodies the most. To my mind, *everyone* can benefit from greater pliability and a balanced body that allows more oxygen-rich blood circulation and increased vitality. The amount of pliability that will benefit you the most depends on the intensity of your activity, and the type of sport or activity you engage in. Swimming, for example,

is different from playing baseball, which is different from cycling. Obviously, playing football as I do, my body needs to absorb a lot of force every week. As I go into my eighteenth season, I now do pliability training four days a week, and among strength, conditioning, and pliability, I spend roughly one-half of my time on pliability training. Many athletes spend no time on pliability—in fact, many athletes don't know what pliability is!—and others might spend only a few minutes. A person who works behind a desk and isn't stressing his or her body every day needs a different level of pliability—say, once a week—whereas a high school athlete who works out for two hours a few times a week needs higher levels. A simple way to think about it is that strength training, playing sports, and working out create denser muscles. And the denser the muscles are, the more pliability they need.

It can be hard for younger athletes to wrap their heads around the concept of pliability, because they have natural pliability. They recover quickly, and don't want to waste their time preventing an injury that hasn't happened yet. Many of them aren't thinking ahead to pain, soreness, or worse in the future. As I said, younger bodies are naturally pliable, which is why in high school and college, young athletes *need* more strength than they do pliability. As athletes hit their twenties, their strength increases as their pliability decreases. As their pliability goes down, their injuries go up. And as their injuries go up, their careers get cut short. *Ability* allows athletes to achieve. *Durability* allows them to continue achieving. And *pliability* makes both possible. This is why coaches and parents need to take the lead by incorporating pliability training as early as possible in the lives of younger athletes. If I'd begun pliability training when I was fifteen or sixteen years old, I wouldn't have had to endure so many years of unnecessary pain, as so many athletes do.

If you want proof that pliability, and the TB12 Method, works, I'm it. I was the kid, as you'll learn in the pages ahead, who was the sixth-round NFL draft pick, 199th overall, the athlete who was told he never had the right body for football. No one believed I'd play even one year in college, or one year in the pros. But I just finished my seventeenth season, the Patriots won the Super Bowl, and not a lot of players have ever started at quarterback in the NFL at the age of forty. If you want a great case study for how the TB12 Method can transform someone—including the thousands of men and women whose lives have been changed at the TB12 Sports Therapy Center in Foxborough, Massachusetts—it's standing right in front of you. I'm excited for you to start your own journey.

CHAPTER 1

WHAT I USED TO BELIEVE

I'VE LOVED SPORTS, AND BEEN EXTREMELY COMPETITIVE AT THEM, MY WHOLE LIFE. I MAY HAVE PICKED UP MY FIRST FOOTBALL AT AGE FIVE, BUT THE PATH THAT GOT ME TO WHERE I AM TODAY WAS NEVER REALLY STRAIGHT OR EASY.

I was born and grew up in San Mateo, California, in the Bay Area, the youngest of four children and the only boy. Everyone always called me Tommy. We were a hardworking, sports-centric family with parents who put their kids before anything else. When I was young, my dad was self-employed and on the road a lot, building up his insurance business. He was out the door by seven in the morning and gone till six at night. My mom was in charge of the house, washing our clothes, cooking our meals, always keeping the domestic side of the family going. My dad was tired when he got home from work, but he never let that get in the way of our time together. He'd still be in his dress shirt when he drove me to the baseball field or the driving range, where the two of us would hit, or field ground balls, or practice throwing as the day grew dark. I loved those times with my dad, and on the drives back home, I remember that good feeling of *I'm hitting the baseball better* or *I think I may be fielding better.* (I still feel that way today, for example with my throwing mechanics; I'm still always improving and learning.) My parents were just as involved in my sisters' lives and sports. My dad would coach their teams sometimes, with my mom serving as the team mom, getting pizza and sodas for all the players.

My parents also had four season tickets to the San Francisco 49ers games at Candlestick Park, ten rows from the top of the stadium on the southwest side—basically in the south end zone. On Sundays we all went to church in the morning, then made the forty-five-minute drive to Candlestick and the 49ers game, and when it was over, back at home my mom would start getting dinner ready while the rest of us gathered around to watch the game highlights on TV. Those four season tickets usually went to my dad and mom, one of my sisters, and me, since going to a game was always the high point of my weekend. I can't say I have that vivid a memory of it, but on January 10, 1982, when I was four years old, I was at Candlestick Park during one of the greatest games in football history. On the final drive of the NFC Championship game, the 49ers were down by six points with fifty-one seconds left to play when Joe Montana, the 49ers quarterback, got around a three-man rush and threw the pass that became The Catch—a perfect ball that his receiver Dwight Clark leaped up to grab just inside the end zone. Everyone in the stadium jumped up. People were crying, including me—though, to be honest, I'd been crying during the whole first half, too, since I wanted a foam finger with 49ERS ARE #1 printed on it. (I think my dad finally bought me one at halftime just to shut me up!)

Clark's touchdown tied the score, and when the kicker, Ray Wersching, made the extra point, the game ended with the 49ers winning 28–27. The Catch put an end to the Dallas Cowboys' 1970s domination of the NFL and started a new era for the 49ers, who went on to win the Super Bowl that year against the Cincinnati Bengals. To be four years old and watching that game (with a foam finger) was, I have to say, pretty incredible.

It's no surprise that, for a kid growing up in the Bay Area and loving football and sports in general as much as I did, Joe Montana was one of my

I was probably three or four years old, sporting a typical haircut my mom used to give me. I was always a happy boy, growing up in the Bay Area with three older sisters and great parents. Life was good. It still is.

Little League baseball was always a fun thing for me. I was eight years old, and I would wear my Royals uniform all day. If we had a game at three in the afternoon, I would put on that uniform at 7:00 a.m. It was the beginning of my playing team sports—the Royals were the first team I think I ever played on.

earliest idols. That wasn't so unusual; everyone loved Joe Montana. He was Joe Cool, after all. He had a knack for coming through in the clutch, the same way Michael Jordan or Wayne Gretzky always managed to make the winning play at the right time. By the age of ten, I remember playing outside on the street with my friend David Aguirre, drawing up simple football plays on a sheet of paper. *Okay, you run to the fire hydrant. Now you break out. Then you go deep.* We even made up our own plays, which we memorized. My favorite was called the Secret Weapon—*You run up, you break out . . . and then you run back to the post!* By the time I entered my freshman year at Junipero Serra High School in San Mateo, my natural love for football had kicked in, and the summer after that I started attending football camp at the College of San Mateo, where I was a staple for the next four years. My size—by my senior year in high school I was 6'4",

210 pounds—probably played a part in my ability to play as many different sports as I did, not just football but also basketball and baseball.

Despite my size, though, the thing I remember most about those days is how so many of the teammates I played alongside were just plain *better* than I was—faster, stronger, with superior natural physical abilities. I always felt I was being left behind. However, whatever I lacked in skills I tried to make up for with a work ethic I'm pretty sure I picked up from my family and environment. Early on, my family instilled in me a drive to always learn to do better, and discipline came pretty naturally to me, too. When I was in fifth grade, my oldest sister, Maureen, who was already a very good athlete, began getting seriously involved in high school sports. My dad would get up early to train alongside her at the local athletic club, and I tagged along with them every morning at 6:00 a.m. The club trainer was a guy named Glenn. One of the great things about Glenn was that he didn't just hold Maureen accountable—he held *me* accountable, too. Thirty years later, I still remember Glenn saying, "I want you to do one hundred jumping jacks, twenty-five push-ups, and twenty-five sit-ups every morning. On the days you don't come to the gym, I want you to do them at home. And when you're all done with your workout, leave me a message on my answering machine." For every message I left him, Glenn promised to pay me a dollar. For every day I didn't leave Glenn a message, I would owe him *five* dollars. For whatever it's worth, I ended up owing Glenn money. Discipline needs to be reinforced daily as well.

This same work ethic and discipline instilled in me by Glenn, and to a bigger extent by my family, inspired me from the start to seek out every last bit of extra help I could get from coaches, trainers, and

(Top) Looking over the line of scrimmage before the snap of the ball during my senior season at Serra High School. We were playing Sacred Heart Cathedral, and we lost the game. I was crushed. It was an especially tough defeat for my family. My uncle was the principal at Sacred Heart, and my dad had made a bet with him that whichever side won would host Thanksgiving dinner that year. When I walked in that night, my uncle had a bunch of pictures from the game covering the walls!

(Bottom) Surrounded by my teammates, standing in the pocket during a typical Serra High School home game during my junior season. We won the game, I remember!

Me, flanked by two great friends and Michigan teammates, Pat Kratus (L), the Wolverines' defensive lineman, and Jeff Potts (R), an offensive tackle. It was the end of my second year at Michigan, and I was still growing and developing as a player. We always had a blue-versus-white scrimmage to end the spring season, and the games got pretty muddy!

Michigan's four quarterbacks in December 1997—a great bunch. That's Brian Griese on the top left, Scott Dreisbach on the top right, and Jason Kapsner to my left. This was during my third year at Michigan, just before our team played in the Rose Bowl.

basically anyone who pushed me to push *myself* to the next level. Football camp, for example, was where I met the great Tom Martinez, coach of the football program at the College of San Mateo, as well as the college's women's softball and basketball teams. From that point on, even after joining the New England

Patriots, I always tracked Tom down for advice whenever something didn't feel right, or if I had any questions about throwing mechanics. I can't say how many pro quarterbacks my age, who've played as long as I have, would do this, but during every NFL off-season, up until his death in 2012, I called on Tom for his counsel. He's a mentor I think about often. I would be remiss if I didn't mention another throwing mentor, Tom House, who has also taught me a tremendous amount over the past five years. I sought out Tom to help me continue to understand throwing technique—but he has taught me so much more, and I am very grateful. Like I said, in order to achieve goals, it takes a great support system. I'm so blessed to have just that.

Throwing was one thing, but early in my career, I knew I needed to improve my strength, too. That's why, when I was playing college football at the University of Michigan, I did extra weight lifting with the head strength coach there, Mike Gittleson, and when the New England Patriots drafted me, I found another strength coach in Mike Woicik. From the beginning of my athletic career, I also worked extremely hard at improving my footwork and my conditioning. Whatever I was told to do—jump rope, practice my quarterback techniques, etc.—I always did *more*. No matter what sport I was playing, I wanted to get *better* at it. I still do. John Wooden, the famous UCLA basketball coach, once defined success as "the peace of mind which is a direct result of self-satisfaction in knowing you did your best to become the best of which you are capable." I believe any one of us can always do more, and better, if we work to develop the right mind-set. Competition is tough—and the further you go in athletics, the tougher both mentally and physically you need to become.

> As an athlete I was a late bloomer. I was a solid all-around athlete, but not an extraordinary one. Few watching me play high school football or baseball or basketball would ever have predicted I would someday end up in the pros.

Still, the fact is, it took me a while to find my stride in sports at both an amateur and an elite level. Once I did, I wanted to make sure I did everything possible to perform at a peak level for as long as possible.

Playing the way I am today, after seventeen seasons in the NFL, requires focus, discipline, and an openness to doing things differently, and that's been true ever since the Patriots won our first Super Bowl in February 2002. If you're going to achieve and sustain peak performance, you need that same focus, discipline, and openness.

But let me back up first to talk about how things began to take shape in my athletic career.

As an athlete, I was a late bloomer. I also wasn't someone who put a lot of effort into school, though I was a B, B-plus student who did well in math, statistics, and finance. The thing is, I never really applied myself to academics, since reading books would have taken time away from my much greater passion and time commitment for sports. As far as those sports went, I was a solid all-around athlete, but not an extraordinary one. Few watching me play high school football or baseball or basketball would ever have predicted I would someday end up playing in the pros. My first year at Serra High School, I played freshman football, and we ended the season 0-8. The reality is that I never actually played—although I was the backup quarterback, I actually played more as a linebacker and tight end (which didn't turn out very well, either). During my sophomore year, the freshman quarterback, Kevin

Krystofiak, quit, so I tried out for JV football, which was basically a team made up of sophomores. We improved a little, but our record was still only 5-4. Not great, but I had so much fun, and I loved my coaches.

In my junior year, I made the varsity football team; we finished 6-4, and in my senior year, our record was 5-5. When I joined the varsity team—by that point I wasn't playing basketball anymore—I was up doing 6:00 a.m. workouts most of the year, doing runs and rope drills and running over bags and up hills. But no matter how much work I put in, most of the time I still came in last place. The effort was always there, but better athletes were still running by me, jumping higher than I did, and testing better than I tested.

Still, if I hadn't found my full identity and potential at football yet, I shined at baseball, which I played throughout high school as a catcher and left-handed hitter. In addition to playing football, I was on the varsity baseball team my junior and senior years, and the Montreal Expos picked me in the eighteenth round of the 1995 MLB draft. But by then I didn't want to play baseball anymore. Ironically, the punishment it inflicted on my body, and my knees especially, was probably the biggest reason I ended up losing my love for the game. It was the pain I coped with day after day that led me to focus exclusively on football—though by that point, my love of the game had overtaken my love of baseball anyway.

In my senior year, my dad decided to put together some game-reel highlights to see if we could garner any football interest from colleges. Even though we weren't a very good high school team, and I was extremely low on the scouting radar, I'd gone to a football combine at St. Mary's College, where, for the first time ever, a few of the scouts watching just might have thought, *Hey—maybe this guy can eventually be decent.* My dad had videotaped a lot of my games,

and the school had some footage as well, and in the fall of my senior year, when football season ended, we brought the best of what we had to a local editor in San Mateo, who spliced together some reels. We ended up making fifty or so VHS tapes (remember those?) of my playing highlights. I remember my dad and me flipping through a college book of Division I and II schools and asking, *Should we send a tape to this place? What about that place?* We sent packages to the dozens of colleges I was interested in, and that I thought I had a shot at getting into, and we got a few responses back. Army wrote something like, *Thanks for sending us your tape, but it doesn't look like your skill set fits our offense.* (Well, they did run the triple option at the time. Funny, and true.) I would have loved to attend the University of Southern California, which recruited me, but the University of Michigan was interested enough to send a recruiter, Bill Harris, out West, and in April of that year Michigan offered me a scholarship, and USC didn't.

Michigan was and still is, in my opinion, the best Division I school in the country, combining athletics and academics, and the three coaches who recruited me—Bill Harris, an assistant coach; Gary Moeller, the head coach; and Kit Cartwright, the quarterback coach—were all on board when I chose Michigan in the spring of 1995. They knew me, and they also knew my parents. But by the time I arrived in Ann Arbor, Coach Moeller had been let go, and Bill Harris had left Michigan to become defensive coordinator at Stanford—which meant that two of the three guys responsible for recruiting me, and who knew me and my family pretty well, were gone. It's a dynamic that I'm sure happens in a lot of professions. The people who bring you in generally act as your mentors and champions and want you to do well, but when I first came to Michigan, there weren't a lot of people invested in my success. No one was actively rooting against me—they just didn't know me, and there were other players to think about. It was nobody's fault; it was just the way it was. Looking back, it was a great, positive lesson at an early point in my career that made me more determined than ever, and I wouldn't change anything about it.

Michigan recruited me as the fourth or fifth quarterback on the depth chart, which is a diagram showing where all the starting and backup players rank on the team in any given year. I was competing with another true freshman, DiAllo Johnson, who showed up at Michigan the same time I did. The starting QB for the Wolverines was Scott Dreisbach, who was a year older than I was. The second quarterback was Brian Griese, who was two years my senior and who later went on to play very well in the NFL, and in third place was Jason Carr, the son of the new

Michigan football coach, Lloyd Carr. Four games into the season, the Wolverines were 4-0, when during one of our practices Scott Dreisbach dropped back to throw a pass, released the ball, and unluckily caught his thumb on another player's helmet. It turned out that he needed thumb surgery and was out for the rest of the year. Everyone moved up one slot. Brian Griese started, Jason Carr was his backup, and I moved into the third position.

Brian Griese had a good season in 1995, but we didn't finish the year very well. We beat Ohio State 31–23, I remember, but lost our bowl game 22–20 to Texas A&M. Then, when the 1996 season got under way, we lost Kit Cartwright, who became the offensive coordinator at Indiana. Everyone assumed Dreisbach would come back and start as our QB—Michigan hadn't lost a game before Scott injured his thumb the season before, after all, and Jason Carr was gone, even though his dad, Lloyd, was still the head coach—but I still began competing to become the starting quarterback. It wasn't going to happen. Everyone loved Scott, and I started to realize that he would play through his senior year, which meant I'd be sitting on the bench for the next three seasons. During a meeting with Coach Carr, I told him I wasn't seeing many opportunities and that where I was and where I wanted to be were two different places. Coach Carr told me I had the potential to be a very good player and that I should just go out there and compete and worry about the things I could control, and not worry about the things I couldn't. He reminded me that I'd chosen Michigan for a reason, which was true: Michigan *was* the best school for me. It was just disheartening not being able to play. What's more, the prospects of starting looked daunting, as I was mentally and physically behind Scott.

As time went on and my frustrations grew, I was lucky to find—or be found by—our team's sports psychologist, Greg Harden. Greg had been at Michigan for many years and counseled many of the university's great athletes. One thing that impressed me was that Greg had also worked with Desmond Howard, one of the Wolverines' previous superstars. Howard, a return specialist and wide receiver, won the Heisman Trophy in 1991 and later played for the Redskins and the Packers. One time Desmond came into Greg's office

Every day during practice I was competing as hard as I could, because I knew that if I didn't, there was no guarantee anyone would ever allow me to see any game time. I thought: *If I don't treat practice like a game, there's no way the coaches will let me play in an actual game.*

and said, "Greg, I'm never getting the ball thrown to the right place. I'm always breaking my routes, the ball is all over the place, and I'm being forced to make all these diving catches." Greg's response was, "You know what, Desmond? That's why you're *Desmond Howard. Desmond Howard* can make all those diving, one-handed catches no one else can make. If the quarterback was on the money all day long, every single play, no one would have a chance to see what you can really do." Those words have always stayed with me. And the lesson was, when things don't go your way—or, rather, what you don't *think* of as your way—there can be a variety of opportunities that may not be obvious in the moment but that through hard work, preparation, and persistence can present themselves over time and make you better.

"I'm never going to get my chance," I used to tell Greg. "They're giving me only three reps" (meaning practice snaps). Greg would say, "Three reps? Three reps is a heck of a lot better than zero reps. I want you to do the best you can with those three reps that they give you, Tommy. If you do anything less, then shame on you. Now go out and do those three reps *well*." His words further jump-started my own competitiveness. They empowered me, actually—now I had a plan. I would leave Greg's office and go to practice and do those three reps *well*. A week later, the coaches gave me four reps. Then five. Then six. As time went on, I was getting the majority of the reps. Every day during practice I was competing as hard as I could, because I

knew that if I didn't, there was no guarantee anyone would ever allow me to see any game time. I thought: *If I don't treat practice like a game, there's no way the coaches will let me play in an actual game. So I'm always going to treat practice like a game.* It's a rule I still live by today.

My second year at Michigan, Scott Dreisbach was our starting QB, and as the season went on, I competed with Brian Griese for the second position. After a few weeks, Brian had slowly but surely beaten me out. Overall, we didn't have a great year, and late in the season against Penn State, the coach pulled Dreisbach from the game and put Griese in. Long story short, Griese finished the rest of the season, and we ended up beating Ohio State 13–9, though unfortunately we lost our bowl game again, 17–14, to Alabama. By now the coaches were more neutral about Dreisbach. Griese was doing a solid job, but no one was really standing out, which is why when the 1997 season started, there was something of a free-for-all quarterback competition. It was never nasty, and there were never any bad feelings—all the QBs had good relationships with one another—plus I've never believed that entitlement has any place in team sports. If another guy is more capable of doing the job, it's his right to play. By that point, I was competing for playing time with Brian Griese, Scott Dreisbach, and a new guy, Jason Kapsner, a highly recruited player out of Minnesota. In the end Coach Carr chose Brian, who was by then a fifth-year senior, as starting QB,

At Michigan, versus Purdue, 1999.

and Brian deserved that spot. I became the second quarterback, beating out Scott, who ended up third or fourth on the depth chart alongside Jason. That year, 1997, we were undefeated, and it was a magical season, with Brian playing great and us winning every game and finishing off with a Rose Bowl victory over Washington State. Brian taught me a lot about drive and determination. Nothing was going to get in his way, and I was lucky to be able to watch him play. Looking back, I can see that he was a man on a mission, and he taught me what mental toughness really is.

Going into my fourth year, I felt that I was in a position to be the starting QB, having beaten out Dreisbach and Kapsner the previous season. With Brian Griese gone—he had graduated, been drafted, and moved on to the Broncos—a new freshman, Drew Henson, came in. Drew was one of the highest-rated recruits in the country, a multisport athlete who'd been drafted that same year by the New York Yankees. In Drew, all the coaches thought they might have found the next John Elway. Coach Carr had been heavily involved in Drew's recruitment process, and a lot of people were really eager to see what he could do on the field. The thing is, over the previous three years, I'd grown as a person and as a player, gained more experience, and learned to compete really, really hard. I didn't mind the competition; competition brought out the best in me. During training camp that year, I worked more intensely than I ever had in the weight room and on the practice field. I really tried to take it to another level, and it paid off when Coach Carr chose me for the starting job.

Unfortunately, we lost our first game to Notre Dame 36–20, and a week later we were blown out, 38–28, by a great Syracuse team led by Donovan McNabb. Two games in, both losses; it wasn't what you'd call an auspicious debut on my part. At this point, almost everyone wanted Drew to come in and replace me. But Coach Carr kept me in for the next game and, as it turned out, for the rest of the season, because after those first two losses we won nine straight games to finish the year at 9-2. Then we went on to Ohio State, where, despite our team breaking a Michigan record by making thirty-one completions, we lost the game 31–16. Still, we won our bowl game, 45–31, over Arkansas, and finished the season 10-3. Overall it was a pretty good year, and a memorable one.

In 1999, when I began my fifth season, the rivalry between Drew Henson and me had intensified. Everyone—the coaches, the fans—wanted to see Drew out there on the field, and why not? He was very talented, and he'd forgone playing baseball for the Yankees to play college football at Michigan. Still, our team was coming off a solid 10-3 season. Four days before our opening game, Coach Carr called Drew and me into his office. He announced that I was the team captain and would be starting the game, with Drew playing the second quarter. On the basis of that, Coach Carr would decide at halftime which one of us was playing better and would play the second half.

At Notre Dame, 1999.

Early the following day, I remember telling my dad about Coach Carr's decision. Somehow, a member of the media got hold of my dad on the phone and asked for a comment. I think the reporter was trying to bait him—and he succeeded, too! "How do you feel about your son starting against Notre Dame?" the reporter asked. "Well," my dad said, "I spoke to Tom, and he's really excited to play the first quarter, and then Drew will play the second quarter." Thanks to my dad, the media broke the story. After that incident, one of my sisters gave my dad the nickname "Loose Lips." That nickname still fits him quite well!

Drew and I played it out, as Coach Carr had said. During our first game against Notre Dame, I played the first quarter and Drew came in for the second quarter. Coach Carr decided I would play the second half, and we won that game, 26–22, scoring a touchdown in the last two minutes. The second game, against Rice, I played the second half, and the third game, against Syracuse, Coach Carr decided to have Drew play the second half. Midway through the season, against Michigan State, a team that also hadn't lost a single game so far that season, I played the first quarter and Drew played the second quarter—and Coach Carr again decided to have Drew play the second half. But only a few minutes into the second series, Drew threw an interception, and Coach Carr told me I was going back in. We finished the game strongly, scoring four touchdowns on our last four possessions. But Michigan State was on fire, too, and we couldn't slow them down. We lost, 34–31. It was our first loss of the season. I remember thinking, *I played really well when I came back in, so maybe they won't rotate Drew and me anymore.* Even so, a few days later Coach Carr announced he was continuing the rotation. I didn't think too much about it, because at least I was playing.

The following game, against Illinois, we played at home as heavy favorites. As usual I played first, followed by Drew, and then Coach Carr picked me to play the second half. Halfway through the third quarter, the big lead we'd built up was undone by a bunch of crazy things: Illinois scored four unanswered touchdowns; a high snap flew over my head; I threw an interception; and we ended up losing a game we should have won, which meant two straight losses. After the game, Coach Carr called me in to tell me he was giving up the rotation and that I would be

playing the whole game next week. As if that weren't good-enough news, we then won our next four games against Indiana, Northwestern, Penn State, and Ohio State, before beating Alabama in the Orange Bowl and finishing the season 10-2.

Looking back, I can understand why all those other quarterbacks were playing before I was. I also understand why Coach Carr wanted Drew Henson and me to rotate. Still, it made for a tricky college experience, considering I was still learning a lot about who I was and how competitive college football could be. During my time at Michigan, I was fortunate to be in a competitive, team-first environment. I met lots of great friends and mentors. I'd shown up on campus in 1995 as an athlete who was soft of mind and heart. Learning how to fight for what I wanted was a great experience. But with my college years behind me, it was time to see if I could make it to the next level.

In 2000, the New England Patriots and their then quarterback coach, Dick Rehbein, chose me as the NFL's 199th draft pick, which, if you do the math, means that I was passed over by every team in the NFL somewhere between four and six times. The scouting report said I was tall, poised, smart, and alert. Able to read coverages. I had good accuracy and touch, and I was potentially a team leader. But the positives were buried under a landslide of other stuff: *Poor build. Very skinny and narrow. Can get pushed down more easily than you'd like. Lacks mobility and ability to avoid the rush. Lacks a really strong arm. Can't drive the ball down the field and does not throw a really tight spiral.* The report ended by calling me a "system-type player who's not what you're looking for in terms of physical stature, strength, arm strength, and mobility," and "Could make it in the right system but will not be for everyone." And these reports were right. I needed to get better in a lot of areas.

In my first season with the Patriots, I was mostly the fourth quarterback on the depth chart. As usual, it was because I *didn't* have the natural ability some athletes had at that age. In order to compete, I had to work harder than ever before. Fighting to be able to play is something I've carried inside me my whole life, and it wasn't any different when I joined the Patriots. From my college experience I picked up a lot of great lessons, the biggest one being the importance of competition and of the need to earn my role on a team. That lesson—that attitude—has always mattered a lot to me. When I arrived at Michigan, no one ever promised I'd be the starting quarterback by my second year. Compare that with today, when some student-athletes make it a condition of accepting a college scholarship offer that they'll see game time in their first or second year. My first year with the Patriots, our head coach, Bill Belichick, said flat-out that he wanted only one thing: competition. My response was, *Hell, I know how to compete. I've been doing that for the last nine years. Nobody ever gave me anything. You want competition? Okay, great, let's compete.*

I approached it just like I had at Michigan. I worked my butt off every day in practice, knowing that if I didn't make the extra effort to treat every practice like a game, it was unlikely that the coaches would ever let me play in an actual one. I wanted to gain the respect of my teammates. Again, my mind-set back then was to *always treat practice like a game*, and

> Physical pain was something I'd been dealing with since high school. Not knowing any better, I assumed that was just the way it was. So I did what I'd always done: I iced my arm and shoulder, rested for a day or two, and waited for the pain to come back. It always did.

it's still my mind-set today. During my first Patriots season, if I scored a touchdown during a two-minute practice drill, I celebrated as if I were in front of seventy thousand people. I have to believe this had a positive effect on my teammates, who thought, *Oh my God, this guy* wants *to practice, he* wants *to compete; there's no entitlement here, this is all about the team.*

Still, I had never achieved anything without the intensity and discipline I brought to practice, and a mind-set increasingly focused on making sure my body stayed healthy and uninjured. The scouting reports weren't totally off base. I didn't have a natural body for football. Yes, I always had a pretty good arm, but my footwork was below average, and just like in high school and college, when I would run last or next to last before working my way back toward the middle of the pack, I was the slowest guy on the field. It took me at least a year to catch up and be able to compete with the older guys. At twenty-three and twenty-four years old, my only goal in life was to make the team, and I kept putting in the extra effort because I had to. With every level you reach, everyone gets faster, stronger, and better, and I had to work really hard just to be competitive. That's why every Friday at 6:00 a.m., when no one else was around, I worked with our strength coach, Mike Woicik, doing speed and footwork drills, trying to close the gap between me and my teammates.

It was around this same time that I started becoming more and more aware of what was changing in my body.

There's a big difference between playing college foot-ball and playing football in the NFL. I didn't know it at the time, but at Michigan I was doing half the work-load the NFL demands, and at half the intensity, too. When you play college football, the season is only twelve or thirteen games long, and you practice and work out no more than four hours a day. Also, there are probably only four or five games during the college season that are truly intense, in which the two teams are of the same caliber and are evenly matched. The NFL is different. The job begins at 7:00 a.m. every day and goes until 6:00 p.m. *Every* game is a heavyweight brawl, and the inten-sity never lets up. An NFL season has four preseason and sixteen regular-season games, and the Patriots have made the playoffs almost every year since I've been the starting quarterback, which adds up to between twenty and twenty-four games per season. In short, when I be-gan playing for the Patriots, it was double the practice and double the intensity. Until 2011, NFL teams had what they called two-a-days—twice-daily practices with very intense throwing. After a couple of years of two-a-days, plus the pounding my body was taking every day on the field, I got to a point where the tendonitis in my right elbow was so bad I could barely throw the football.

Physical pain was something I'd been dealing with since high school. Back then, almost every day after baseball practice my elbow hurt so much that I would go home and drop it into a big bucket of ice. I didn't know anything different. If my shoulder was sore—which it was most of the time—I'd put a big bag of ice across my neck and upper shoulder. Playing catcher meant that I spent most of my time in a squat, which brought pain to my knees, which meant even more ice packs. The pain followed me to college, where my arm and shoulder ached after almost every practice and game. Not know-ing any better, I assumed that was just the way it was. It was football's fault. I blamed the sport. So I did what

I'd always done, and what every trainer and coach had always told me to do: I iced my arm and shoulder, rested for a day or two, went back onto the field, threw again, and waited for the pain to come back. It always did.

Basically, I followed the same systematic strength-ening and conditioning approach that athletes at all levels and in all sports have followed for decades, and still follow today. Strength training, in which you use free weights, machines, or your own body weight at higher and higher levels of volume or intensity, mixed with shorter and shorter periods of rest, is designed to increase muscular strength and endurance, which in turn allows your muscles to handle even more weight; whereas conditioning focuses on aerobic ex-ercise, plyometrics, calisthenics, and exercises based on real-life motions—basically any way to elevate your heart rate and make you break a sweat in order to prepare you for competition. You do cardio and lift weights and do your best to find the right bal-ance between them. If you get injured while training or playing, you assume it's because your muscles are weak. Your first instinct is to strengthen that per-ceived weakness by lifting weights. But lifting more weights isn't the solution. The core problem is an im-balance among strength, conditioning, and *pliability*. So adding heavier weights to that injury and existing imbalance only makes things worse. *Heavier loads lead to even more imbalance and more muscle compensation, which lead to more injuries.* Strengthen, condition, get injured, go to rehab—that was and still is the nature of the age-old performance-training regimen.

I never questioned that model or way of thinking, and no one else I knew did, either. I also didn't con-sider any alternatives, because as far as I could tell, there weren't any. Not to mention, ever since I was young, coaches and trainers had always told me that playing sports was all about dealing with pain. It was just a fact, it seemed to me, that playing sports—one of the great joys and opportunities of my life—strained and pounded and broke down my body.

That's when I began exploring better ways to train. The reason for this book is to educate others to take a more preventative approach to injury. In the health and medical worlds, there's been plenty of talk about the benefits of wellness and preventative measures to keep people from getting sick in the first place. Why don't we do the same thing in sports training? Why hasn't the science of preventative health measures translated into the world of sports? This book and the TB12 Method are my attempts at an answer. To me, the only way to break the age-old strengthen-condition-injury-rehab model is to incorporate the most important missing leg: *pliability*.

As I said, playing sports has been one of the many joys and privileges of my life. But I've also seen how the grind of training and the punishment that sports inflicts on our bodies takes away that joy for too many athletes. Along with the championships I've been fortunate to be a part of, I'm also proud of the mind-set and approach I've taken to push myself to a different model of training that creates and enables my own sustained peak performance. This regimen is one I want all athletes of all ages to experience, and the principles that fuel the sustained peak performance I've enjoyed over the years are, I believe, also the future of sports training. The TB12 Method that Alex and I developed allows me to feel, play, and perform every week at levels as high as—or higher than—they were back when I was first given the opportunity to step onto the field as the Patriots' quarterback. This is borne out by my own experience: I've been faster every year for the last six years, and have also broken my own personal bests in agility and functional strength tests. Over the same period, according to conventional wisdom, this doesn't happen to athletes in their thirties.

But back in 2000, before I knew what pliability was, my love for football, together with my innate determination and competitiveness, got me through whatever pain I was experiencing and pushed me to give the game my absolute best effort whenever I was given the chance. It was in my second year as a Patriot, in 2001, that I finally got an opportunity to play and to prove to everybody what I'd been preparing for, and what I'd always believed I could do.

It was the second game of the season—the first after the September 11 terrorist attacks. A hot, humid night in New England. The Patriots were playing the New York Jets, and the Jets were up 10–3. I wasn't expecting to play that day; we had a great leader in Drew Bledsoe, our starting QB for the previous nine seasons. But five minutes before the game ended, on third and ten, Drew was chased out of the pocket by Jets defensive end Shaun Ellis and collided on the sidelines with their linebacker Mo Lewis. It was one of the loudest hits I can ever remember hearing. When Drew left the field, Coach Belichick called me into the game. Everything was happening fast, and the only thing I could do was react to the moment. Despite the fact that I had played only minimal minutes the prior season, it just felt like *football*—like something I'd done many times before. Although I was sad to see Drew hurt, I didn't want to let down the team by playing poorly.

During my rookie season, and even during the 2001 season, I never could have imagined the injury to Drew and how that would affect my opportunity to play. All I knew for sure was that if I got a chance, that was all I was going to need—even though the only reason I got that chance was that one of my teammates got hurt. It wasn't until a few days later that we all learned Drew had suffered a very serious injury and would be sidelined for most of the season. We lost that game against the Jets, but it turned out to be a Cinderella

Celebrating our comeback at the 2017 Super Bowl. I was pretty fired up!

season for the Patriots organization, and for me as well. For the next fourteen games, I was the quarterback, and we went 11-3. During the playoffs that year, our placekicker, Adam Vinatieri, made a few unbelievable field goals—two during a game we played in a blizzard against Oakland, and a third, game-winning one when, as underdogs, we beat the defending Super Bowl champions, the St. Louis Rams—aka the Greatest Show on Turf—in Super Bowl XXXVI.

That part was good, and even amazing. But as time went on, three or four years into my Patriots career,

I'd gotten more conditioned than ever to the fact that no matter what I did, my arm and shoulder were going to be hurting. By 2004, at age twenty-seven, I was pretty much constantly aware of the wear and tear on my body. Twenty-seven may sound young, but by their late twenties, most athletes who've played contact sports their whole lives come up against injuries and imbalances in their bodies among strength, conditioning, and pliability.

We're all born naturally pliable, which is why we focus on strength building and conditioning in our teens and twenties. But as our natural pliability diminishes with age, we become more aware of the toll that maximum—versus *optimal*—strength training takes on our bodies. In my case, that meant more pain. More soreness. More stiffness. Longer and longer recovery times. Why? I was plenty strong, but my pliability was running out— and running out to the point where the pain I was experiencing wouldn't allow me to play the sport I loved to play.

Sometime during the 2004 training season, one of my teammates, Willie McGinest, saw me taking time off practice and took me aside. Like me, Willie was from California, and he'd played college ball at USC. He was a linebacker, one of the most talented players on the team, and a major contributor to our Super Bowl wins in 2001, 2003, and 2004. Willie had a certain aura and charisma about him—he was "the Godfather" of the locker room—and he'd always been like an older brother to me. Seeing what was happening, Willie suggested I meet with his body coach, who at the time was Alex Guerrero. Without that meeting, the TB12 Method would never have come to exist.

When Willie recommended that you do something, you did it. Still, to be honest, I didn't expect much of anything. Alex may have come highly recommended, but what could any trainer or coach do that was different from what I'd been doing since high school, which is to say use ice and rest, then play and do everything I could to avoid injury and rehab, all while keeping up my strength and conditioning, while getting the same unsatisfactory results every time? I had nothing to lose, but still, it took a lot of nudging. I thought I had all the answers already. A sore throwing arm didn't necessarily mean the end of my career, but I was beginning to wonder whether I could continue to play in pain until the day my body just gave out. But was that any kind of real solution? Looking back, I wasn't in *enough* pain to realize I needed to change what I was doing. Finally, when Willie said to me, "Dude, you can't practice; you can't even move your elbow," I said okay and booked a session with Alex the next time he was in town.

Alex grew up in California and studied traditional Chinese medicine in college. Since 1996, he'd been working at his rehabilitation facility in Los Angeles, where he worked with a wide range of athletes across all sports. He came east for six days every month to work with Willie and other players, and on one of those trips the two of us met up at Willie's house. In those days, nobody was doing anything close to what Alex was doing. Sports medicine and athletic performance went hand in hand but were segmented, with a strength trainer doing one thing, a position coach doing another thing, and a massage therapist doing something else entirely. Alex, on the other hand, had spent his life and career studying and combining Eastern and Western perspectives and creating a holistic, mind-body approach to sports performance and well-being. His commitment to his clients was obvious. If I got hurt, it hurt *Alex* to see me hurt. The recovery he and I later engineered following my ACL injury really cemented our relationship, and over time we developed a set of principles that have become the foundation of my performance training.

When we met, Alex immediately began zeroing in on my tendonitis by using targeted, deep-force muscle work in a way no one ever had before. Mind you, I had been getting massage, cold treatments, hot treatments, ultrasound, electrostimulation treatments, ART, chiropractic work, stretching, and everything else in between for more than fifteen years from various athletic training staffs. The first treatment with Alex began my understanding of what pliability was. Explaining that my elbow tendon was inflamed, Alex spent the next hour lengthening and softening the muscles surrounding my elbow joint, as well as icing only my inflamed elbow tendon, using a mixture of instinct, know-how, and experience. As he continued lengthening and softening my muscles, the pain and tension in my elbow slowly dissipated. Why? Because by lengthening and softening my biceps, my triceps, and the muscles of my forearm that were tugging on my tendon, Alex was removing the tension from that tendon. My tendon no longer had to work so hard to stabilize my elbow joint. My muscles could now work in a more relaxed, optimal state. If I kept on with this form of treatment during the upcoming season, Alex promised that my tendonitis would continue to improve. It made so much sense to me. I began to wonder why this wouldn't be true for *all* the muscles in my body. By removing tension from *all* of my joints, by lengthening and softening *all* of my muscles, my whole body would function in a more optimal way, and would be better able to disperse the forces I faced on and off the field.

Twenty-four hours later, after another treatment, I could feel the difference in my elbow. Forty-eight hours later, after two more treatments, the improvement in my elbow was even more noticeable. Over the next two weeks, as I kept working with Alex in a methodical way that soon became a routine, the pain and soreness in my elbow and shoulder was better by half. Anybody who was in tune with his or her body and had experienced the intensity of pain I had in my elbow and shoulder year after year, and felt the pain go from a 10 (max) down to a 5 (moderate) after only a few treatments, would have told you the same thing. Alex's goal was to eliminate the pain completely.

Until that point, I hadn't really realized how accustomed I'd gotten to my body hurting as much as it did, or how I'd just accepted pain and soreness as part of the job of playing sports. Playing football for a living was like getting into a car crash every Sunday—a *scheduled* car crash—and I began developing a whole

Me and Alex at the TB12 Sports Therapy Center, 2017.

new understanding of what I was putting my body through every week, and the amounts of trauma my body was experiencing. I also started seeing Alex less as a body coach and more as a body engineer, someone who's able to determine the optimal balance between the stresses and loads placed on my body. In my case, Alex was in the business of designing, building, and maintaining my sustained peak performance in the most holistic way possible. The following year, once I modified my training program to incorporate more of the targeted, deep-force work of lengthening and softening my muscles, Alex told me I'd gotten to a point where I might never have any elbow or shoulder problems again. And I haven't to this day.

Adding resistance bands to my rotational movement improves my strength and maintains my pliability.

TB / CHAPTER 2

WHAT I NOW BELIEVE

I SPENT THE 2004 AND 2005 SEASONS WORKING WITH ALEX. THAT IS TO SAY, WE WORKED INFREQUENTLY, TWO DAYS EVERY OTHER WEEK, AS ALEX WAS CONTINUING TO TREAT HIS OTHER CLIENTS. THAT SCHEDULE WORKED FOR ME BACK THEN, SINCE I HAD MORE NATURAL PLIABILITY AND COULD GET THROUGH A COUPLE OF WEEKS WITHOUT SEEING HIM, VERSUS TODAY, WHEN HE AND I DO PLIABILITY TRAINING FOUR DAYS A WEEK. TOGETHER WE CREATED THE STRONGEST FOUNDATION OF WHAT WE HAD STARTED CALLING PLIABILITY—THE DAILY LENGTHENING AND SOFTENING OF THE MUSCLES IN MY SHOULDER AND ELBOW, AND, AS TIME WENT ON, ALL THE OTHER MUSCLES IN MY BODY, TOO, THROUGH TARGETED, DEEP-FORCE MUSCLE WORK. THINK OF A DEEP, RIGOROUS MASSAGE, BUT MUCH MORE FOCUSED, AND IN MY CASE USING COMPLEX TECHNIQUES BASED ON AN UNDERSTANDING OF THE BIOMECHANICS OF WHAT IT TAKES FOR ME TO THROW A FOOTBALL AND FUNCTION AT PEAK LEVELS AS AN ATHLETE WHO ACCELERATES, DECELERATES, RUNS, CUTS, AND MORE, AS WELL AS THE DAILY ACTS OF LIVING THAT COMPLEMENT MY OFF-FIELD LIFE.

The concept of pliability treatment as a key component of my training regimen didn't arrive in one day, or one week; it has been an ongoing evolution. In effect, I had replaced injury and rehab with pliability and prehab. I began to take preventative measures against being in pain, or getting hurt, rather than waiting to get hurt before I did something about it. Pliability treatment, as I later saw it, wasn't just a way of reeducating my body to understand that it could sustain impact while my muscles remained long, soft, and primed. Most important, it was a primary defense system against the cycle of injury and rehab that every athlete fears or experiences personally. I also knew that when the 2005 NFL season got under way, my shoulder and my elbow stayed pain-free; the more I threw, the better I felt; and

I was absorbing hits a lot better as well. Why were Alex and I the only people who knew about this and were using it? I knew I had never seen it used in any locker room or training room I'd ever been in.

Until 2005, I never questioned the age-old strengthening-and-conditioning model—basically, lifting weights and sprinting. I never asked why coaches prescribed one shoulder exercise over another, or why I had to rest my arm for twenty-four or forty-eight hours after a game, or why weight training improved my on-field performance. Most athletic programs are built on that model—so why should I challenge it? For all I knew, the coaches and trainers were the experts. It didn't occur to me, either, that something might be *missing* from that model.

Strengthening and conditioning work—I'm not saying they don't—but if you asked coaches or trainers to explain *why* they work, few of them could give you a consistent answer, though they would all probably agree that it increased performance. It is just what athletes have always done. It wasn't until I started working with Alex that I began thinking about the subject in a new way. Over the course of the following few seasons, everything changed for me, including a lot of my own entrenched belief systems. This is where discipline is important. As I say, I still believed in the importance of muscle strengthening and conditioning. We all need to focus on that daily or weekly. Athletes especially need it. But as I thought about creating a regimen that would lower the incidence and risk of injury over the long term and ensure sustained peak performance, I knew pliability treatment was the missing leg of the traditional model of strengthening and conditioning, and that it needed to be incorporated at every level. In fact, the more I committed to what I'm now calling the TB12 Method, the better my on-field and off-field results have been.

"Why doesn't everyone know about this?" I kept asking Alex. The answer was that there was no education around it. Years and years of conversations with Alex ultimately led to the creation of our TB12 Sports Therapy Center in Foxborough, Massachusetts, in September 2013—our first location—and the focused, holistic regimen known as the TB12 Method, which for the past dozen years has transformed the way I train, work out, play football, eat, hydrate, supplement, recover, rest, manage my health, and live my life. The TB12 Method, which is geared toward a single purpose—achieving sustained peak performance—*is* my life, and I'm so happy to be sharing it with you.

———

Let me take you back a few years, though. I had an MVP-type year in 2007—the Patriots went 16-0, and we won the AFC Championship, though we lost the Super Bowl to the New York Giants—but in September 2008 I injured my knee. Players do whatever they can to steer clear of contact injuries, but that one I couldn't have avoided. It happened during the Patriots' season opener against the Kansas City Chiefs, on the second drive, fourteen plays into the game. On the fifteenth play, I dropped back, intending to throw the ball deep. I took a stride into my throw, and a defensive back on the ground lunged to tackle me. His helmet made contact with my left knee. My knee met with more force than it could absorb and disperse. The collision ended up shredding my ACL and MCL, and causing multiple bruises and a lot of swelling.

An ACL tear is a common football injury, and a tough injury for any athlete. Mine was a direct hit. My surgeon, Neal ElAttrache, who gave me the best possible care, told me I needed surgery, followed by anywhere from nine to twelve months of rehab and recovery in order for me to feel "back to normal." On top of that, after the surgery I developed an infection in my knee that made my rehab even more of an uphill battle. It was a tough, challenging point of my career. Based on my injury and infection, I faced long odds of getting back to being the player that I was.

My ACL surgery and staph infection made it a challenging October, but Alex oversaw my rehab and recovery as well as my routine check-ins with Dr. ElAttrache and the Patriots' training staff. Many hospitals, surgeons, and physical therapists have protocols they believe anyone recovering from ACL surgery should follow. No matter how old you are, how much you weigh, or what your level of athletic

(Opposite page) Working out at the TB12 Sports Therapy Center, 2017.

ability is, the procedures are really pretty similar: *This is what we want you to do during Week 1. This is what we want you to do during Week 2,* and so on. But Alex and I decided to complement what the doctors and trainers were telling us with our own methodology. Before long we were doing more than was recommended, plugging suggestions from, say, Week 6 into Week 4, and seeing how well my body felt and responded. More important, we resumed practicing the movements I make on the football field, those things I was rehabbing *for*—dropping back, handing the ball off, play-action passing, and throwing on the run. Mentally, it felt good to be back and preparing. Physically, it felt good to begin practicing what I would need to work on once the season started.

When you get injured, who is ultimately responsible for your return to full strength? The doctor? The trainer? The sport? The answer is none of the above. No—in the end, it's *your* body, and *your* life. How you take care of yourself and maintain your health and avoid injury is up to *you.*

To illustrate what happens during an injury, let's look at what happened to me with my ACL. When I took a helmet to the knee, tearing my ACL and MCL, blood and lymph rushed to my injured knee. The muscles surrounding my knee contracted and tightened, creating a kind of natural splint as they tried to stabilize my knee and protect it from pain when I moved it. But they couldn't, as it was already beyond natural repair. At that point, the damage was done. Over the next seven months, Alex and I focused on pliability to help reduce the discomfort I was feeling. We wanted to get back full muscle pump function—100 percent contraction and relaxation—in order to have my muscles support all the actions I was asking them to make as part of my rehab process, which helped reduce the swelling and, in turn, the pain. Through pliability sessions, my

brain and body were able to relearn how the muscles surrounding my knee are supposed to work. Eight weeks into my recovery, I was running in the sand, and six months later—not twelve months—the discomfort in my knee was gone. I should add that during my recovery I checked in regularly with Dr. ElAttrache, who told me my knee was coming along great. That's one of the many things I've learned, and which is now a big part of the TB12 Method: we tailor our program to the individual. Yes, there are core principles, like balancing strength and conditioning with pliability, but the ratio, intensity, and types of exercises are customized to the person, depending on his or her age, strength, and fitness, the sports they play, the lifestyle they lead, and other factors, including what their goals are.

Since my ACL recovery—nine years ago—my knee hasn't bothered or limited me a single day. In fact, two years ago I took a hit on my knee during a practice, requiring an MRI. The doctors who read the MRI joked afterward that my knee looked so healthy, they seriously doubted I played professional football. At that point, I'd been playing for almost twenty-five years. Why was my knee in such good shape? In my view, it was because my muscles—and not my tendons, ligaments, or joints—were handling the forces and stresses placed on my body, just as God intended them to. If muscles are not balanced, loads and stresses go to unintended places, like joints, tendons, or ligaments—and over time, that's not sustainable.

The ACL tear was the most intense injury I'd suffered, and is still the only one that's kept me from playing a game. Up until then, I'd played my whole life without getting seriously hurt. For the first time in my life, I found out I could get badly injured. But through that process, I began to ask questions, like *What can I do to prevent something like this from happening again?* From working with Alex, and realizing

I wasn't a victim of my injuries and that I was a very active participant in my own health and wellness, I understood there were some injuries I couldn't avoid. I also understood that the choices I made off the field would help determine whether or not I got hurt, or stayed hurt, as well as the degrees and severities of injuries. In the months during and after my ACL injury and recovery, I began looking at all the lifestyle choices I was making that could affect the way I got injured, and how I could recover. If incorporating pliability was so important, what were some of the other things I could do to extend my peak performance and help me recover faster? I couldn't do everything as described in this book at once. I went forward line by line, precept by precept. I'm hoping you do the same.

For as long as I could remember, like most athletes, I ate and drank whatever was in front of me—pizza, beer, soda, whatever. Now I began exploring the role of hydration. Pliability and hydration go hand in hand, and one can't really exist without the other. What does proper hydration mean? How does hydration affect muscles? How does hydration help keep muscles soft—looking and feeling like pieces of tenderloin instead of beef jerky—and what should my nutrition look like to allow my muscles to maintain that optimal look and feel? Once I began understanding that the things I put inside my body had a direct effect on my performance on and off the field, I took a long look at my diet and the nutritional choices I was making or not making. Hydration and nutrition are the foundation of healthy muscles, and if your muscles aren't healthy, it's that much harder to attain optimal pliability. Ignore either or both, and it will take you longer. Again, not sustainable. Knowing that almost every NFL player took some sort of supplement to support or increase muscle strength, I also got interested in vitamins and supplements.

As time went on, and with the goal of continuing to reduce inflammation in my body, Alex and I also began exploring the role of bioenergetic apparel and sleepwear. In January 2017, after spending two years researching the best materials, TB12 launched our first bioceramic recovery wear. To me, tech-enabled apparel and sleepwear isn't all that different from virtual reality, meaning that what seemed far-fetched a few years ago will soon become part of the mainstream, contributing to how we do both prehab and rehab. I'm happy to say TB12 is at the forefront of this movement.

As I've said, pliability and the TB12 Method aren't a replacement for strength training and conditioning. But I've come to believe that strength and conditioning at the expense of pliability is a sure recipe for injury. By incorporating pliability into their daily regimens, athletes at any level will find they have a much higher probability of preventing injury and extending their careers almost indefinitely—not to mention bettering their performance. Not least, by limiting their risk of injury, pliability increases their ability to practice. In the NFL there are one hundred practices per season. I take part in almost all of them—let's say ninety. The average would be seventy. If practice makes perfect, this means I have a 20 percent advantage to improve through practice, and more opportunities to get ahead of the competition.

Sometimes I like to think about how amazing the quality of NFL football would be if players managed to avoid injury and stay healthy not just for two years or five years but for twelve years, fifteen years, or, in my case, seventeen years and counting. In pro football, health equals productivity equals durability. If you're a wide receiver who makes 7 catches a game but who plays only eight games because of an injury, that works out to 56 catches a year—and that's a below-average stat. But if you play sixteen games,

Strengthening and conditioning work—I'm not saying they don't—but it wasn't until I started working with Alex that I began thinking about the subject in a new way. As I thought about creating a regimen that would lower the risk of injury over the long term and ensure sustained peak performance, I knew pliability was the missing leg that needed to be incorporated at every level.

averaging the same amount of catches, making 112 in total, that turns your season into a Pro Bowl year. The difference? Productivity and durability. If you're playing in the NFL, you've already shown the world how good you are. The question now becomes, how often can your body get out there on the field to prove it? Only by incorporating pliability into your workout can you reach a place where both your brain and body are working toward the goals you've set for yourself. What *are* your goals? How do you define success in your life? Only you can answer that! I'm positive the TB12 Method can support you along the way.

Durability also makes for a better game. I have game log after game log of information stored up in my head, based on years of problem solving and pattern recognition. As a quarterback, my ability to adapt to change is crucial. The game never stops evolving, so why should I? By this point in my career, I've seen virtually every situation and scenario that exists. I've always had great coaches and mentors, but experience has trained me, too, and the answers to multiple scenarios that come to me on the field show up quickly. The ability to couple experience with a healthy body creates better players, better performances, and a much better game. During a game last season against the Buffalo Bills, with four minutes left in the first quarter, I stepped up into the pocket, got

past a defensive lineman, and threw the ball to Danny Amendola, our wide receiver, who was running to the right front pylon, for a touchdown. It was your basic pitch-and-catch. But before I even threw the ball, my brain cut to the moment I had made the same play four years earlier when we played the New York Jets. I knew what I was going to do because I'd done it before. The difference maker, again, is durability. *That's* what seventeen years of sustaining peak performance feels like for me, physically *and* mentally, and I love it.

Over the years, there's been a misperception in the media that the TB12 Method has to be done one particular way, and that unless you reach a secret Ninja Level, you won't see the benefits. That's not true. The TB12 Method can benefit men and women of any age and any level of fitness or performance or ability. At the TB12 Sports Therapy Center, our body coaches see a wide range of people who are drawn both to the holistic and attitudinal components of what we do. Our mission is to create comprehensive, customized programs for clients that reflect their goals and biomechanics. A lot of athletes come to us because conventional methods haven't worked for them. Some come to train, others are more focused on performance, and still others are trying to recover from injuries. We see professional athletes, elite amateurs (including high school athletes), college students who

Me and Alex working at the TB12 Sports Therapy Center, 2017.

want to make the team or have their eyes on the pros, weekend warriors, and men and women from eight to eighty who just want to unlock their own sustained peak performance, whatever that may be, and increase their vitality through all stages of their lives. What we try to create in our clients is genuine change and new patterns of behavior that go beyond simply showing up at the gym a few days a week. Even if you take away only four or five things from this book, whether it's how to improve your diet, or work out smarter, or the half dozen supplements everyone should take,

I guarantee you'll start to see huge differences in your life.

At the same time—contrary to what the media thinks—I won't always turn down a cheeseburger or an ice cream cone. I just won't have one every night, and I won't have ten of them, either. Last year, my wife and I went to Italy, a country that presents a lot of temptation. Yes, I brought along my electrolytes, as well as my protein, nutritional supplements, and TB12 Snacks—I had to be ready to play football two weeks later—but in Italy I definitely ate some things that were *not* TB12-compliant! My brain and body needed that downtime. Too much of a bad thing is bad for you, but too much of a good thing isn't a good thing, either.

Personally, as I've said before, we all have different goals. I want to play until my mid-forties, and I realize that requires a focused, disciplined approach. I've always been motivated to target and improve on my deficiencies, and I still am. Coach Belichick says, "You pay the price in advance," and a teammate of mine liked to say that "The only place where success comes before work is in the dictionary." The reason I got a chance to play pro football in the first place back in 2001 was that one of my teammates got hurt. I never want to see someone else do my job—which is one reason why I need to stay healthy. Other players are always asking me about the "one thing" they should do to improve their performance. Well, there isn't any "one thing." Sustained peak performance isn't about changing one or two habits in your life. It *is* your life. It requires commitment. It requires discipline. It requires openness. My career as an NFL quarterback and my life aren't two separate things. Every hour of every day in my life revolves around my job. That includes what I eat, what I drink, when I plan my vacations, my travel destinations, and the training equipment I bring along with me. As a pro quarterback, I train about four hours per day—and I'm committed to making every hour of every day count.

> A lot of athletes come to us because conventional methods haven't worked for them. What we try to create in our clients is genuine change and new patterns of behavior.

I've written this book in hopes of educating and inspiring a very different lifestyle for maximizing performance and increasing vitality. My goal is to help all of you discover what sustained peak performance means to you.

CHAPTER 3

12 PRINCIPLES OF TB12

Resistance-band core work.

THE TB12 METHOD ISN'T JUST A TRAINING REGIMEN—I SEE IT AS A HOLISTIC LIFESTYLE. IT'S BUILT UPON TRUTHS AND PRINCIPLES THAT UNDERPIN WHAT WE DO EVERY DAY AT THE TB12 SPORTS THERAPY CENTER IN FOXBOROUGH. BUT BEFORE DIVING IN DEEPER, I WANT TO SUMMARIZE THESE PRINCIPLES, SINCE THEY MAKE UP THE FOUNDATION OF WHAT WE AT TB12 BELIEVE IS THE OPTIMAL APPROACH TO EXERCISE, TRAINING, AND LIVING A LIFE OF VITALITY. ANY ONE OF THESE PRINCIPLES CAN BE TAKEN ALONE, OF COURSE. BUT ALSO UNDERSTAND THAT THEIR EFFECT IS CUMULATIVE, SO THE MORE YOU CAN IN-CORPORATE, THE BETTER YOUR RESULTS WILL BE. WE DON'T VIEW THE BODY AS AN ASSORTMENT OF PARTS. IT'S A CONNECTED SYSTEM THAT FUNCTIONS AS A WHOLE, AND YOU SHOULD TREAT IT THAT WAY. BY PRACTICING AND LIVING ALL TWELVE OF THESE PRINCIPLES, YOU'LL BEGIN TO SEE GREAT BENEFITS.

Band-resisted push-up.

12 PRINCIPLES OF TB12

1. **PLIABILITY IS THE MISSING LEG OF PERFORMANCE TRAINING—AND THE MOST UNDERUTILIZED AND LEAST UNDERSTOOD.** Everything begins with pliability, the daily lengthening and softening of muscles before and after physical activity. Without pliable muscles, you can't achieve long-term health. Every athlete needs to find a balance between strength, conditioning, and pliability. The balance will change based on what your age, sports, needs, and goals are.

2. **HOLISTIC AND INTEGRATIVE TRAINING.** Nothing works in isolation. Everything we do at TB12 is interdependent, and we believe that a holistic approach works better than a divided one. The body is one system. Treat it well. It is the only one you have.

3. **BALANCE AND MODERATION IN ALL THINGS.** We subscribe to the precept of balance and moderation in all things. Too much of a good thing isn't a good thing. Too many bad things are just plain bad.

4. **CONDITIONING FOR ENDURANCE AND VITALITY.** Conditioning is about having the energy, endurance, and vitality to perform the activities you love in a healthy, pain-free way. Good health is about how you *feel*. We've been educated around how we look. But *feeling better*—that's the key.

5. **NO-LOAD STRENGTH TRAINING.** Muscles aren't for strength or for show. Their function is to protect your bone structure and to support the acts of daily living. You should train to develop the optimal strength to do the job your body needs to do, while limiting the load—especially the *overload*—you put on your joints. Make your muscles work every day, and load them appropriately for what you're asking of them in your daily life.

6. **PROMOTE ANTI-INFLAMMATORY RESPONSES IN THE BODY.** Anything that reduces inflammation in our bodies, including hydration and nutrition, maximizes pliability and accelerates recovery. Try to avoid self-inflammation—whether it's in your mind, body, or spirit.

7. **PROMOTE OXYGEN-RICH BLOOD FLOW.** The blood that flows to your brain is the same blood that flows to your feet—and everywhere in between. The more ways you can foster the circulation of oxygen-rich blood and 100 percent muscle pump function—full contraction and relaxation—in every part of your body, the better. Oxygen-rich blood rejuvenates and regenerates, leading to optimal health.

8. **PROPER HYDRATION.** Drinking enough water every day, preferably with electrolytes, is essential for muscle pliability and optimal health.

9. **HEALTHY NUTRITION.** No training or exercise program is effective unless complemented by proper nutrition. You can't train or recover well when you deprive your body and muscles of the right nutrients. What you put in your body is often what you will get out of your body.

10. **SUPPLEMENTATION.** Healthy nutrition is amplified by the right vitamins, nutrients, and minerals, based on your current diet, age, and activity levels.

11. **BRAIN EXERCISES.** Neuroplasticity is all about generating and regenerating neural connections—which happens only when we train our brains the same way we do our muscles.

12. **BRAIN REST, RECENTERING, AND RECOVERY.** The body and the brain need recentering, rest, and recovery via sleep, meditation (or other balancing techniques that encourage the right mind-set), and recovery innovations such as tech-enabled sleepwear.

Below and in the chapters ahead, I'll go into each of these twelve principles in more detail. They form the foundation of performance, productivity and durability.

PLIABILITY IS THE MISSING LEG OF PERFORMANCE TRAINING— AND THE MOST UNDERUTILIZED AND LEAST UNDERSTOOD

Most athletes grow up learning to lift weights and run wind sprints in order to accomplish their athletic goals in their off-season training. It's simply part of their coaches' and trainers' belief system. And it works, too—to a degree. But I believe the traditional strength and conditioning model also leads to countless injuries, rehabs, and careers cut short. Consider that the average career in the NFL is 3.3 years, the average in pro baseball is 5.6 years, in the NHL it's 5.5 years, and in the NBA it's 4.8 years. Even outside elite athletics, our bodies begin a general decline beginning in our mid to late twenties. But by incorporating pliability into your strength and conditioning regimen, it doesn't have to be that way. Of course, you'll still get older, but with pliability you're less likely to age poorly, or in a compromised state. My goal is to teach people to maintain a prime physical state for as long as they can commit to the core TB12 principles I mentioned on the previous page.

Bottom line: you can't sustain peak performance solely through strength and conditioning. You can perform well, often great, for a short period of time, but you won't be able to sustain it. Ask yourself what it might mean to not get hurt, or not be in pain, or at least to begin creating a stronger, more effective "body immune system" to counteract pain and injury.

Nobody plans for a two-year career, after all! That's where pliability plays a major role. By rhythmically contracting and relaxing your muscles in a lengthened, softened state through pliability sessions, you make connections between the brain and the body, which is known as neural priming. Why is that important? Because the body begins to associate muscle function and movement with long, soft, primed muscle contractions. One of the critical keys is doing pliability treatments both before and after your full workout or physical activity. (Think of pliability as the new "warm-up" and "cool-down.") This is the essence of the brain–muscle connection—creating the right neural priming, muscle memory, and conditioning that enable your muscles to work in ways that lower the risk of injury during physical activity.

Contrast this to an athlete who does daily weight lifting with *no* pliability. The only way he can absorb force is by making his muscles tight, dense, and stiff. Those muscles can't disperse force appropriately for two reasons. First, they're already contracted, which means they don't have the ability to absorb any excess stress; and second, they're working alone, rather than as part of a whole muscle group that's integrated into a *system* of muscle groups. What will happen when an athlete with tight, dense, stiff muscles goes out onto the field and tries to make a tackle, or runs and makes a sharp cut? If these functions overload a muscle, bone, tendon, or ligament, he will get injured. In fact, I believe his muscles, which aren't pliable, are more likely to be overloaded through negative trauma—meaning trauma that's unintended and beyond his control—and injuries. Later he'll blame the injury on "weak muscles." He may think he didn't work out long enough. But I believe that's wrong. By continuing to lift weights, he's telling his brain—and therefore his body—that his muscles should remain tight, dense, and stiff. Unfortunately, *tight, dense, and stiff* is the enemy of pliability and will increase his risk of injury even more.

As I said, the goal of pliability is to reeducate your brain–body connection, which continually sends messages to your muscles to stay long, soft, and primed, no matter how you're asking your body to perform. When an athlete needs to contract and relax his muscles, they're ready to fire *appropriately* as they do the jobs he's asking them to do. As an NFL quarterback, I can't predict when I'll sustain trauma from a hit or a tackle. But I've trained my muscles to stay pliable as I stand in the pocket. The moment another player's helmet makes contact with my body, my muscles are pliable enough to absorb what's happening instantly. My brain is thinking only *Lengthen and soften and disperse* before my body absorbs and disperses the impact evenly and I hit the ground. In this way, it is difficult for any one part of my body to get overloaded, as many muscles are acting to support the forces placed on it. That's the key.

> The goal of pliability is to reeducate your brain–body connection, which continually sends messages to your muscles to stay long, soft, and primed, no matter what you're asking your body to do. One of the critical keys is doing pliability both before and after your full workout or physical activity. (Think of pliability as the new "warm-up" and "cool-down.")

HOLISTIC AND INTEGRATIVE TRAINING

At TB12, we believe that everything we do with regard to our bodies is interconnected and interdependent. Just as you can't do strength training without conditioning, you also need to find the right balance between strength, conditioning, and pliability, depending on your sport or activity, and the intensity with which you do it. It also depends on your age and physical condition. The older you are, the more you need to incorporate pliability—and commit to it, too, as younger athletes have a hefty supply of pliability that starts to dissipate with age. There are great benefits to strength and conditioning—you need a baseline of both to do the job you are trying to do. More important is *how* you do it, functionally, and whether you do it alongside pliability.

Holistic means only that your health and performance are intergrated. You need to consider every detail of your exercise and training regimen and reduce or cut out the things that negatively affect your pliability. Time is an asset for us all, which is why adopting a holistic, integrative approach to your exercise and workout routine is so important. Among strength, conditioning, and pliability, at my age I spend roughly one-half of my time on pliability sessions. Many athletes spend *no* time on pliability—and a few might spend only a few minutes. I believe that at a minimum, most younger people should dedicate 20 percent of their workouts to pliability. As you get older, and depending on what sport you engage in (for example, contact versus noncontact), you'll need to increase the percentage of pliability in your workout. Why do golfers today experience more back pain than they did in past decades? Why do baseball pitchers today need Tommy John surgery on a regular basis? Too much overload, and not enough muscle pliability!

Resistance-band core work.

One keyword of the TB12 Method is *balance*. Each of us needs to figure out the meaning of that concept in our lives, based on our innate strengths and weaknesses, and on external factors, too. At TB12, balance is as much about creating the right mixture of strength, conditioning, and pliability as it is about lifestyle choices—what we eat, how much rest and recovery we get, and what daily activities we engage in. The more balanced we are, the better.

BALANCE AND MODERATION IN ALL THINGS

One keyword of the TB12 Method is *balance*. All season long, football players work hard to improve their weight lifting, sprinting, jumping, and agility. Many often gain recognition for their efforts—but their bodies can possibly be out of balance. Working too hard at one thing, even if you work harder than anyone else, may not lead to improved performance, especially if you have imbalances. Most likely it just means you're getting better at that one thing.

Each of us needs to figure out the meaning of balance in our lives, based on our innate strengths and weaknesses, and on external factors, too. At TB12, balance is as much about creating the right mixture of strength, conditioning, and pliability as it is about lifestyle choices—what we eat, how much rest and recovery we get, and what daily activities we engage in. The more balanced we are, the better. In my experience, most athletes like to work on things that they're already good at. It reinforces their confidence in their own abilities. Strong athletes like to work on strength, and fast athletes like to work on speed. But that doesn't create balance. To create balance, we need to work on our deficiencies as well.

CONDITIONING FOR ENDURANCE AND VITALITY

Why do we work out, and what does "good health" really mean? If you're like most people, you measure your health based on what a scale says, or on your blood pressure or cholesterol or BMI levels, or how you look in the mirror. (Maybe you've even had your body fat measured.) You probably also assess other people's health using those same criteria.

I define good health and being healthy as *vitality—and feeling it*. That means I have the energy to do the things I want to do and love to do: Play professional football. Work out. Ski. Surf. Play basketball. Play soccer in the yard with my kids. Interact with my teammates. Focus on my game plan in the team meeting room. It also means doing all those activities without pain, and with energy, enthusiasm, passion, and endurance.

The bottom line is that the conditioning and endurance that clients do at TB12 helps create the energy and vitality they need to do the things they want to do. Exercise, working out, and engaging in physical activities are all parts of a joyful life.

NO-LOAD STRENGTH TRAINING

Strength training allows you to do your job well, whatever that job is, and helps your muscles contract appropriately for the daily acts of living you ask of them. But the emphasis on more weight, greater reps, and longer workouts wears down our bodies' natural pliability and creates tight, dense, stiff muscles that aren't appropriate for the jobs we ask them to do or for our daily acts of living. Quarterbacks, pitchers, and golfers are all what are known as "rotational athletes." That means they need to rotate their trunks or arms as they do their jobs. If rotational athletes do only "linear" workouts, such as running and lifting weights, they're confusing their bodies. They need their muscles to be long, soft, and primed, which allow those muscles to rotate efficiently as they do their jobs. This can't happen if their muscles are tight, dense, and stiff.

At TB12, about 90 percent of the time clients work out with resistance bands. Most are surprised to find that resistance bands work their bodies functionally better than weights do in terms of elasticity, resistance, versatility, and efficiency. Bands also allow for a bigger, more fluid range of motion, and build strength and power without overloading muscles or creating excess inflammation. By targeting accelerating and decelerating muscle groups at the same time without putting stress on your joints, bands can also mirror your body's normal, everyday movements.

A lot of people work out with resistance bands or do water aerobics or practice tai chi. Not many young people do these things. They've grown up believing that good health is synonymous with big muscles. But despite what the culture markets to us, the goal of strength training isn't bulking up. It's training your muscles to work appropriately for the job you're asking them to do or how you're asking them to support your movements throughout the day, without creating undue risk of injury.

PROMOTE ANTI-INFLAMMATORY RESPONSES IN THE BODY

Chronic inflammation is the enemy of pliability. Chronically inflamed muscles are working in a suboptimal state and are more resistant to lengthening and softening. That's why pliability and nutrition work together to decrease the amount of chronic inflammation in our bodies. Why would a body be chronically inflamed? Simple: Dehydration, poor nutrition, poor recovery, and tight, dense, stiff muscles.

Some degree of chronic inflammation is inevitable as we get older. But to gain optimal pliability and promote faster recovery, consider adopting lifestyle changes that combat inflammation. They include proper hydration, a nutritional regimen made up of real food—preferably organic—and adopting methods that reduce stress, re-center the brain, and accelerate recovery.

38

PROMOTE OXYGEN-RICH BLOOD FLOW

Few things can survive on this planet without oxygen. Why are our bodies and muscles as oxygenated as they are when we're young? Because younger muscles expand and contract at 100 percent—what we call *100 percent muscle pump function*—and haven't yet sustained many negative traumas such as falls, collisions, injuries, or overloads.

As we get older and experience years of muscle contractions and negative traumas through just plain living, our muscles get stiffer, shorter, and more dense, limiting full muscle pump function, which in turn limits oxygenation. That's one reason why, as we age, we don't recover as quickly. Athletes often say, "I'm not young anymore." Why? Because they don't have pliability. Pliability helps us achieve a state of 100 percent muscle pump function. This allows full oxygenation in every muscle of our body, helping us reach a state of optimal health and vitality. In contrast, over time, tight, dense, stiff, dehydrated muscles *lose* their optimal pliability—and therefore their optimal oxygenation. Without full oxygenation, muscles begin to degenerate. *That*'s why athletes say they're not young anymore.

As I said, we are all born with optimal pliability. We had to *work* on strength and conditioning. Which came first? Pliability. We need to be pliable *first*.

The moment another player's helmet makes contact with my body, my muscles are pliable enough to absorb what's happening instantly.

PROPER HYDRATION

Most of us aren't close to being properly hydrated. Hydration, in fact, is one of the easiest, most important things we can all do *right now* to enhance our pliability. Drinking enough water helps our bodies maintain good metabolism and digestion, lubricates our joints, and keeps oxygen and nutrients circulating to our muscles. Even more than nutrition, proper hydration is essential to maintaining healthy, pliable muscles.

At the TB12 Sports Therapy Center, we recommend that everyone, even nonathletes, consume at least one-half of their body weight in ounces of water every day. At 225 pounds, that means I should be drinking 112 ounces a day, minimum. If it's an especially active day, I'll drink anywhere from 200 to 300 ounces of water. Sometimes I think I'm the most hydrated person in the world.

HEALTHY NUTRITION

Eating poorly undoes many of the benefits you get from exercising, and risks endangering healthy muscles. The more nutrient-dense food you eat, the better your body can generate energy. By adopting the proper nutritional regimen, you create a healthy inner environment that allows your body to thrive.

From my perspective, eating well means eating mostly plant-based whole foods, foods rich in fiber and essential fatty acids. No processed or fast foods, sugars, or fats. Minimal amounts of caffeine and alcohol. In the same way pliability complements and completes the traditional strength and conditioning model, nutrient-rich food allows our cells to absorb what they need. Find what works best for you.

SUPPLEMENTATION

It would be great if everyone had the benefits of a mostly plant-based, real-food nutritional regimen, but that often doesn't happen, because of our busy lives. That's where supplements come in. At TB12, we define the word *supplement* literally—as an add-on, or supplementation, to the foods we eat. The right supplements can't take the place of proper nutrition, but they can help ensure that you get the daily vitamins, minerals, and nutrients your body may be lacking.

Through intense workouts, and a lot of running and throwing, I push my body to its limits. Since 2000, I have used supplements as a way to help my body work hard and recover quickly. Along with electrolytes and trace mineral drops, every day I take a multivitamin, vitamin D, vitamin B complex, an antioxidant, essential fish oils, protein powder, and a probiotic. I'll talk about supplementation more in a later chapter.

BRAIN EXERCISES

In the past, brain exercises were reserved mostly for people with brain injuries, or those facing diseases like early-onset dementia or Alzheimer's. But the research we at TB12 have done reminds us that the brain is an organ that we need to exercise in the same way we train our bodies. To my mind, I need to get ahead and stay ahead of brain injuries, especially in the off-season, and I try to keep my brain as healthy as possible by ensuring it gets the right amount of cognitive exercise, along with proper hydration and the right nutrients.

TB12 brain exercises are based on what we now know about neuroplasticity, or the brain's ability to keep changing and learning over a lifetime. The exercises I do increase the amount of sensory information my brain takes in and improve my ability to process and store that information. They improve my fast-recognition abilities, narrow my focus, and increase my pattern recognition.

BRAIN REST, RECENTERING, AND RECOVERY

No real peak performance training can take place in our bodies unless we do it in conjunction with our brains. Our brains are our control centers. We can exercise our brains to create greater neuroplasticity and generate new neural connections. Another way to keep our brains as healthy as possible is to ensure they get the right amount of exercise through cognitive training.

Creating a healthy inner environment through hydration and nutrition isn't enough. Does it matter what you eat if your mind-set is negative or angry, or you have poor self-esteem? At TB12, we encourage clients to focus on the right mind-set, and also to make the time to reflect and recenter. So many people have written books on how to achieve the right state of mind, and I have read many of them. I am an optimistic person who chooses to focus on things that bring me joy. More important than formal meditation is developing a positive mind-set that allows you to achieve everything you want to achieve.

One of the simplest things anyone can do is create a regular routine for sleep. My general discipline and pattern is to sleep from 9:00 p.m. to 6:00 a.m., which gives me nine hours of uninterrupted therapy and regeneration. I also want to make sure my body remains in a state of recovery even at night. I do this by wearing bioceramic-infused functional apparel and sleepwear. The advantages? It increases energy, promotes recovery, and improves performance. If my opponents aren't wearing what I wear, I'm getting the edge on them even when I'm sleeping.

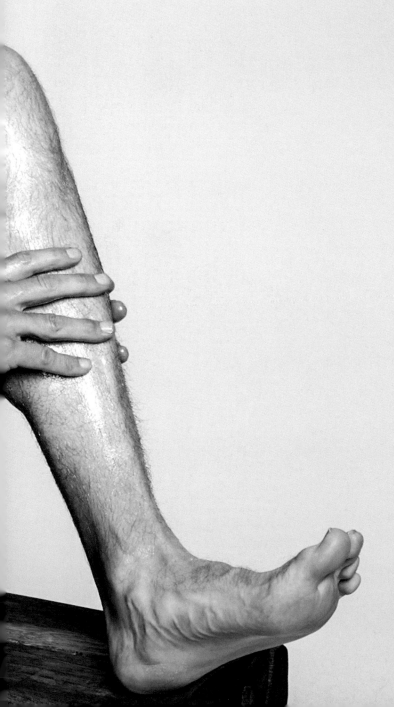

Doing self-pliability on my left calf, always stroking toward the heart.

THE MISSING LEG

At the core of the TB12 Method is our belief that injury prevention and wellness through pre-hab is achievable and necessary for athletes and active individuals. If injuries occur, we believe that there are faster, better, and more sustainable ways to recover than traditional rehab.

The key is in complementing traditional strength and conditioning training with muscle pliability. Pliable muscles are softer, longer, and more resilient: they help insulate the body against injury and accelerate post-injury recovery.

WITH CONVENTIONAL TRAINING, REHABILITATION IS A NECESSARY EVIL

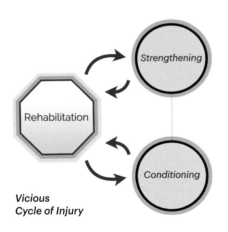

Vicious Cycle of Injury

Conventional training focuses on traditional strengthening and conditioning exercises. While this can help achieve performance goals, it is usually short-term oriented and inevitably incorporates rehabilitation as a "necessary evil."

Traditional rehab, in turn, leads directly back to strengthening and conditioning, often without fixing the underlying problem. This can create a vicious cycle of strengthening, conditioning, and rehabilitation—a cycle in which rehab treats the symptoms but not the causes. You may *feel* better, but you don't *get* and *stay* better.

IMPROVED MUSCLE PLIABILITY TRANSFORMS VICIOUS CYCLE INTO VIRTUOUS CIRCLE

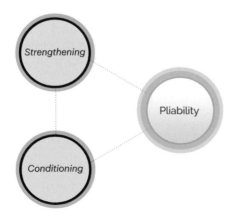

Proper pre-hab and whole-body wellness can significantly lower the risk of injury—and enable sustained peak performance. Our methods complement strengthening and conditioning with a critical missing leg of athletic preparation: pliability.

Pliable muscles are long, soft, and capable of full muscle pump function. They improve strength and promote circulation of blood and lymph to facilitate healing. We improve pliability through deep-force muscle work and further promote it through hydration and nutrition. Together with the right strengthening and conditioning, our program helps break the vicious cycle of injury and creates a virtuous circle of sustained peak performance.

IT GOES WITHOUT SAYING THAT ALL ATHLETES WANT TO ACHIEVE THEIR GOALS. IN MY EXPERIENCE, MOST ATHLETES ARE GREAT AT FOLLOWING THE SYSTEMS OR DISCIPLINES THAT ARE IN PLACE, AND OFTEN DO NOT QUESTION RULES AND DIRECTIONS. A LOT OF THE TIME, THAT'S A GREAT APPROACH FOR ATHLETES. BUT SOMETIMES IF THAT SYSTEM OR DISCIPLINE IS MIS-GUIDED OR INCOMPLETE, IT LIMITS THE ULTIMATE POTENTIAL OF THOSE ATH-LETES. UNFORTUNATELY, BAD SYSTEMS ARE OFTEN BUILT ON EARLIER BAD SYSTEMS, AND ATHLETES ARE OFTEN TRAINED WITHIN THOSE SYSTEMS. BELIEVE ME—I'VE SEEN IT. BUT OUR HEALTH IS OUR RESPONSIBILITY.

This is especially true for younger athletes. Not knowing any better—and why should they?—they buy into the system and discipline of strength and conditioning over and over again. That isn't a bad thing, necessarily; the problem is that they rarely give any thought to why the system exists, or what exactly they're being disciplined around. If the strength coach says, "Do fifty reps," you do fifty reps. If the trainer says, "Six laps around the field," you start running. *Which brick wall do you want me to run through now, coach?* You do what you're told, and the positive feedback and affirmation you get keep you following the pack. After all, if you challenge the system or ask why you're doing that press or lifting that load, you risk getting sidelined or kicked off the team. *Why am I bench-pressing four hundred pounds?* you may wonder, or *Why am I lifting weights three times a week?*, but you keep those questions to yourself. In that way, an embedded system and discipline only gets more embedded.

Many athletes also grow up equating great workouts with working out *longer* and *more often* than anyone else. They also believe that the best workouts require lifting the maximum amount of weight.

Why lift two hundred pounds if you can lift three hundred? Why run a half marathon if you can run twenty-six miles? Even people who don't play a sport but who want to keep fit go to the gym and work out, say, forty-five minutes on a stair climber or stationary bike, followed by another half hour doing the maximum number of weight or circuit-training exercises possible.

This idea—focus on the *most* workouts and the *longest* workouts and you'll get better at all the things you want to improve—makes sense up to a point. In football, for example, there's a widespread belief that working hard in the off-season means you should do wind sprints and weight lifting. And yes, by doing those things you can improve your general athleticism. The mistake comes when you believe that by working hard and being able to run and jump, you'll become better at your job, which I don't believe is entirely true.

There's a difference between a strong or a fast athlete and a well-rounded athlete. At football combines, for example, coaches ask players to lift weights, sprint, and jump. To them, that's what being a good athlete means. Now, those are three specific linear skills—but are they really a measure of great athleticism? To my mind we shouldn't define athleticism only one way. Athleticism has *something* to do with speed and strength, but not everything. It also requires coordination and mental toughness. Ask people to list the world's greatest athletes, and most will name someone who has *all* those attributes versus, say, the world's strongest man or the world's fastest human.

In short, our ideas about how to train to become a great athlete are out of balance. A coach may work a player hard at one thing, and a player may work harder than anyone else at that thing, but in the end, that player is getting better at only one or two things. And all too often his improvement comes at the expense of pliability, if he doesn't commit to that as well.

The *most/longest* model has been in place since I was in high school, and before. Again, that model may seem logical. Sometimes it even yields benefits in the short term—but it won't work if you want to sustain your peak performance. Why? Because most sports don't require those extremes of effort or exertion, or those skills. In my job—throwing a football—there's no need for me to bench-press three hundred pounds. It's not even about diminishing returns—it's actually detrimental to my performance. The same is true for long-distance running. Why would I ever train to the point where I could run a marathon? That requires a different physical makeup and configuration than I need for my job, and one that

would put a lot of unnecessary strain on my feet, ankles, and knees. That's why one of our twelve TB12 principles is creating a balanced, optimized training program for the sport or activity you need to do or the daily acts of living you're asking your body to perform.

To use an analogy, just because you're standing at a buffet, that doesn't mean you're supposed to eat everything. You should eat just enough so that you feel full, and no more. Sports training is no different. If you're an athlete, instead of focusing on the *most* or the *longest*, you should be training your muscles to work appropriately for the actions you ask them to do. If you do daily squats with a four-hundred-pound load on your back, the only thing you'll get better at is squatting with a four-hundred-pound load on your back. Outside professional weight lifting, when is anyone asked to do that? The answer: rarely, and then it's probably sports-position specific. Again, that may be gratifying personally, but without the right amount of pliability, I believe it comes at the expense of your long-term health. To repeat, most of what you train for should be focused on *making your muscles work appropriately for the actions you're asking them to do*. Put another way, *your strength workouts should follow the function of your sport or activity*. We focus too much on *maximum* strength—and not enough on *optimal* strength.

Most athletes don't know this. As I said, if they play a coached sport, they do what they're told. Now, in defense of the age-old strength and conditioning

> You don't strain or tear a muscle because it's too weak. You strain or tear a muscle because it's overloaded. Don't mistake muscle soreness, or a muscle tear, for muscle weakness. You need to *lengthen* and *soften* that muscle in order to restore balance and efficiency.

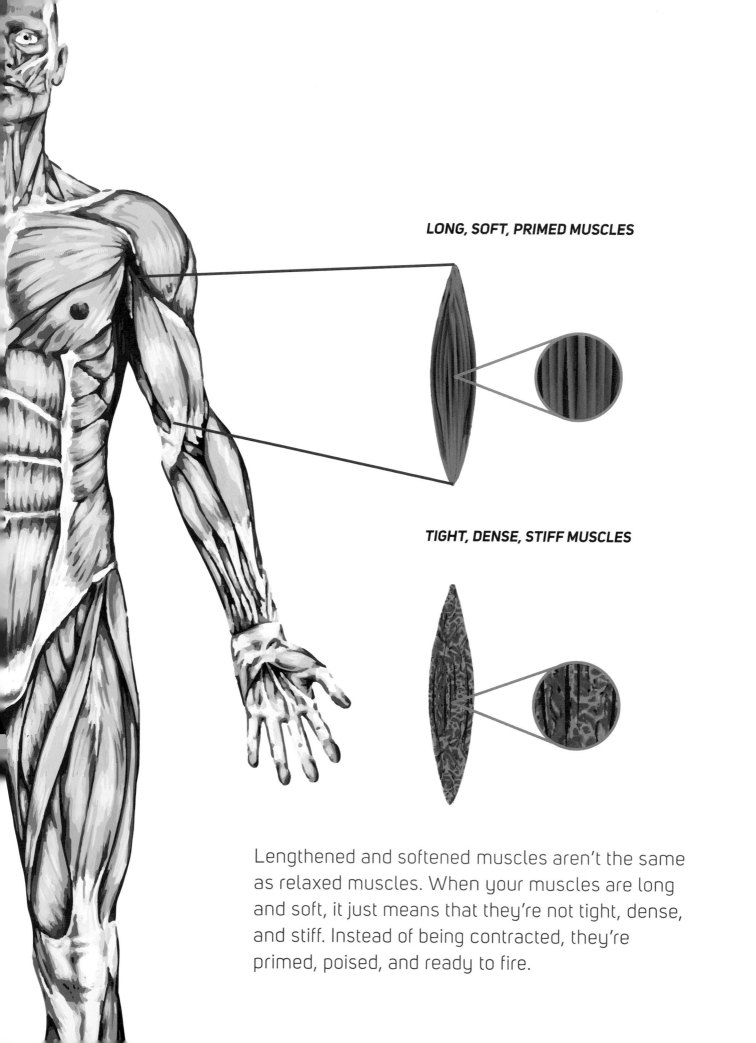

LONG, SOFT, PRIMED MUSCLES

TIGHT, DENSE, STIFF MUSCLES

Lengthened and softened muscles aren't the same as relaxed muscles. When your muscles are long and soft, it just means that they're not tight, dense, and stiff. Instead of being contracted, they're primed, poised, and ready to fire.

model, throughout professional sports history, no one has given much thought to what it means to "play for a long time." The focus has always been on "playing." Athletes just want to make the team. If they get injured a few years later, instead of pointing fingers at the training they've done their whole lives, they blame the sport.

But being a professional means taking responsibility for your body, your health, and your career. If *you* don't, who will? It means you ask *why* you're doing what you're doing. If elevating your heart rate and lifting weights works so well, then why are the statistics around them so bad?

Consider that every year in the United States, two million high school athletes are injured, which leads to more than 500,000 doctor's visits, which lead to way too many surgeries. College players are just as prone to injury, and so are adult amateur athletes. Seventy percent of all college athletes say that they've played through an injury at least once, and more than a million adult amateur athletes get a sports-related injury every year. A good pro football career lasts around 10 years, but the average NFL career today is 3.3 years, with most of those careers cut short by injury. Younger players are leaving the game earlier, too. In 2014, nineteen players age thirty or younger retired from the NFL, versus five players back in 2005. Players say the biggest reason is their fear of the long-term effects of playing while injured. I don't have that fear. Bottom line: Playing sports increases the likelihood of injuries because you more regularly confront excessive loads and forces. That's why, as an athlete, if I want to live a healthier life on and off the field, I have to make great choices that are aligned with my goals.

But first, let's go back to high school, where most athletes are introduced to strength training. In order to get better at their sport, they're urged to lift weights, and to increase the amount of weight they lift as time goes on. *Without incorporating pliability, their muscles become tight, dense, and stiff. They lose their muscle pump function—which leads to imbalances in their bodies. Imbalances lead to muscle compensation. Muscle compensation leads to muscle overload—and muscle overload leads to injury. Here a balance of strength, conditioning, and pliability needs to take place—but all too often doesn't. Once you determine how much strength you need, that's when you should determine how much pliability you need as well.*

This same cycle (and training system) follows athletes into college, which is where a lot of athletes keep getting injured without understanding why. It continues into professional sports. If a player is already lifting, say, 225 pounds for fifteen reps on a bench press—for whatever reason, bench presses and squats are the most common criteria for strength—he feels he should lift even more. Every day I see players bench-pressing 300 or 400 pounds, and when they tear a muscle, they tell themselves it's because they didn't stretch enough beforehand. They don't realize that nine times out of ten, their muscle tear had nothing to do with stretching—tears happen because muscles are not absorbing and dispersing the amount of force placed on them. How do you change that? By putting an emphasis on pliability in order to create a balance that can help absorb those extreme forces.

It isn't only healthy players who feel the pressure to lift more, and harder, and longer. Even injured players gravitate toward a set of corrective exercises that involve improving strength. As I said, there's a widespread belief that injury is the direct result of muscle weakness—that an injured muscle needs to be *re*strengthened. But muscle soreness or pain is mostly the result of muscles that are *over*loaded. The last

The movements of everyday life—standing, sitting, walking—can cause our muscles to become tight, dense, and stiff. Pliability in any form helps lengthen and soften them. In this picture I'm doing self-pliability on my right triceps. Again, the forceful stroke I'm making is in the direction of the heart.

Working on my right forearm, targeting all sides of the muscle. The brain and body won't learn new behaviors unless it's through positive and intentional trauma. As I do self-pliability, I'm targeting the front, middle, and back of my forearm while rhythmically contracting and relaxing it.

PLIABILITY: A DEEPER DIVE

51

In this book I often say that during a pliability session you should *contract and relax your muscles rhythmically*. But how fast is *rhythmically*? The answer depends on the sport you play or the activities you engage in in your daily life. The movements you make should ideally mimic the speed of your sport or activity. If you practice yoga, your muscle contractions should be at the speed of yoga—or faster. A road-biker doing pliability treatment on his calves should mimic the muscle movements that he makes on his bike—or, again, slightly faster. I train fast, because in the sport I play, I think fast and move fast, which is why during pliability sessions, I try to make two muscle contractions every second—and I'm still trying to improve on *that*.

thing athletes should do is strengthen an injured muscle more than they already have without first bringing it into balance through pliability training. Once balance is restored, *that's* when restrengthening should occur. In addition, a lot of athletes still believe that the only thing they need to do to keep themselves fit is to stay strong and conditioned while maintaining low body fat. They don't want to hear that all the work, energy, and sweat they've put into their workouts could be damaging. They've spent years doing things one way. And until they discover pliability, they have no idea they can have a body or a career free of the pain that athletes of the past have endured.

What most athletes don't ask and should be asking is: *How can I train to* not *get hurt? Why is strength important, but only up to a point? What are the things I need to do, and the decisions I need to make, to keep myself from getting hurt, or from injuring myself without meaning to, in the future?*

From high school through college and today in the pros, I've seen over and over again the impact that injuries have on players and teammates. I've also seen more athletes than I can count navigating a system that emphasizes short-term solutions that target symptoms, not causes. Hurt your hamstring? Then let's just focus on the hamstring. Why don't we instead ask *why* you hurt your hamstring—and what you can do to keep it from getting hurt again? If an injury is the result of excessive force, why don't we figure out ways the body can absorb that force? But we don't. When something breaks, we try to fix it and then we move on, without addressing the root causes. But surgery for durability is an oxymoron. Having surgery doesn't *lengthen* your career—it *shortens* it. The result is more injuries and more broken athletes, not just across pro football but in all sports, and at all ages and levels.

Another problem created by the traditional strength and conditioning model? The one-size-fits-all philosophy. Let's look at football. A pro football team has around seventy players, and trainers typically track player data over the course of the season. Again, most athletes grew up believing that the stronger they get, the better their overall performance will be. That's just not true. *Strength matters, but only as it relates to the function of the job an athlete is being asked to do, or the position he or she is playing.* In my case, my friends all know that I'm not going around carrying heavy dumbbells. During my workouts, I'm focused instead on doing the things that can help me to do my job better. What *is* my job? As an NFL quarterback, my job is to stand in the pocket, cut, run, throw, and generally withstand the tough nature of the sport I've played for more than two decades. How strong do I need to be? How much weight do I need to lift? The answers are based on a variety of factors, including my weight, my body fat percentage, and the stability of my core.

What's the job of an offensive lineman? Well, an offensive lineman needs to be strong, and to develop dense muscles, and to push and brace against a lot of incoming weight. How about a wide receiver, whose job it is to run and catch the ball? How much strength does *he* need, and how much weight should *he* lift?

We're all born with natural pliability—and strength. When we're in our teens, we begin strengthening and conditioning to balance our natural scale. By our mid-twenties, we've begun to lose our natural pliability. But believing that strength is what helped us achieve our goals, we strengthen even more. In fact, what we need to help restore our natural balance is *pliability*.

Certainly not as much as the offensive lineman. In the end, a wide receiver *needs to get his muscles to work appropriately for the actions he's asking them to do.* Once you determine how much strength you need, that's when to determine how much pliability you need to do.

Day after day I see players working extremely hard at doing the wrong thing. I'm talking about some of my own teammates, too. They're committed to greater strength and conditioning, but often they're doing it at levels that won't ever pay off for them. It's a system of diminishing returns. So why do they keep doing it—and why do trainers keep teaching it? Because it's all they were ever taught. If you're doing the wrong thing, and working hard at it, you're just getting a lot better at getting worse—and at a faster rate, too. Imagine you have a faulty golf swing. If you keep practicing the same way you always have, you'll only end up reinforcing your own bad form. Why not focus instead on what will get you to where you want to go? We've all heard the definition of insanity—doing the same thing over and over again and expecting different results. Well, sports training is the apotheosis of that. Way too often, we get trapped in the same old routines.

Doing sprints, lifting weights, and the pain, rehab, and recovery that follow make up a vicious cycle that injures and spits out athletes year after year. It's not only institutionalized but it's also extremely profitable for a lot of people. There's not a lot of money to be made from healthy athletes, or, for that matter, from healthy people. The sports training system today is also linked to a mind-set that's focused on short-term gains. Coaches, trainers, and athletes all want big wins *now*. Most of them don't have the patience to develop the mind-set it takes to achieve consistent, continuous results. Still, if I've learned one thing as I go into my eighteenth NFL season, it's how important it is to devote yourself to an attitude of sustained peak performance that never wavers in its longer-term perspective. Playing sports, especially professionally, is a multiyear commitment and endeavor. Would I want to play sports for only a few years, or would I want to play at the highest levels for a decade, two decades, or longer? The answer is obvious.

As I said in the introduction, it can be hard for younger athletes to wrap their heads around the concept of pliability. Few of them are thinking long-term—and the same goes for most of us. It's a human bias to focus on short-term gains without factoring in their longer-term consequences. When you're younger, you feel invincible. You haven't experienced years and years of muscle contractions, overloads, and injuries. You also don't feel the impact of poor lifestyle choices or habits as much as you do when you're older. I tell younger athletes they have all the tread on their tires right now—but what do they want, and how do they see themselves, in the future? Still, their motivation may not be there. Given a choice between spending hours per week doing pliability or being with their friends, most of them will choose their friends. Then there are those athletes who've been working out one way for a long time and don't want to change their routine, out of fear they won't achieve the same results.

What does it mean to not get hurt? It means I've given myself the opportunity to be the best I can be, year after year, mentally and physically. And once you incorporate pliability into your strength and conditioning regimen, along with the other amplifiers this book goes into, I know it will take you where you want to go.

Nine years ago, I strained my right groin tendon (a very common football injury). One of the doctors I consulted recommended surgery, saying there was a 99 percent chance the strain would bother me during the entire season. He also warned me that my *left* groin muscle would probably need the same surgery sometime within the next twenty-four months. After weighing my options, I decided on a more holistic approach. Alex and I decided to work on it differently— through pliability training over the next three weeks. After lengthening and softening my right groin muscle, along with the other muscle groups in my leg that correlated to my movements, the tension was removed from my tendon, and I felt zero pain. In the eleven years since, I've never had another right groin problem. It's understandable that a doctor would recommend surgery, based on his own experience and training—without understanding the benefits of pliability.

SUSTAINED PEAK
PERFORMANCE

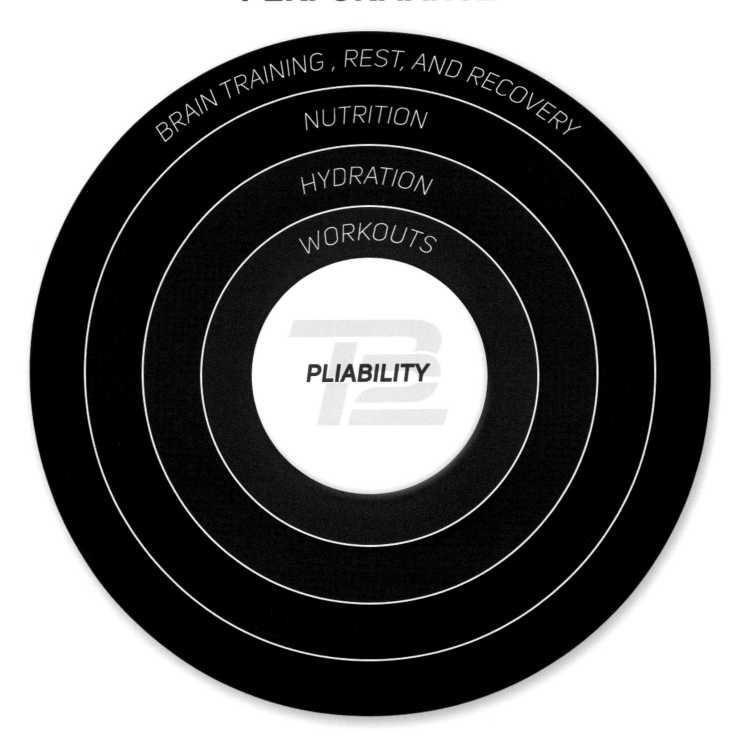

BRAIN TRAINING , REST, AND RECOVERY

NUTRITION

HYDRATION

WORKOUTS

PLIABILITY

Achieving sustained peak performance doesn't happen through pliability alone. The amplifiers you'll be reading about in the pages ahead—hydration, nutrition, and brain training, rest, and recovery—accelerate pliability and ensure that your inner environment is just as healthy and balanced as your outer environment.

WHAT IS PLIABILITY?

Pliability is the name Alex and I give to the training regimen he and I do every day. Using his hands and elbows, Alex performs targeted, deep-force muscle work to lengthen and soften every muscle of my body as I rhythmically contract and relax that muscle. We almost always focus on my entire body, unless one area takes up more of our time. He and I do this twice—once before a full workout and again after—for reasons I'll explain in a moment.

Pliability is different from massage. But for the sake of visuals, imagine that I'm lying on a table. Instead of lying there passively, I'm rhythmically contracting and expanding my muscles as Alex works on them one at a time. My calf, my hamstring, my quad, my triceps, my biceps—up to twenty muscle groups in all. As I contract and relax each muscle, Alex, using optimal pressure and forces similar to those I experience playing, training, or carrying out the daily acts of living, strokes *through* that muscle, in isolation and always toward the heart, for twenty seconds on average. Rather than working all the muscles of my body simultaneously, he focuses on each part of each muscle—the outside (lateral), the inside (medial), and the middle. The pressure he applies is intense—again, trying to mimic what I experience in my life. Once, when a team at the Massachusetts Institute of Technology tested us, the researchers found that Alex was applying anywhere from fifty to one hundred newtons (a unit of force) of pressure using just his finger. When he uses the point of his elbow, the pressure can approach four hundred newtons or more. That's almost *ninety pounds* of force. That means Alex is applying ninety pounds of force to individual areas of my muscles. The sheer amount of pressure he exerts trains my brain to create neuropathways—and neural-primes my muscles

for the extreme amounts of impact I face over the course of a practice, a game, or my life in general. Alex is educating my brain *and* my muscles to stay lengthened, softened, and primed, which is a big reason why I'm able to absorb and disperse hits well.

As Alex and I do pliability training, a number of critical benefits are taking place in my body and brain.

As he forcefully strokes through each muscle, always toward the heart, while I contract and relax it, Alex is educating that muscle to fire at 100 percent capacity— or, as we say at TB12, with *100 percent muscle pump function*. He's educating my muscles to stay lengthened and softened, as well as primed, while doing their functions. By giving each of my muscles a positive and intentional "traumatic" experience as he lengthens and softens it, Alex is helping forge the connection between my brain and body. He's teaching my brain and body that long, soft, and primed is how I want my muscles to respond to the movement my brain is asking of them. Together, our goal is to help my muscles reach the same lengthened, softened, primed state I need them to be in while carrying out the acts of daily living, which for me include training and playing.

I undergo many of the exact same treatments every time. The process of lengthening and softening my muscles is predictable and repetitive. The only time the routine varies is if I've been traveling or doing things that have made my muscles tighten, stiffen, and grow dense, or if I'm focusing on a muscle that's been damaged from impact (say, my shoulder) or a body part such as my leg. Otherwise, the process of pliability is very routine. If I'm overbuilt, or dense, in one area, that's when I know I need to lengthen and soften the muscles in question. If I've done a lot of chest workouts with bands, that will make my muscles dense. When I start to throw, I can tell that I'm not as fluid as I should be, which means that I've overbuilt those muscles. The solution is to rebalance those muscles by lengthening and softening them.

As I said, I do pliability both before and after a full workout, but each session is slightly different in its purpose. In the before part of pliability, I'm training my muscles to stay long, soft, and primed during the workout I'm about to put them through. If you think about it, a runner doesn't just show up on a track and run a 100-yard sprint. First he primes his muscles—and the *before* part of pliability does the same thing for me.

Next comes the point where I stop doing pliability and begin my actual workout. I may work on drop-backs or throwing mechanics. I may run or swim or do strength training. If I'm at the TB12 Sports Therapy Center, I'll do a full-body workout using resistance bands, trying to activate 100 percent muscle pump function in every part of my body—feet, ankles, shins, quads, glutes, core, shoulders, arms, neck, and so on—maintaining full muscle pump function through full range of motion.

Right at the point in the workout when my arm or leg muscles start to tire, I'll stop working out and finish with another pliability session—but there's a small difference. During the *after* session of pliability, I'm focused mostly

on flushing out lactic acid to facilitate lymph movement, allowing more oxygenated blood to rejuvenate my muscles. The strokes are similar, but there's less force and less speed as I contract and relax my muscles. Again, I'm training my brain to store what my muscles have just learned. What have they learned? They've learned to be long, soft, and primed through intense training movements—the same movements I use in games. That's what ideal training looks like to me.

I go through this process again and again. In this way, my brain learns new habits and responses, and by remaining in a lengthened, softened, primed state, my muscles are much less likely to get hurt. Why? Because when my body comes up against force—say, two defenders trying to tackle me—my muscles can more easily absorb and disperse that force. Imagine the alternative, where, say, three of my muscles are responsible for absorbing force, but two of them are so dense that they can't contract and relax fully, and therefore can't evenly absorb and disperse the impact. That means the remaining muscle, the weakest in the chain, so to speak, takes the full brunt of the impact. This muscle becomes overloaded with force—and that overload often results in an acute injury.

As I've stated repeatedly, pliability is the game changer and should be incorporated by all athletes at all ages if they want to try to avoid injury and sustain their own peak performance. In the end, doing pliability is about training *smarter*. Over the years, I've made a proactive choice to reallocate the time I used to spend doing wind sprints, running up hills, and lifting weights to getting daily pliability instead. I credit the pliability I've done with the fact that, except for my 2008 ACL injury, I've played the past seventeen seasons without significant injury.

Now I'll explain pliability step-by-step, beginning with what our brains and our bodies store, and why.

At TB12, we look at things through four different lenses.

1) Am I increasing oxygenation?
2) Am I reducing inflammation?
3) Am I optimizing pliability?
4) Are my goals aligned with my training regimen?

HOW A BRAIN LEARNS

Our brains are the central processing centers for what our bodies do and how we live. That includes how our muscles move, respond, and behave. Our brains communicate with our muscles via nerve cells called neurons. Neurons connect to a specific muscle—the glute, the hamstring, the biceps, and so on. When I pick a football up off the ground, it may look straightforward, but the act of picking up a ball is the result of a lot of brain–body coordination. Before I reach down, a neuron in my brain fires, causing a neuron in my spinal cord to fire. My spinal cord relays a series of impulses that travel down one side of that neuron to my shoulder, arm, and hand muscles. My muscle fibers shorten and grow dense. Once I pick up the ball, they go back to their relaxed position. The whole operation—impulse to pick up the ball, neuron firing, chemical impulses, short, dense muscles—takes place in an instant.

Human behavior is either innate, or instinctual—like smiling, laughing, or crying—or else it's learned, meaning it comes from our personal experience. In both cases, our brains and bodies memorize and store that behavior or those patterns.

When we're young, and in our teens and early twenties, we're at the peak of good health. Our bodies are extremely pliable. They have plenty of collagen, which helps our muscles contract and relax fully and evenly. We also recover quickly. As time goes on, our brains and bodies begin accumulating both negative and positive habits, experiences, and traumas, which our brains store in their neural pathways. Imagine that you fell off your bike when you were a kid, or you injured a muscle playing a sport in high school. Your brain stores that traumatic event in its neural pathways, and the memory of that event, conscious or unconscious, determines how your body responds to any future movement related to that muscle or bone or tendon. It doesn't matter whether the event took place one year ago or ten years ago. It's now a muscle memory.

That's why if you start running up hills and doing wind sprints and lifting heavy weights in high school, as most athletes do, over time the brain locks in these habits and movements, and they become learned behaviors that teach your body how you want your muscles to function—reinforced by the fact that every other athlete is doing the same thing. You won't change those behaviors until the negative trauma is replaced by the positive traumas of pliability training. Say that you ask your body to lift heavy weights. Then you ask it to run and cut. Then throw. Then rest. By training your body to do a lot of different things, it can get confused. That's why the more we train our bodies to do the tasks specific to the sports we play, or to our daily acts of living, the less our brains have to learn, and the less our bodies have to adjust.

LYMPHATIC SYSTEM

The lymphatic system is a network of tissues, vessels, and organs that serves as a kind of vacuum cleaner inside our bodies. The lymph system cleanses and helps eliminate toxins, wastes, and other unwanted substances by draining a colorless, clear fluid, known as lymph, from our tissues and funneling it back into the bloodstream, always in the direction of the heart. It also helps our bodies maintain fluid balance and absorb fats and nutrients. Pliability—as well as optimal muscle pump function—facilitates the expulsion of lymph from our body's tissues, leading to healthier, stronger muscles.

BODY IMBALANCES

Many of the clients who come into the TB12 Sports Therapy Center for the first time have no idea their bodies are imbalanced, and that their muscles aren't contracting evenly, at 100 percent. Often the underlying issue is an imbalance.

Body imbalances, which can come from the acts of everyday life—walking, running, working out, wearing the wrong shoes, and so forth—are extremely common. Bear in mind that the muscles in our body are designed to support our structures. Muscles aren't for strength, and they're not for show. Their function is to protect our bones and to contract, which gives us the strength to move. Imagine you get a charley horse, in which your muscles go into spasm for several seconds, accompanied by severe pain. Or, in my case, imagine that during a game an opponent runs at full speed and smashes his helmet into my thigh (it happens!), injuring my quad muscle. Aware that something is wrong, my brain sends a message to the muscles surrounding my quad muscle. It tells them to contract and become tight, dense, and stiff. In effect, my brain is telling those muscles to create a natural splint to support and protect my injured quad, and to keep it from hyperextending even more, at least until the bruise in my quad goes away.

The problem is, with my quad muscle no longer firing, and the other muscles in my body stepping in to compensate for that injured quad, my body becomes imbalanced. With my quad muscle no longer firing, it goes flat. It won't contract and relax at 100 percent. As a result, that nonfunctioning quad muscle—and the coordination of my right leg—can end up impairing my hip, my knee, my ankle, and my foot. Basically, all the other muscles in my body, with the exception of my quad, have to work harder to accomplish what my brain is asking my body to do.

As with the example I gave earlier of a child falling

There are certain players who just love being in the weight room. Picture a guy who's getting ready to do his last squat. The music is blaring. The whole team is huddled around him. When he gets underneath the bar and does that squat, the whole weight room is cheering. By lifting that weight, basically that player is saying to his teammates, "I'm going to get the job done, whatever it takes." That's great for everyone's mental toughness, and it's also great for team camaraderie. It's almost embedded in who we are as athletes. But if a player really loves doing those kinds of exercises because they make him feel good and he gets rewarded for them, he'd better work just as hard on pliability.

Working with a medicine ball to improve strength and conditioning.

Working with Alex to absorb forces and stresses that can be unpredictable.

It's important to engage your core in *all* aspects of life at *all* times. In this exercise, I'm strengthening my core by adding band resistance through rotation.

Many of the workouts I do are specific to the things I want to really excel at. The key is doing pliability before and after any workout, sport, or activity. If you skip pre- and post-pliability, you increase your chances of getting hurt. Doing pliability is like creating a built-in immune system for sports injuries.

off his bike, imbalances are often the result of unhealed injuries. Imagine a time when you hurt your back lifting a heavy box. You are told to rest by not lifting anything for the next few days and applying ice until your back starts to feel better. You probably *will* feel better—but the question is, do you ever actually *get* better? No, because you haven't changed your brain's response in relation to how you hurt your back in the first place. You hurt your back lifting that heavy box because your back muscles became overloaded by the excess amount of force you were exerting on them. Unless you retrain your brain and your muscles through pliability to understand that your back muscles should respond to lifting the box in an optimal, more efficient way, your back will *still* be overloaded—and you'll have a greater chance of reinjury. To try to avoid reinjuring your back while lifting the same heavy box, you need to balance all the muscle groups that are supposed to work through that particular movement. The point is, the only way to create a change in your brain is by creating a positive and intentional traumatic experience through pliability sessions. Bottom line: no real healing will ever take place in your body unless the brain and the body work together.

Most people with imbalances have gotten *good* at doing things *badly*, whether it's walking, running, or playing football. Some daily acts of living are unconscious. We walk, run, and sit with imbalances. Multiply that by thousands, or millions, and that's a lot of compensation and overload, often resulting in injury. For example, before I met Alex, the muscles in my throwing arm had

lost their natural pliability. They'd lost optimal muscle pump function. They were contracting and relaxing at, say, 50 percent. It was a vicious cycle: My arm muscles were so tight that they could no longer fully contract and relax. Deprived of sufficient blood and oxygenation, they couldn't heal. Why weren't they getting sufficient blood and oxygenation? Because they couldn't contract and relax. The only solution was pliability, the lengthening and softening of my arm muscles, which gave that arm the ability to fully contract and relax, with 100 percent muscle pump function, and allowed for great recovery.

LACTIC ACID

Whenever we exercise, our muscles require greater amounts of oxygen. Sometimes we exercise so hard that our circulatory system can't keep up with our body's demands. In order to maintain the oxygen that our muscles need, a switch takes place. The body transitions from what's known as aerobic metabolism to another state, known as anaerobic metabolism. That's when our bodies begin breaking down our stored glucose and converting it to lactic acid, otherwise known as lactate. This lactate is then used to replenish muscular energy. Even after intense exercise, lactate normally leaves our bodies over time, naturally or through perspiration—but pliability expedites the elimination of that lactate and helps restore the body to a less acidic, more naturally alkaline condition.

Over the years, a lot of quarterbacks have told me they want to change their technique. The thing is, their brains may want to change, but until they make a brain–body connection with pliability, their muscles won't allow it. A big part of my ongoing improvement with throwing mechanics comes from the daily pliability work I do. Because I'm making those connections between my brain and my body, my muscles can make the mechanical changes that help me throw the ball better and move more efficiently in the pocket. The bottom line? Whatever changes I want to make in my throwing mechanics, I can. I train my brain to ask my muscles to work differently. This can only be achieved through pliability treatments—positive, intentional trauma that causes new learned behaviors.

MUSCLE MEMORY

Aerobic activity, or sprinting, followed by weight lifting, is the core of the traditional strength and conditioning model. In strength training, when you bench press two hundred pounds, what exactly are you training your muscles to do? The answer: to contract hard, to remain tight, dense, and stiff, and to brace the heavy weight that your body is up against. Not only are you training your body but you're also teaching your brain that *tight, dense,* and *stiff* is the optimal condition of your muscles, based on the function of lifting weights. The problem is, if you are playing in a game a few days later and a lineman tackles you, it's possible that those same tight, dense, stiff muscles will lead to a torn muscle or a broken bone, because your body couldn't absorb the forces in a balanced way. Those two hundred pounds that you've been bench pressing have come at the expense of lengthened, softened, primed muscles that could have dispersed that hit. As it stands in the weight lifting example above, an arm or a leg in a constant state of contraction, which won't bend easily, has very little function on the field—except for, say, certain positions that brace against a lot of incoming weight. That's not to say we don't need strength—we need *optimal* strength to remain balanced—but more than that, we need pliability to complement that strength, in order to increase our *durability.*

Bottom line: Whatever messages our brains send to our muscles, and that our muscles send to our brains, will be stored in the brain's neural pathways. *Negative traumas are stored there until they are challenged and replaced by the positive traumas we experience through pliability treatments.*

NEGATIVE VERSUS POSITIVE TRAUMA

Trauma is a loaded word, and I want to explain what I mean by it. I don't believe the body differentiates between kinds of trauma. All it knows is that it has experienced an external force that's causing a response in the body and the brain. Most players will say there's a difference between positive and negative trauma. One happens in practice, or in the weight room, when you incur excessive amounts of force from running, cutting, or lifting. This can also happen in a game. Still, the only thing your muscles know is that they're contracting to absorb forces—and contracting hard.

The body may not discriminate between kinds of trauma, but for the purposes of pliability, I do.

Of the two kinds of traumas, the one I describe above is called *negative-unintentional*. It's usually the result of an injury that is sometimes beyond a player's control—slipping and falling, a bike crash, etc. The second kind of trauma, which creates pliable muscles, is called *positive-intentional*. During both negative-unintentional and positive-intentional cases, the brain and the body experience forces that are unfamiliar. And the brain stores these forces as muscle memory in order to protect its structure.

However, the positive-intentional trauma exerted on me through targeted, deep-force muscle work during pliability trains my body and brain to deal with the negative-unintentional traumas that I face in games, practice, or any other environment that's beyond my control. Through positive-intentional trauma, I create neural pathways that improve my body's ability to deal with the stresses of the sport I play.

As a result of the positive-intentional trauma I get from doing pliability, my muscles learn to stay

Over several occasions at the MIT Media Lab, researchers measured the amount of force Alex and I both exerted during a typical pliability session. They found that when Alex uses his hands, he exerts anywhere from fifty to one hundred newtons of pressure—newtons are a unit of force—and when he uses his elbows, it goes up to four times that amount. (Certain muscles may require fifty newtons, others four hundred. It depends on the density of the muscle.) In response, I make two muscle contractions every second. Four hundred newtons is the equivalent of *ninety pounds of pressure* on one muscle group at a time. *That's* pliable.

long, soft, and primed, and are able to handle what-ever comes my way on or off the field. Why? Because they're in a balanced state, which absorbs and dis-perses the force any one of my muscles takes at any one time. As I said earlier, when I stand in the pocket, I never know when I'm going to be hit. The moment an opposing player's helmet makes contact with my body, my body is able to absorb that hit thanks to daily pliability. Throughout the movement my mus-cles remain long, soft, and primed. Whatever impact I experience is absorbed and dispersed evenly through-out many muscle groups, and not just the specific area where I got hit.

When athletes get injured, they shouldn't blame their sport— or their age. Injuries happen when our bodies are unable to absorb or disperse the amount of force placed on them. If our bodies can handle that force, it doesn't matter what sport we play or how old we are. That's why age isn't my problem!

TRAINING THE BRAIN

The brain is composed of tens of billions of cells called neurons, which make connections with other neurons. These connections are called synapses, and our brains contain hundreds of trillions of them. Whenever we learn something new, these synapses thicken, increase, and connect to other neurons to strengthen what we've just learned. The stronger those synapses, and the more neurons they call on, the better our brains can store and retrieve information. To create stronger, faster connec-tions in our brains, we need to practice a habit, skill, or behavior again and again. In turn, our brains generate synapses linked to that habit, skill, or behavior, and call on them anytime we do that thing. The more we prac-tice that habit, skill, or behavior, the more automatically our brains recognize it. Thanks to neuroplasticity—that is, the brain's ability to keep growing, changing, and learning throughout life—pliability retrains the brain by introducing new behavior patterns—in this case, the lengthening and softening of our muscles. Over time, the brain and body realize that this is how we want our muscles to behave as they carry out the jobs we're ask-ing them to do.

TRAIN YOUR BRAIN, CHANGE YOUR BODY

Earlier I wrote that pliability is different from massage. In what way? The key to pliability is stimulating and reeducating the brain by creating new neural pathways. Massage by itself doesn't do that because it's passive. There's no contraction of your muscles through movement, which means the brain doesn't understand that your muscles need to stay in a long, soft, primed state. Therefore, no muscle pump function takes place. After getting a typical massage, for a few hours or possibly a day most people feel better, thanks to increased blood flow and a big rush of endorphins. Then they go back to doing what they were doing before. Their brains and muscles haven't learned anything, because no real education has taken place. Static massage doesn't educate muscles. Only positive-intentional trauma through pliability does that.

The goal of pliability is to evoke a positive neural response in my body before a workout. This process is called *neural priming*. When I receive targeted, deep-force work on one of my muscles, I'm forcing my brain to create connections between its neurons and to forge new neuropathways. By doing this again and again, the amount of input my brain neurons need in order to fire up my muscles—whether I do that through working out, running on a treadmill, or using resistance bands—becomes automatic. That's why Alex likes to quote the axiom *Neurons that fire together wire together*.

Thanks to pliability, as the season goes on, I actually begin to feel better, since my brain–body connection gets stronger around the daily functions I'm asking each of them to do. In the off-season, by contrast, with my workouts varying from week to week,

it's harder, and my body is actually more sore than it is during the season. My muscles never get good and truly primed for movement. My guess is that the off-season is when many football players neural-prime their way to getting injured *during* the season. That's why I've changed my own off-season training to replicate, as best as I possibly can, what I do during the season.

Whether you're eighteen or eighty years old, you can attain a higher state of pliability. This means that your muscles are firing at 100 percent, evenly, and that there's reduced load in your muscles. If a college athlete comes into the TB12 Sports Therapy Center looking for sustained peak performance, in general Alex will tell him it takes about thirty days to notice a difference. After twelve months, that athlete will notice huge leaps. I just turned forty, but I *feel* like I'm thirty.

PLIABILITY BASICS

Most of us are born with adequate amounts of pliability, and some people are born with more pliability than others. As I said earlier, in childhood, adolescence, and into our twenties, our bodies and muscles keep generating plenty of collagen, and this innate pliability accelerates our recovery from exertion and injury. Our blood is oxygen-rich. Our muscles contract and relax evenly, at 100 percent. We're pliable pretty much all the time.

But as our bodies undergo one negative traumatic experience after the next—falls, scrapes, and injuries, as well as heavy weight training and overload—our natural pliability begins to deteriorate. We focus on strength and conditioning, not realizing that our pliability is slowly running out. Even if we've been active our whole lives, we all notice a decrease in our pliability starting when we're in our mid-twenties. It becomes harder and harder to work out the way we once did. Our bodies may still be creating and storing collagen, but they're less able to break down and metabolize the lactic acid that begins to accumulate and calcify in our muscles. By the age of fifty or sixty, we have roughly 50 percent less pliability and muscle function than we did when we were in our twenties. And unless we do pliability training, we won't ever get 100 percent muscle contraction, which circulates oxygen-rich blood from muscle group to muscle group.

COLLAGEN

Collagen is the most abundant protein in the body. Found mostly in our skin, bones, and connective tissue, it gives our bodies strength, structure, and elasticity. When we are young, our bodies create and regenerate collagen easily. But as we age, our collagen production declines, and the proteins that make up collagen become more rigid. The result is less elasticity in the skin, organs, and muscles, longer recovery times, and muscular stiffness and soreness. Thanks in part to our natural collagen levels, we don't need as much pliability when we're young as we do when we're older—which explains why younger athletes naturally focus on building up their strength. But beginning in our mid-twenties, we need to find a balance between strength, conditioning, and pliability to compensate for the collagen that we lose over time.

Right now, at this point in my career, and speaking structurally, I'm as balanced as I've ever been. I feel like my muscles fire evenly and at 100 percent. I'm not overbuilt in any one area, which gives me huge advantages on the field. A lot of the time I'll be playing against athletes who are structurally imbalanced. They have traded pliability for overstrengthening or overconditioning, and I believe they have a higher probability of getting injured. I'm blessed to have both experience *and* durability.

PLIABILITY BY AGE

Our need for pliability depends not just on our job or function but also on our age and our goals. There are big physical differences between a twenty-two-year-old and a forty-year-old. For example, at age forty, I have eighteen years of strength on the average twenty-two-year-old player. But the twenty-two-year-old has more natural pliability than I do in the form of collagen, which gives his body strength, support, and structure—basically, he has more tread on his tires. Ideally, athletes should begin pliability at the same time they begin strength training. In general, a twenty-two-year-old athlete needs more strength and conditioning than a forty-year-old athlete, and a player my age needs more pliability than he needs strength and conditioning. That's why today my workouts consist of 25 percent strengthening, 25 percent conditioning—and 50 percent pliability. If I were twenty-two again, I would devote a quarter of my workout to pliability and the rest to strengthening and conditioning.

One of the advantages I have over younger athletes is that at age forty, I'm pliable *and* I have experience. Younger athletes have natural pliability but fewer seasons under their belts than I do. If I can negate their natural advantage, I'm in a great competitive position, both physically and in terms of experience. As long as I remain pliable, they can't catch me—and *that's* why I made the shift to the workouts I do today.

The good news for athletes who aren't twenty-two anymore? You're never too old to get the benefits of pliability: 100 percent contraction in all your muscles,

NATURAL PLIABILITY BY AGE

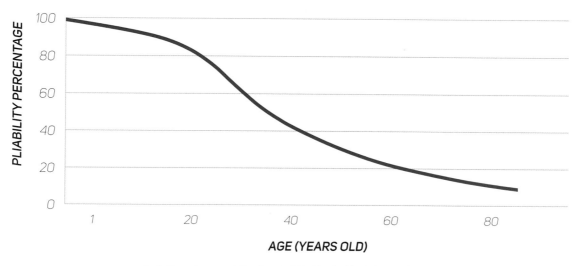

Illustrative: not representative of any individual involved but indicative of natural pliability trends.

Reflecting in my office, 2017.

which in turn allows for greater blood oxygen levels. The greater your blood oxygen levels, the more fully your muscles can expand and contract. The better your muscles can expand and contract, the better your lymph system is able to flush toxins from your system. The result will be healthy—and pliable—muscles, along with energy and vitality.

You'll also be surprised by the effects pliability can have on everyday injuries and conditions. Thanks to oxygen-rich blood infusing every muscle in your body,

optimal pliability allows for ongoing regeneration. Strength training (without pliability), on the other hand, creates tight, dense, stiff muscles, limited muscle expansion and contraction, less oxygen-rich blood, and overall degeneration. Over time, this unhealthy environment leads to injury—which in turn leads to less muscle pump function, less oxygenation, and less rejuvenation. Unfortunately, this is what aging currently looks like for 99.9 percent of the world.

Some injuries are just part of the job, and beyond the control of any athlete. Take, for example, a hip pointer, when you get a direct blow to your hip bone. That's a line-of-duty injury, and often difficult to avoid. But some other injuries, like muscle strains, are, in my experience, most likely avoidable if you are committed to pliability and its amplifiers. If you play football or another sport in which you know you'll get hit every week, before getting into that collision, you'd better start thinking, *How am I going to prepare my body* before *it gets hit?* What you do on and off the field in terms of developing and maintaining your pliability is critical to helping prevent injury and lowering the chances of injury when you *do* get hit.

INFLAMMATION: A PRIMER

In the sport I play, I know I'm going to get hit. There is going to be trauma, and my body will naturally create trauma responses to ease the pain and soreness after every game. Even if our thoughts and emotions play no part in generating inflammation—but in fact they do!—if you play any kind of sport at any level, it's a given that you'll end up with some degree of inflammation. So let's take a closer look at what inflammation means.

There are two kinds—*acute inflammation* and *chronic inflammation*. Acute inflammation, which lasts only a few days, is a natural response of our bodies' immune system. When we get injured, the body sends in small proteins, known as cytokines, that fence off the affected area and clean away the damaged cells while circulating oxygen, nutrients, and antibodies that help our bodies deal with infection and accelerate healing and recovery. Along with helping our blood clot, these natural proteins trigger the pain, swelling, and high temperatures that go along with recovery.

Chronic inflammation, on the other hand, happens when the body is continually sending out the same white blood cells and cytokines in response to what it perceives as a threat. These white blood cells and cytokines have no idea they're targeting healthy muscles or their tissues. They're only doing what they're supposed to do. The thing is, our bodies aren't designed to deal with everyday inflammation responses, and over time our white blood cells can begin degrading our organs and our bones. Low-level everyday inflammation is thought to play a part in some long-term diseases and conditions. There's also the inflammation that takes place in the gut that can interfere with how we absorb nutrients like calcium and vitamin D, which help keep our bones healthy.

Inflammation is inevitable when you do what I do for a living. Every workout I do causes microscopic damage to my muscle fibers that typically goes away after a period of recovery. At forty, my goal is to reduce inflammation in my body any way I can through pliability, and with the help of other amplifiers I'll be talking about later in this book. Stacking inflammation in the form of poor nutrition, alcohol, etc., is in my mind not sustainable if your goal is to maximize your potential.

Alex and I believe pliability can meaningfully help cure a lot of common sports injuries, including tennis elbow, plantar fasciitis, lower back pain, and many others—including breaking down scar tissue or preventing it from building up in the first place—and minimizing inflammation from surgeries.

TENNIS ELBOW occurs when a player strains the tendon that connects the forearm to the elbow joint. Why has the tendon been strained, generally? Because an accumulation of excess tension has been placed on it. Therefore, the tendon becomes overloaded over a period of time. The solution is pliability, and the lengthening and softening of all the muscle groups in the arm to create balance. Once the muscles are balanced, as well as soft, long, and primed through the daily functional movements the brain asks the elbow to perform, the tension goes away.

PLANTAR FASCIITIS is the inflammation of the ligament band connecting the heel bone to the toes, which causes a lot of pain and discomfort. (It can result from simply wearing shoes with bad heels.) Doctors often prescribe wearing a boot to stretch out the fascia. At TB12, the problem can usually be solved by the lengthening and softening of the plantar fascia through pliability sessions. We have seen this injury very often, and have been successful in treating it and getting our clients back to full strength after only a few sessions.

Then there's **LOWER BACK PAIN**. Doctors and therapists usually prescribe rest, ice, and back-strengthening exercises. But strengthening tight muscles that cause compression, and that result in lower back pain, is not the solution. What they rarely do is target the psoas muscles, or hip flexors, that correlate to lumbar compression. Again, by lengthening and softening the psoas muscles and the muscles of the back, pliability will usually get rid of back pain entirely.

In all three of the examples above, the answer to relieving pain is through pliability. Long, soft, primed muscles will not cause elbow pain, foot pain, or back pain. Once the muscles are pliable and balance is restored in those muscle groups, that's when you strengthen them.

Doing self-pliability on my right triceps—again in the direction of the heart. As you may realize, I always spend adequate time on my right arm.

Q & A

Does Pliability Hurt?

Some people who try pliability for the first time say that they experience a degree of discomfort during and after their first few sessions. A good analogy is weight lifting. If you've never lifted weights, after the first weight training sessions, you'll probably be sore. But over time, that soreness goes away. (Weight lifting, I know, is a bad example, but it's a good analogy that most people can relate to.) In general, whether or not you feel discomfort after pliability depends on how healthy your muscles are—or how dense they are. If they're dry and dehydrated, pliability may take some getting used to, since without adequate hydration, or optimal muscle pump function, the muscles of the body are tight, dense, and stiff. That means it's harder to lengthen and soften them. But the more you lengthen and soften your muscles through pliability, the easier it gets. You can't lengthen and soften your muscles in one day. It takes time, and you need to go step-by-step. It's not about adding yet another time commitment to your day—it's about dividing up your time more intelligently. The key to pliability is repetition and consistency.

Are Women More Naturally Pliable than Men?

No. The idea of pliability is to get the body's muscles to function and fire at 100 percent so that they can perform as well as possible the acts you're asking them to do. Whether you run twelve miles every day, play tennis, or do yoga, the inflammation rates for men and women are the same.

How Long Does It Take to Turn Muscles into Pliable Muscles?

It depends on the person, their age, and on how dense their muscles are. The denser your muscles, the harder it is to make them pliable. In general, a consistent regimen will take anywhere from a week to a month. At a TB12 Sports Therapy Center, we would expect to see significant change in two treatments.

Should I Wait Until I Get Injured to Start Pliability?

No. I understand why some athletes might believe that pliability is a post-injury thing, but you should begin doing it now to prevent injuries—or strains or tears that could lead to injury—in the future. After all, I met with Alex only when the pain in my arm and shoulder was becoming

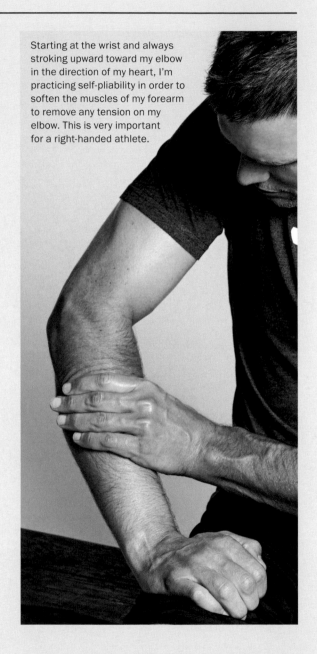

Starting at the wrist and always stroking upward toward my elbow in the direction of my heart, I'm practicing self-pliability in order to soften the muscles of my forearm to remove any tension on my elbow. This is very important for a right-handed athlete.

intolerable. Most of us don't want to spend time preventing things that haven't happened yet. But the foundation of pliability is that it prevents athletes from getting hurt in the first place. We have learned to strengthen. Now we need to learn to lengthen and soften in order to create balance.

Why do I continue getting daily pliability? Because I want to play football for as long as possible. I love my sport. I love my teammates. I love what I do. Ever since I was a kid, my first love was always football, and to me, sustained peak performance means doing what I want to do, and what I love to do, for as long as I can.

TWO FAQS ON PLIABILITY VERSUS FLEXIBILITY AND STRETCHING

What's the difference between pliability and flexibility? Couldn't I get the same effects of pliability from stretching?

It's easy to think that people who've been stretching for the past twenty years would be pliable. That is not necessarily true. Stretching promotes flexibility, but you can't equate flexibility with pliability. There are a few important differences.

Pliability is all about lengthening and softening the muscles. Flexibility, which often comes as a result of stretching, may *lengthen* the muscles to some degree, but it doesn't *soften* them. Lengthening and softening the muscles relieves tension on them. Stretching doesn't.

Second, pliability training always involves—and requires—some level of proactive positive trauma to stimulate the muscle and train the brain to contract and relax the muscle in its fullest state. Throughout our pliability work at TB12, we focus on the brain–body connection. Stretching doesn't do that.

Another issue is that people who are extremely flexible can stretch their ligaments to the point where their ligaments become too loose. This makes it hard for their muscles to contract back to an optimal state. In some cases, it can increase the risk of injury. Whenever people stretch out their back or their legs, they risk creating microtears in the fibers of those muscles, like ropes that have been pulled too tight and begun to fray. To heal microtears, the body sends in lactic acid, which

hardens and scars the muscles. In response, what do most people do? They stretch their muscles all over again. Over time, this cycle of stretching, tearing, and restretching can lead to injury.

This is why stretching is an activity that would actually *benefit from pre- and post-pliability training*. Doing pliability before and after stretching, as you would with any sports activity, can help minimize the amount of muscle tissue microtearing and muscle scarring that could result in injury. You don't get points for sticking your foot behind your neck! Think of pliability as the pre- and post-routine to *any* physical activity or sport, up to and including yoga.

Can I Do Pliability on My Own?

Yes! But here's a disclaimer. Without a doubt, the highest form of pliability comes through targeted, deep-force muscle work provided by a TB12-certified body coach. Achieving optimal pliability isn't altogether possible without the treatments of a body coach trained in those methods. But you can achieve limited amounts of pliability, and experience some of its benefits, by using other methods, which I'll go into in the next chapter. These include self-pliability with assisted devices, self-pliability unassisted, and partner pliability. But the highest form of pliability will always come from a certified TB12 body coach—and that's what I would recommend.

TB / **CHAPTER 5**

TRAINING AND METHODS

This, to me, is the highest form of pliability—
Alex working on my right shoulder before I
practice throwing mechanics.

FOR THE PAST DOZEN YEARS, AS I'VE SAID, I'VE BEEN FORTUNATE ENOUGH TO WORK WITH ALEX, WHO'S ALLOWED ME TO EXPERIENCE PLIABILITY AT THE HIGHEST LEVELS. JUST AS SOME ATHLETES USE COACHES FOR GOLF OR TENNIS, A BODY COACH IS RESPONSIBLE FOR FIGURING OUT HOW EVERY MUSCLE IN YOUR BODY WORKS, IN ISOLATION AND WITH OTHER MUSCLE GROUPS, AND BRINGING YOUR BODY'S STRENGTHS AND DEFICIENCIES INTO BALANCE. I CERTAINLY REALIZE THAT OUTSIDE PROFESSIONAL SPORTS, MOST PEOPLE DON'T HAVE THE LUXURY OF A BODY COACH. BUT THERE ARE MANY WAYS TO INCORPORATE PLIABILITY INTO YOUR STRENGTH AND CONDITIONING REGIMEN THAT COME CLOSE TO REPLICATING THE BENEFITS I GET FROM ALEX'S TARGETED, DEEP-FORCE MUSCLE WORK. THESE RANGE FROM PARTNER PLIABILITY TO SELF-PLIABILITY USING ASSISTED DEVICES SUCH AS VIBRATING FOAM ROLLERS AND VIBRATING SPHERES TO UNASSISTED SELF-PLIABILITY. IN EACH CASE, THE KEY IS TO DO PLIABILITY BOTH BEFORE AND AFTER EXERCISE.

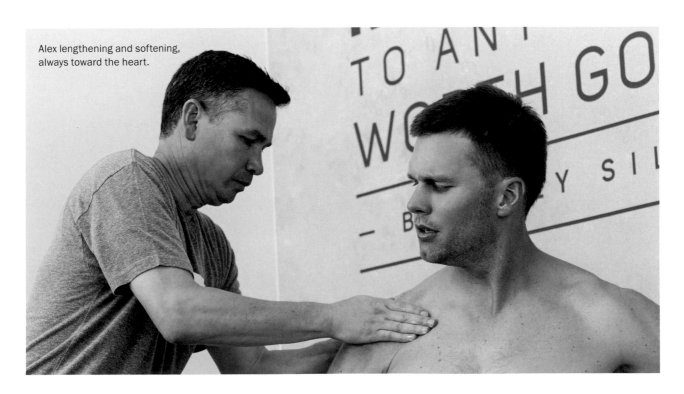

Alex lengthening and softening, always toward the heart.

Whatever form your pliability takes, all methods can fit together. I believe that any method of incorporating optimal pliability into your strength and conditioning regimen will help transform your health, performance, and longevity. The more pliability—and the more balance—the better. However, I want to make it very clear that the best method of achieving optimal pliability is through a certified TB12 body coach.

SELF-PLIABILITY USING ASSISTED DEVICES: VIBRATING FOAM ROLLERS AND VIBRATING SPHERES

Outside of working with a TB12 body coach, to my mind, one of the more useful devices out there for creating and maintaining limited pliability on certain muscles is a vibrating foam roller. Foam rollers target the body's trigger points, as well as larger muscle groups. Trigger points are small patches of tightly contracted tissue that can keep our muscles from getting the blood circulation they need. The regular use of a vibrating foam roller can help muscles recover and revert to more natural states of pliability—but only to a certain degree.

The thing is, foam rollers by themselves don't create optimal pliability. Pliability is as much about neurostimulating our brains as it is about lengthening and softening our muscles—again, the brain–body connection—and to do that, you need some kind of vibrating function. At the TB12 Center, we exclusively use a high-intensity *vibrating foam roller*. When it's used as part of a comprehensive strength, conditioning, and pliability regimen, the roller we use has been clinically proven to improve users' range of motion by 40 percent over traditional rollers. Our goal is to get people to experience a degree of pliability if they can't make it to a TB12 Sports Therapy Center. But optimal pliability requires a certified TB12 body coach.

Along with the vibrating foam roller, we also use a *vibrating sphere*. Before and after workouts, some athletes use a lacrosse or squash ball to stimulate their muscles. But again, unless the ball has a vibrating function, it won't activate the nervous system and therefore won't lead to any pliability. By contrast, both the vibrating foam roller and the vibrating sphere affect the nervous system. When you use one or the other, your brain learns new patterns and habits *as* your muscles are contracting and relaxing.

Remember always that our brains and bodies learn through trauma. The nerves in our muscles are in constant communication with our spinal cord, which is the seat of our nervous system. The spinal cord and brain take in and process the information that comes from our muscles—and send that information right back out again to those muscles. This ongoing cycle of exchange keeps our pliable muscles firing evenly, at 100 percent.

MUSCLE GROUPS

As everyone can see, the body's muscle system is
extremely dense, complex, and interconnected.

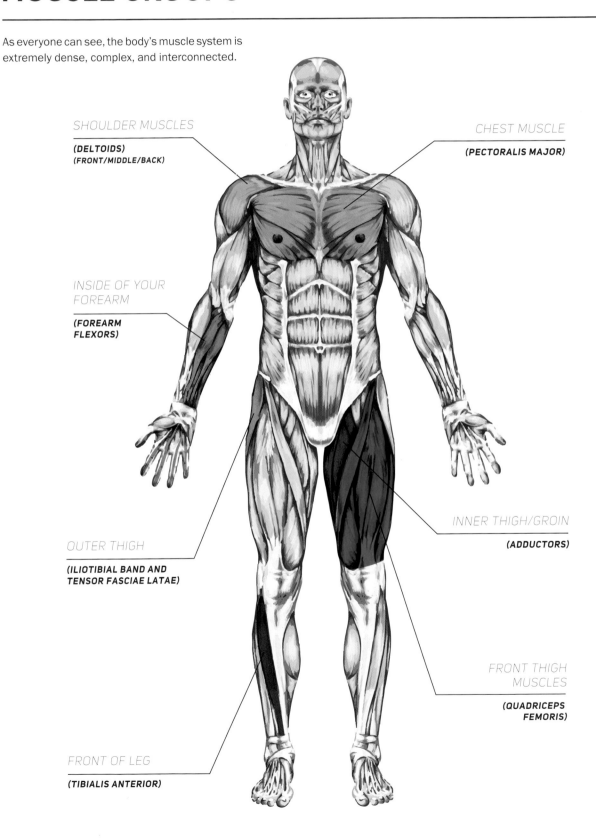

SHOULDER MUSCLES

(DELTOIDS)
(FRONT/MIDDLE/BACK)

CHEST MUSCLE

(PECTORALIS MAJOR)

*INSIDE OF YOUR
FOREARM*

**(FOREARM
FLEXORS)**

OUTER THIGH

**(ILIOTIBIAL BAND AND
TENSOR FASCIAE LATAE)**

INNER THIGH/GROIN

(ADDUCTORS)

*FRONT THIGH
MUSCLES*

**(QUADRICEPS
FEMORIS)**

FRONT OF LEG

(TIBIALIS ANTERIOR)

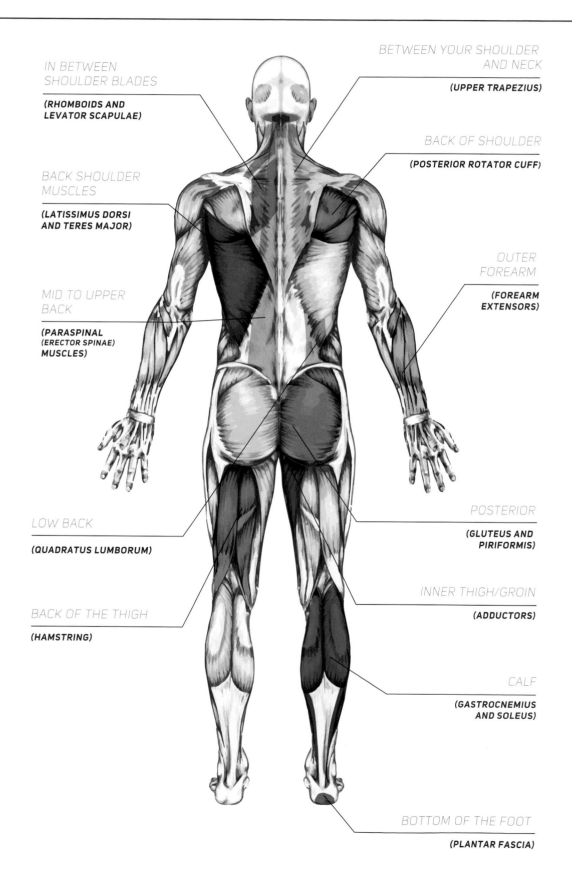

IN BETWEEN
SHOULDER BLADES

**(RHOMBOIDS AND
LEVATOR SCAPULAE)**

BACK SHOULDER
MUSCLES

**(LATISSIMUS DORSI
AND TERES MAJOR)**

MID TO UPPER
BACK

**(PARASPINAL
(ERECTOR SPINAE)
MUSCLES)**

LOW BACK

(QUADRATUS LUMBORUM)

BACK OF THE THIGH

(HAMSTRING)

BETWEEN YOUR SHOULDER
AND NECK

(UPPER TRAPEZIUS)

BACK OF SHOULDER

(POSTERIOR ROTATOR CUFF)

OUTER
FOREARM

**(FOREARM
EXTENSORS)**

POSTERIOR

**(GLUTEUS AND
PIRIFORMIS)**

INNER THIGH/GROIN

(ADDUCTORS)

CALF

**(GASTROCNEMIUS
AND SOLEUS)**

BOTTOM OF THE FOOT

(PLANTAR FASCIA)

CHOOSING BETWEEN A VIBRATING FOAM ROLLER OR A VIBRATING SPHERE

Are a vibrating foam roller and a vibrating sphere interchangeable? For many muscle groups, the answer is yes. But if you're doing pliability on your legs, for example, the stability of the roller can be better. For muscles or body areas that are harder to reach, like the neck, arms, or back, a vibrating sphere can work better, and you can also use the sphere against a wall. The sphere is also more compact and easier to transport in a suitcase if you travel. But more important than whether you choose the vibrating roller or the vibrating sphere—or both—is the fact that you're getting started with degrees of pliability, and the ways it can help improve your performance.

SELF-PLIABILITY WITH ASSISTED DEVICES

In the section ahead, I'll be showing you eighteen muscle groups you can target using self-pliability with assisted devices.

A full-body pliability session should take about twenty minutes. Once you experience a difference in the muscle you're working on, and it feels softer than it did when you started, move on to the next muscle. In some cases, if you're doing pliability and you feel like your hip flexors or your arms are especially tight, focus most of your effort and attention on those muscles.

If you're using a roller with multiple speeds, begin with the lowest speed and work your way up to higher speeds once you get comfortable with the vibration. (If the highest speed feels too intense, that's an indication you should drop down a speed or two.)

In the pages ahead, I go through the best ways to work with the vibrating foam roller and sphere. An illustration of the muscles you'll be working on using assisted devices or doing partner pliability can be found on pages 78 and 79. Again, achieving pliability with assisted devices takes time. You'll begin to feel a difference after two weeks, and a more noticeable difference after about a month.

LOWER BODY

BOTTOM OF THE FOOT (PLANTAR FASCIA)

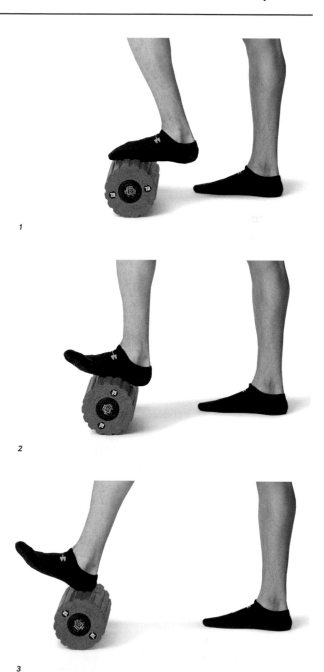

WHAT IT IS: The *plantar fascia* is a dense tissue band that runs across the bottom of your foot and connects your heel bone to your toes.

REASON FOR PLIABILITY: It all starts with your feet! Runners, walkers, and people with flat feet are at higher risk for developing issues with the plantar fascia, ranging from foot pain to problems with their Achilles tendons. If the bottoms of your feet aren't pliable, you'll have less range of motion with your toes, which can lead to reduced motion in your ankles, which in turn places more load on your calves.

1. Flex your left foot and position it on top of the foam roller. *2.* Make sure to keep your weight on your standing leg and foot, without hyperextension. *3.* Maintaining this same stance, curl your toes inward as you roll the roller toward your toes, then extend your toes as you roll the roller backward toward your heel. Then switch to the other foot.

CALF (GASTROCNEMIUS AND SOLEUS)

1

2

WHAT IT IS: The *gastrocnemius and soleus* muscle group is made up of two separate muscles and is more commonly known as the calf muscles.

REASON FOR PLIABILITY: We use our calf muscles to walk, run, stand on our toes, and more. The more weight we put on them—especially if we're over forty—the tighter they can become.

NOTE: When foam-rolling your calf muscles, make sure you maintain full knee extension, and roll from the heel (where the Achilles attaches) all the way up past the knee, making sure you hit both the side and the middle of the calf. Consider bending your knee (see photo) to penetrate all sides of the calf muscles more deeply.

3

1. Sitting on the floor, place your left calf on the foam roller, with your right leg slightly aloft and your hands behind you. **2.** Bracing yourself on both palms, roll your calf forward onto the roller, beginning with your heel, as you rhythmically contract and relax the muscle. **3.** As you target your soleus, cross your right ankle over your left to achieve maximum pliability. Repeat for the other leg.

FRONT OF LEG (TIBIALIS ANTERIOR)

1

WHAT IT IS: The *tibialis anterior* is a long, slender muscle located in the front of your lower leg that leads down to your ankle and foot.

REASON FOR PLIABILITY: When the tibialis anterior tightens, it can lead to shin pain, imbalances, poor biomechanics, and a decreased ability to support weight, which in turn makes you more susceptible to injury.

2

1. Maintaining a crouching "frog" position, with straight arms and both hands placed in front of you, position both your ankles on top of the foam roller. **2.** Still bracing your weight on your arms and hands, and using your right leg as a launcher, begin rolling back and forth on your left shin. **3.** Target your tibialis anterior muscle more deeply by angling your shin against the roller, following the same directions as above. Repeat on the other side.

3

FRONT THIGH MUSCLES (QUADRICEPS FEMORIS)

1

WHAT IT IS: The *quadriceps* is a group of muscles situated in the front of your thigh.

REASON FOR PLIABILITY: Quads that aren't pliable can lead to poor biomechanics and increased stress on surrounding muscles, leading to decreased athletic performance.

NOTE: When foam-rolling your quadriceps, make sure you roll the entire length of your muscles. Starting from the top of the knee, roll all the way up to the top of the hip bone. It's also important to get the inside, middle, and outside aspects of your upper leg, making sure you hit all four of the major muscles that make up the front thigh muscles. To add more neural input and lengthen and soften even more, flex your knee as you trace up the length of the muscles.

2

1. Begin in a modified plank position, with your elbows under your shoulders and the foam roller positioned an inch above your knee bone. *2.* Roll up and down your quad, allowing the foam roller to move toward your upper thigh. *3.* As you move the foam roller up and down, rhythmically contract and relax your quad muscles. Repeat on the other side.

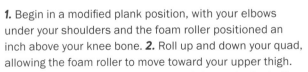

3

INNER THIGH/GROIN (ADDUCTORS)

WHAT IT IS: The *adductor* muscle group, otherwise known as the inner thigh or groin, helps us control and stabilize our legs and feet.

REASON FOR PLIABILITY: Reduced pliability can lead to tight, dense, stiff movement, leading to poor biomechanics, increased strain on surrounding joints and muscles, and decreased athletic performance.

NOTE: When foam-rolling your inner thigh, roll down your inside upper leg to the inside part of your knee. To increase neural feedback as you lengthen and soften your muscles, extend your knee as you roll up the length of your inner thigh.

1. Begin, again, in a modified plank position, resting on your elbows, with your hands clasped. *2.* Angle your upper left leg so the interior is flush against the foam roller. *3.* Keeping your knee extended, move the foam roller up and down your adductor muscle as you rhythmically contract and relax it. Repeat on the other side.

BACK OF THE THIGH (HAMSTRINGS)

WHAT IT IS: The *hamstring* muscle group includes three back thigh muscles. We use our hamstrings when we walk, run, turn our hips, and bend our knees.

REASON FOR PLIABILITY: Nonpliable hamstrings can lead to poor biomechanics and poor posture, which in turn decrease athletic performance and increase the risk of injury.

NOTE: When rolling your hamstrings, make sure to roll the entire length of the muscles from below your knee on both the inside and the outside of your shinbone. Include both your inside and your outside back thigh muscles in your rolling routine.

1. With both arms behind you and your hands on the floor, begin by placing the foam roller right below where the underside of your left knee meets your thigh muscle. *2.* Bracing yourself on your hands, roll forward on the foam roller as you rhythmically contract and relax your hamstring muscles. *3.* To achieve deeper pliability, cross your right foot over your left as you're rolling. Repeat on the other side.

OUTER THIGH (IT BAND AND TFL)

1

2

WHAT IT IS: The *IT band* and *TFL* are muscles that help our pelvis maintain balance when we stand, walk, or run.

REASON FOR PLIABILITY: Without pliability, other muscles will experience increased burden, potentially leading to groin pain.

NOTE: When rolling out the IT band and the TFL, roll from the knee joint to the top of the hip. (You may want to use the vibrating sphere, which allows for more direct contact with your TFL.) Using the vibrating sphere against a wall is a good way to control how much pressure you place on your muscle.

1. Lie on your right side, bracing your weight on your right elbow, with the foam roller positioned an inch or so below the knee joint. *2.* Roll upward to the top of the hip, and then back down again to below the knee joint. *3.* As you roll, extend both arms to maintain your balance. Repeat on the other side.

3

TORSO

POSTERIOR (GLUTEUS AND PIRIFORMIS)

WHAT IT IS: The *gluteus* (aka *glutes*) and *piriformis* muscles make up our backsides. The glutes are especially important in generating power and explosiveness in athletic performance.

REASON FOR PLIABILITY: Decreased pliability makes you more prone to strain and injury, leading to poor biomechanics, increased stress on joints and soft tissue, decreased athletic performance, and higher risk of noncontact injuries.

NOTE: When rolling out your backside, sit in such a way that your outer hip makes contact with the roller. As you begin to roll, extend your hip so that you deepen the contact between the roller and your hip's external rotator. Next, cross your leg over your knee to target an even deeper area of the muscle. Here the vibrating sphere is a great tool for hip pliability, as it allows you to get deeper into the muscle.

1. With your arms behind you, brace your weight on both hands, with the foam roller positioned directly under your buttocks. **2.** Make sure that your outer hip is in direct contact with the roller, and extend it as you begin rolling. **3.** Target the glutes and piriformis more deeply by crossing your left knee over your right knee. Repeat on the other side.

LOW BACK (QUADRATUS LUMBORUM)

WHAT IT IS: The *quadratus lumborum* is situated in the lower part of your back on either side of your spine, within the abdominal cavity.

1. With both knees bent and positioned in front of you, place the roller on the lower left part of your back, beneath your rib cage. **2.** Place your weight on your elbow as you begin rolling up and down your lower left spine. **3.** Press deeply into the roller, angling and adjusting your lower left back to target tender spots. Repeat on the other side.

MID TO UPPER BACK
(PARASPINAL (ERECTOR SPINAE) MUSCLES)

WHAT IT IS: The large *paraspinal* muscles are a group of muscles on either side of the spine, and are generally referred to as the mid to upper back. From a functional standpoint, the paraspinals help to stabilize the spine so it can perform its normal curvatures.

REASON FOR PLIABILITY: Decreased pliability in the paraspinals may lead to poor biomechanics, imbalances, and even scoliosis. This can lead to increased stress on other joints, muscles, and/or vertebral discs, leading in turn to lower back pain, disc injuries, and increased stress on the knees and ankles.

NOTE: When foam-rolling your mid to upper back, make sure you trace the entire length of the muscles. Start at the base of the tailbone and slowly work your way up through the midback to the top of the shoulder. Adjust your body as needed to get even deeper into the muscle. It's a good idea to work through the range of motion slowly, in order to find trigger points or other specific tight spots.

1. Lie on your back with both legs extended. With your knees bent and your arms crossed, position the foam roller on the base of your tailbone. *2.* Bending both knees, roll forward, making sure the foam roller progresses to the top of the shoulder and back down again. Instead of rolling directly along your spine, angle your body so the roller targets both sides of your spine.

UPPER BODY

CHEST MUSCLE (PECTORALIS MAJOR)

WHAT IT IS: The *pectoralis major* muscle is situated in the front chest, and makes up the most dominant chest muscle.

NOTE: When foam-rolling your chest, there are two techniques. The first is to place the roller or sphere against a wall and roll against the chest muscles by moving your torso side to side and up and down. As with some other muscle groups, moving through the muscle slowly and forcefully allows you to find tight spots. To create the deepest possible contact with your muscle, place the roller on the ground and use your body weight to hit all the tender spots within that muscle.

1. Lie facedown with your left arm on the floor and the foam roller positioned between your elbow and your right shoulder. *2.* Your weight should rest on your body, not on your arm. *3.* Using your left arm as a brace, move your torso side to side and up and down atop the roller, targeting your front chest muscles. Repeat on the other side.

IN BETWEEN SHOULDER BLADES

1

WHAT IT IS: The *rhomboids* are rhomboid-shaped muscles in between our shoulder blades that are vital in throwing and in any overhead arm motion.

REASON FOR PLIABILITY: Decreased pliability in this area can lead to stress on the shoulder and neck and cause asymmetries in the arm and back.

NOTE: When using the foam roller between your shoulder blades, consider adjusting your arms in a variety of positions. This allows access to certain muscles while changing their length. For example, crossing your arms or raising your arms overhead while rolling allows better access to your muscles while extending the length of the muscle. You can then rotate your trunk to find tender points within those muscles.

2

1. Lie on your back, bend your knees, and cross your arms so that your hands are gripping the opposite shoulder. **2.** With the foam roller positioned beneath your left shoulder blade, begin rolling up and down. **3.** Adjust your upper trunk to target your muscles more deeply. Repeat on the other side.

3

(RHOMBOIDS AND LEVATOR SCAPULAE)

WHAT IT IS: The *levator scapulae* is a muscle located at the back and side of the neck, whose main function is to lift the shoulder blades.

---

1. Still lying on your back with your knees bent, position the foam roller under your left shoulder blade. **2.** With your hips elevated six inches above the floor, roll from your shoulder blades up toward your neck. **3.** Cross your arms tightly to access the muscle deeply. Repeat on the other side.

SHOULDER MUSCLES (DELTOIDS) (FRONT/MIDDLE/BACK)

1

2

3

WHAT IT IS: The *deltoid* muscles are located on the upper area of the shoulder and are attached by tendons to the shoulder and upper arm bone.

NOTE: When foam-rolling your deltoids, you can choose between two different approaches. In this case, the vibrating sphere is the optimal tool for this muscle group, as the smaller, more direct surface of the sphere will allow you to get deeper into the muscle. Place the sphere or the roller against the wall, and use your body weight to access the closest possible contact with the muscle. Optimally, you might try a variety of positions to locate trigger points within the muscle. For an even more active release, reach across your body while rolling to get deeper into the muscle.

1. Position the vibrating sphere against a wall, leaning into it to achieve maximum depth. *2.* Begin rolling back and forth between your upper arm and the top of your shoulder. *3.* Angle and adjust your stance—and even raise your arm—to target tender points within your deltoid. Repeat on the other side.

1

2

3

NOTE: The advantage of using the vibrating sphere is that it can access smaller, harder-to-reach points within any muscle group. In this case, as you roll out your shoulder muscle, let the sphere target points of tightness or weakness from the top of your shoulder to below your armpit.

1. Position the vibrating sphere against a wall and press into it to access the muscle. **2.** Roll back and forth between your upper arm and the top of your shoulder. **3.** Angle and adjust your stance and raise your arm to target the deltoid's sensitive points. Repeat on the other side.

BACK OF SHOULDER
(POSTERIOR ROTATOR CUFF)

WHAT IT IS: The *posterior rotator cuff* is a group of muscles and tendons that stabilizes your shoulder joint. It's critical for any and all shoulder movements, including—in my job—throwing a football.

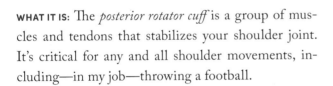

1. Lie on your back with your knees bent and raised, and position the foam roller between the underside of your upper right arm and your shoulder. *2.* Using your knees to elevate your body and lift your hips off the floor, move your body up and down atop the roller. *3.* Contract and relax your arm and shoulder muscles to access tender points. Repeat on the left side.

BACK SHOULDER MUSCLES
(LATISSIMUS DORSI AND TERES MAJOR)

1

WHAT IT IS: The *latissimus dorsi* is a wide, flat muscle that runs through the back and armpits and connects to the upper arm. We use our lats when we're doing pull-ups, chin-ups, or extending or swinging our arms. The *latissimus dorsi* and *teres major* atach to the humerus and are responsible for inward and backward movement of the torso and arms.

NOTE: When foam-rolling your back shoulder muscles, trace all the way up your side from your lower side to your armpits. Continuously flexing and rotating your shoulder will help lengthen the muscle as much as possible. Using the roller against the wall can be an easy, efficient way to locate tender spots within the posterior shoulder.

2

---

1. Assuming the same position as the previous exercise, position the foam roller underneath your armpit. *2.* Angling your knees together and to one side, roll from the armpit all the way down your lower back. *3.* By moving, adjusting, and flexing your shoulder, you can lengthen and soften your muscles even more deeply. Repeat on the other side.

3

BETWEEN YOUR SHOULDER AND NECK
(UPPER TRAPEZIUS)

1

2

3

WHAT IT IS: The *upper trapezius* muscle extends from the upper regions of the back on the posterior side of the neck and trunk. Its functions include elevating, rotating, and stabilizing our shoulder blades and supporting our arms.

1. Position yourself next to a wall, with the vibrating sphere pressed against your right upper back. **2.** Use your upper back to roll the sphere up and down and side to side. **3.** Lean in deeply to target the muscles between your armpit and your upper shoulder. Repeat on the other side.

INSIDE OF YOUR FOREARM
(FOREARM FLEXORS)

1

2

3

WHAT IT IS: The *forearm flexors* are a group of five muscles that are wrist and finger flexors of the forearm. They allow us to move our wrists toward or away from our bodies. Both tennis elbow and golfer's elbow are signs you need to focus on forearm pliability.

1. With your knees bent, lean forward and place your left wrist on top of the foam roller. Your hand should be facing down. **2.** Leaning back onto your hips, roll your wrist forward atop the roller, targeting the entire forearm. **3.** If necessary, use the right arm to steady the left. Repeat on the other side.

OUTER FOREARM (FOREARM EXTENSORS)

1

WHAT IT IS: The *forearm extensors* comprise more than half a dozen muscles on the back of the forearm that allow us to extend our wrists and fingers.

1. In the same position as the previous exercise, place your left wrist on top of the foam roller, this time with the hand facing up. **2.** Leaning back onto your hips, and using your right arm to steady the left, roll from your wrist to your elbow joint. **3.** As you roll out your forearm extensors, rhythmically contract and relax your outer forearm muscles. Repeat with your right outer forearm.

2

3

SELF-PLIABILITY—UNASSISTED

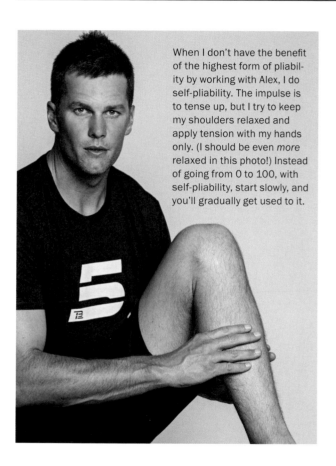

When I don't have the benefit of the highest form of pliability by working with Alex, I do self-pliability. The impulse is to tense up, but I try to keep my shoulders relaxed and apply tension with my hands only. (I should be even *more* relaxed in this photo!) Instead of going from 0 to 100, with self-pliability, start slowly, and you'll gradually get used to it.

Sometimes during the off-season, when I don't have the benefit of working with Alex, I've found ways to do self-pliability. The advantage of self-pliability is that you can lengthen and soften at least some of your muscles, anywhere you are, both pre- and post-workout. The obvious disadvantage is that self-pliability limits the parts of the body you can reach. It can also be tiring! Still, if you're committed to it, unassisted self-pliability is a great thing to be able to do—but you need to start slowly, staying relaxed in your upper body as you stroke through the muscle. I do self-pliability on seven muscle groups—my tibialis anterior, calves, quadriceps, hamstrings, forearm, biceps, and triceps—and in the pages ahead I'll show you the method I use on three of those muscles.

ADVICE TO THE GYM-GOER

I don't play a particular sport. How much pliability do I need?

Whether you're eighteen years old or eighty, the same principles of pliability apply to everyone. If you're not an everyday athlete but you go to the gym to work out, I recommend you do pliability both before you go and as soon as you finish your workout. I would target hamstrings, calves, quads, IT bands, and glutes. The entire self-pliability session should last around twenty minutes.

Even if you don't go to the gym, what are your daily acts of living? Do you stand and sit a lot? Climb stairs? Carry bags? Work in the garden? No matter what your level of activity is, you'll still be contracting your muscles—and without lengthening and softening your muscles through pliability, they will become tight, dense, and stiff. Over time they will lose full muscle pump function and the ability to rejuvenate and regenerate—which, in the end, decreases overall health and vitality.

SELF-PLIABILITY: **CALVES**

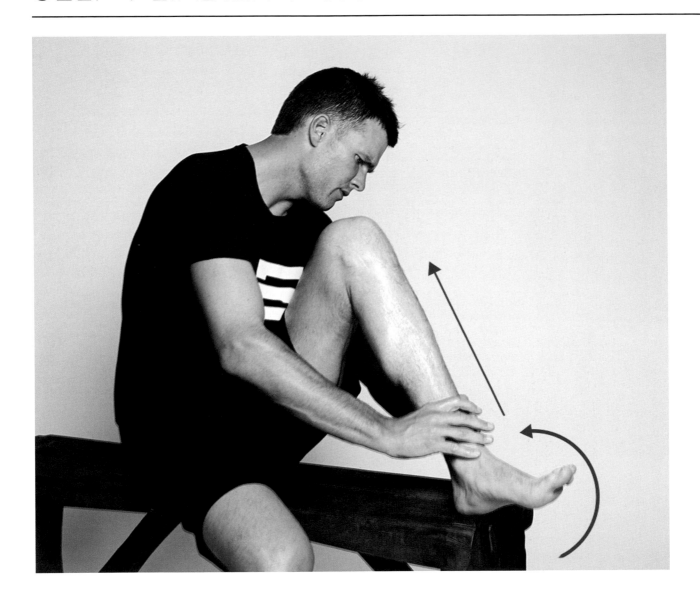

In my job, I'm always on my feet, running and shuffling in the pocket. That's why, when I don't have the benefit of Alex, I maintain a lot of pliability in my calves. You should determine where *you* need pliability based on your daily acts of living.

Apply a nonsticky lotion to your calf. (I recommend lotion for all our self-pliability treatments.) In a seated position, bend your knee in front of you. Using both hands, grab your leg just above your ankle. With both thumbs pressing down on your anklebone, stroke through your calf muscle, toward the heart, for twenty seconds. At the same time, rhythmically point and flex your foot. Repeat on the other side.

SELF-PLIABILITY: **TRICEPS**

Obviously, I need to maintain pliability in my arms—especially my right arm.

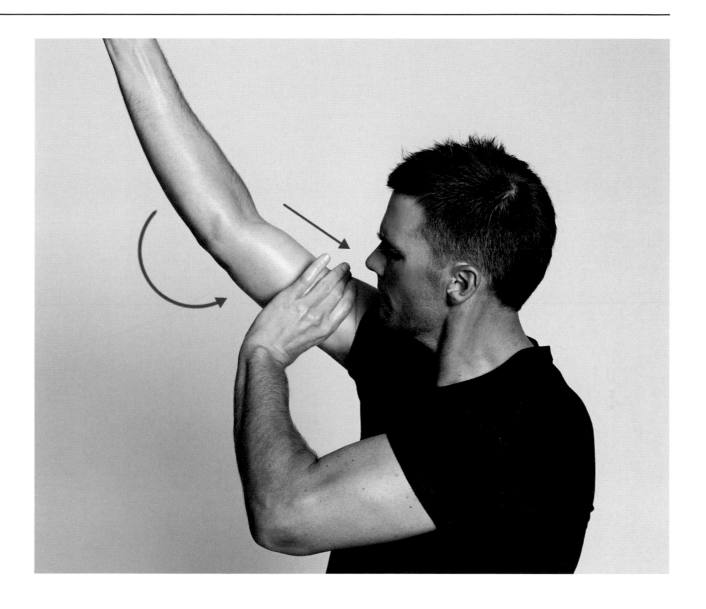

Raise your right forearm and grasp your biceps just above the elbow joint. Press your thumb against the underside of your elbow. Firmly stroke through your triceps muscle with the thumb of your left hand as you rhythmically contract and relax the muscle. Repeat on the other side.

SELF-PLIABILITY:
INSIDE OF YOUR FOREARM

My forearm used to give me a lot of trouble—that's why I developed tendonitis before I met Alex. As I do self-pliability, notice that my left thumb applies pressure as I stroke up the muscle with my hand, always toward the heart.

With the underside of your right arm facing up, grasp the forearm with the left hand. Using consistent pressure, stroke the muscle from the wrist to the elbow joint as you rhythmically contract and relax your forearm. Make sure you target the entire length of the muscle. Repeat on the other side.

SELF-PLIABILITY: **OUTER FOREARM**

More self-pliability on my right forearm, lengthening and softening, always toward the heart.

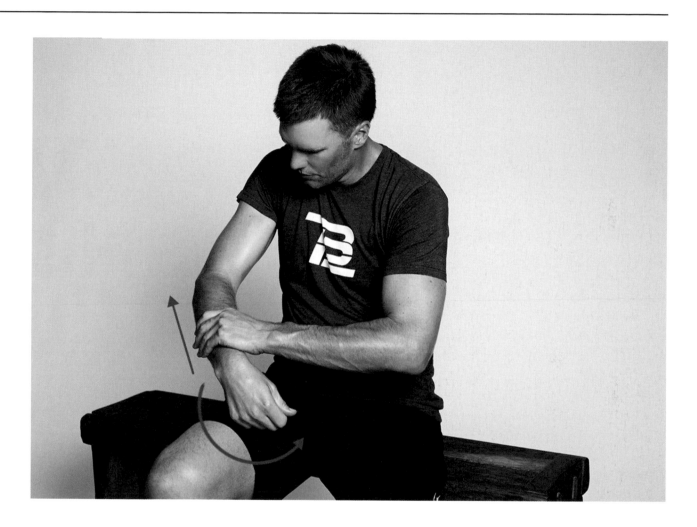

With the outside of your right arm facing up, grasp the forearm with the left hand. Using consistent pressure, stroke the muscle from the wrist to the elbow joint as you rhythmically contract and relax your forearm. Make sure you target the entire length of the muscle. Repeat on the other side.

PARTNER PLIABILITY: THE BASICS

On the rare occasions when I don't have the benefit of working with Alex, I've found ways to do partner pliability. As I've said, the highest levels of pliability come from working with one of our TB12 body coaches, who've undergone a rigorous certification program to master the TB12 Method of pliability through an in-depth understanding of biomechanics, muscle physiology, and proper muscle function. We're also excited to be launching a new training and certification program that we'll be rolling out soon to create a network of world-class TB12-certified body coaches across the country. In the meantime, the methods ahead can offer some of the benefits of in-person targeted deep-force muscle work. While your partner may not be able to replicate the targeted deep-force muscle work I get working with Alex or the same degree of force he exerts to create optimal muscle pump function, he or she can still lengthen, soften, and prime muscles, no matter where you are, both before and after a workout or activity.

By now, you know the technique: Using a consistent but tolerable force, your partner lengthens and softens the muscle, always stroking in the direction of the heart. I repeat: always in the direction of the heart. Meanwhile, the person who's getting pliability contracts and relaxes that muscle rhythmically, up and down or back and forth, for around twenty seconds.

Many muscle groups are optimally done only with the assistance of a certified TB12 body coach. But in the following pages are a half-dozen techniques that you and a partner can perform together safely.

1. If you're wearing shorts, before starting I recommend applying a non-sticky lotion to the muscle you're targeting. You're going to need to be right up against the skin. I use coconut oil, but you should use anything you have on hand.

2. Always stroke upward as you lengthen and soften your partner's muscles, toward the heart, to facilitate optimal blood circulation.

3. Try to target all sides of the muscle, including the inside, middle, and outside.

4. Pliability is active, never passive. As you lengthen and soften a muscle, the person receiving pliability contracts and relaxes that muscle rhythmically, about two times per second. However, speeds will vary, based on the ability and pliability of the person who's getting the treatment.

5. Unless otherwise noted, partner pliability should be done in a relaxed, prone position. If you have a massage table at home, great. If not, you can do partner pliability on a bed or any flat surface, in order to give the person giving pliability the proper leverage.

6. Begin with the lower limbs, then move up to the torso and the upper limbs.

7. Pliability should be done on all the muscles in your body for around twenty seconds. However, if an area of the body is more sore or is giving you trouble, continue with the treatment until the muscle starts to lengthen and soften.

8. The most challenging part of partner pliability is that the person giving pliability is stroking through the muscle in an *upward* direction, toward the heart, at the same time the person getting pliability is contracting and relaxing the muscle rhythmically—sometimes up, sometimes down. With practice, this will become automatic. The goal is to lengthen and soften through the stroke.

BOTTOM OF THE FOOT (PLANTAR FASCIA)

1. The person receiving pliability is in a comfortable seated position, legs and feet extended, as the person giving pliability presses both thumbs against the heel.

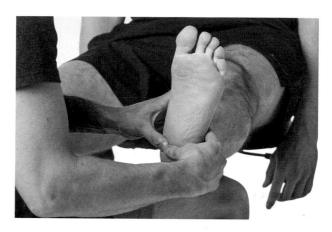

2. The person giving pliability strokes through the plantar fascia slowly and forcefully, always in the direction of the heart.

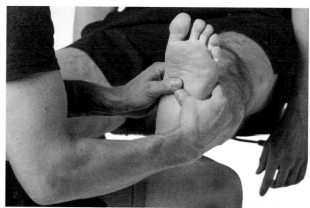

3. The person receiving pliability expands and contracts the muscle rapidly and simultaneously. Repeat on the other side.

CALF (GASTROCNEMIUS AND SOLEUS)

1. The person receiving pliability lies facedown as the person giving pliability grasps the ankle.

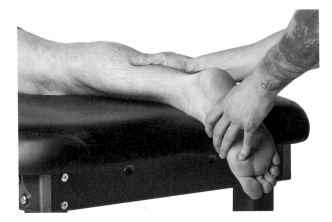

2. Using one or both thumbs, the person giving pliability strokes upward through the muscle, toward the heart.

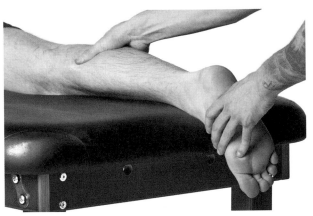

3. As the person receives pliability, he or she rhythmically contracts and relaxes the calf muscle. Repeat on the other side.

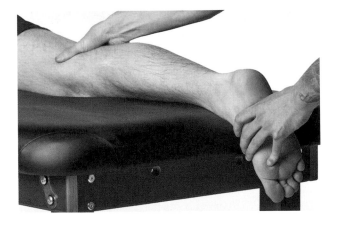

FRONT OF LEG (TIBIALIS ANTERIOR)

1. The person receiving pliability sits with his or her left leg extended, as the person giving pliability grasps the calf just above the anklebone.

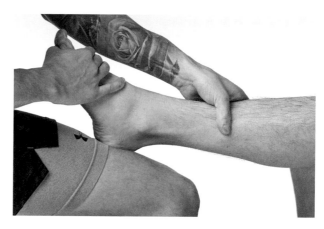

2. The person giving pliability strokes upward through the tibialis anterior muscle toward the heart.

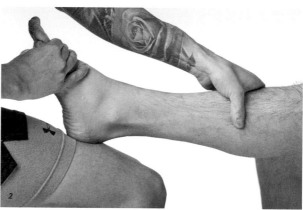

3. As the person receives pliability, he or she rhythmically contracts and relaxes the tibialis anterior. Repeat on the other side.

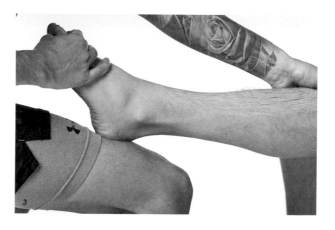

BACK OF THE THIGH (HAMSTRINGS)

1. The person receiving pliability lies facedown with his or her right leg extended. The person giving pliability places both hands just above the underside of the knee joint.

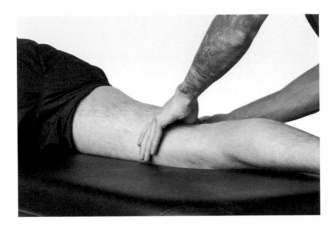

2. The person giving pliability begins stroking upward using both thumbs.

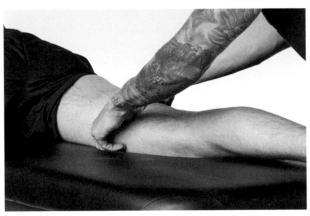

3. As the person receives pliability, he or she rhythmically contracts and relaxes the hamstring muscles. Repeat on the other side.

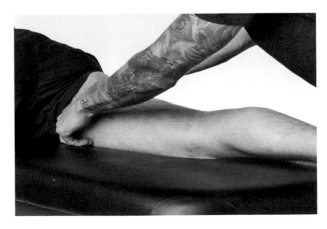

FOREARMS

1. The person getting pliability extends the left arm as the person giving pliability presses his or her thumb against the wrist.

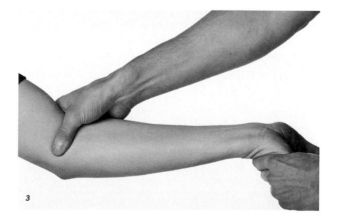

2. Using maximum pressure, the person giving pliability strokes through the muscle all the way up to the elbow.

3. As the person receives pliability, he or she rhythmically contracts and relaxes the forearm. Repeat on the other side.

BACK OF SHOULDER
(POSTERIOR ROTATOR CUFF)

1. The person receiving pliability is in a comfortable seated position. The person giving pliability places both thumbs on the shoulder blade.

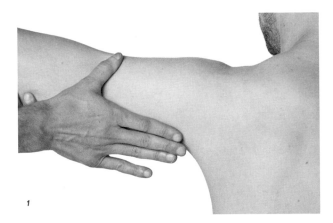

1

2. The person giving pliability strokes through the muscle toward the heart.

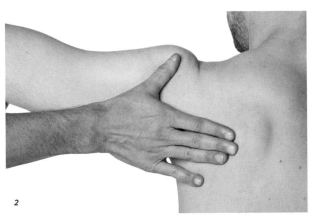

2

3. As the person receives pliability, he or she rhythmically contracts and relaxes the upper arm. Repeat on the other side.

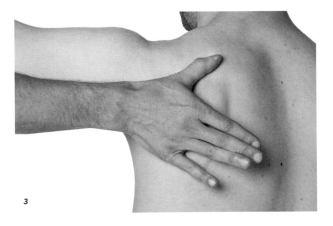

3

A pliability session with Alex, who's working on my right shoulder and applying pressure in the direction of the heart.

CHAPTER 6

WORKOUTS

Resistance-band push-ups are great for strength.

FROM COLLEGE AND ON THROUGH TO THE PROS, I USED TO FOLLOW THE TRADITIONAL METHOD OF WORKING OUT. EVERYTHING WAS WEIGHT BASED. TWENTY MINUTES TO WARM UP AND RAISE MY HEART RATE, FOLLOWED BY FORTY-FIVE MINUTES TO AN HOUR LIFTING WEIGHTS, THEN MORE CARDIO TO FINISH. TWICE A WEEK, ON MONDAYS AND THURSDAYS, I WORKED MY UPPER BODY. TUESDAYS AND FRIDAYS WERE DEVOTED TO MY LOWER BODY, WHETHER IT WAS DUMBBELL SQUATS OR SINGLE OR DOUBLE LEG PRESSES, THREE OR FOUR SETS APIECE. IN BETWEEN THERE WAS CORE WORK—CRUNCH SIT-UPS OR ROLLOUTS—AND BACK WORK.

There's no doubt that lifting weights builds denser, thicker muscles and makes athletes stronger—and my strength numbers showed it, too. Fact is, you'll get better at *anything* in life in which you invest time and energy, whether it's lifting weights, jumping rope, scuba diving, or running marathons. Still, most of the time my workouts left me hurting. Sure, I was getting stronger, but I was a long way away from allocating the right proportion of my workout time to what could allow me to sustain success longer—namely, pliability and its amplifiers.

The goal of traditional weight training is to create maximum strength—which is different from optimal strength. Maximum strength refers to the most/longest model, which I talked about earlier—doing more reps of more weights—whereas optimal strength is the strength that you need to carry out the job you have to do. The goal of pliability is optimal strength.

Once I discovered pliability, I began incorporating different tools and techniques into my workout, including resistance bands.

Football-specific band workouts.

WEIGHTS VERSUS RESISTANCE BANDS

At TB12, around 90 percent of what we do—and *I* do—involves working out with resistance bands. A lot of athletes show up at the TB12 Center with a fixed idea about how resistance bands work, and some even associate them with rehab. Many are surprised to find that resistance bands work their bodies functionally better than weights do in terms of resistance, versatility, and maximizing efficiency. Bands allow for a big, fluid range of motion. They help build strength and power while keeping your muscles longer, and making them less dense, than they would be if you used heavy weights. Bands can also help limit inflammation and overload. They condition you aerobically while complementing your pliability. By targeting accelerating and decelerating muscle groups at the same time without overload, they also mirror your body's normal, everyday functional movements. Together with pliability, they create a balanced approached to staying healthy over a long period of time.

Weights aren't harmful by themselves. What *is* harmful is how most people *use* weights. Imagine your body is a pickup truck. It's weighed down with a thousand pounds of bricks in its cargo bed. This is what weight lifting does to your muscles, ligaments, and joints. Now imagine your body as a pickup truck that's *towing* a thousand pounds of bricks behind it. There's minimal weight on your structure. This difference, between *load* and *resistance,* is the difference between what weights and bands do to our bodies. Sometimes we see older people working out with bands, or doing water aerobics or tai chi. It turns out that they know something the rest of us don't. So, what sense does it make to place excess load on your joints when you're young and healthy, either?

After a lifetime of lifting weights, for the past seven years I've used resistance bands almost exclusively. The difference is profound. My muscles are more balanced and functional, especially for the movements I need to perform as an NFL quarterback. Resistance bands clearly work better for me.

Lifting weights is a man-made phenomenon. Ninety-nine percent of the population doesn't need to lift hundreds of pounds of weight at a time. But often our culture takes its cues from athletes. This weight-lifting model has been glorified and marketed in the culture—but that doesn't mean it's functional, or even that it works very well in isolation. It needs to be complemented to maintain balance.

TRAIN AT THE SPEED OF YOUR SPORT

As a football player, the workouts I do mimic the movements I make over the course of a season. One of our central beliefs at TB12 is that you should train at the speed of the sport *you* play, too. In my job, I need to throw, run, cut, and respond quickly to changing conditions as I stand in the pocket. That's different from the job of a runner, whose workouts may focus on improving his speed or race times and who should be concentrating on speed, agility, and cardiac endurance rather than on leg presses or squats.

Alex always says, *For long-term peak performance, you can't train slow and move fast.* Over a short window of time it may be possible, but lifting heavy weights and moving fast at the same time is not very sustainable. And it's certainly not sustainable if you want to maintain optimal pliability. Maybe younger athletes with natural pliability can—but they'll be sacrificing durability and longevity. Lifting heavy and moving fast is counterintuitive *and* counterproductive. Why? Because without knowing it, you are neural-priming your muscles to work slowly and deliberately, not just during your workouts but when you play your sport, too. If athletes work out slow and heavy, their bodies

can get confused. In our experience, by not connecting on-field work with off-field workouts, athletes will most likely end up overloading, compensating, and getting injured. Basically athletes are training their bodies and brains one way *off* the field and asking them to do something entirely different when they're *on* the field. Why *wouldn't* their bodies get confused? In sports, you need to think fast, and train fast—especially over the long term.

For that reason, my workout consists of quick bursts of exercise using resistance bands. Alex and I will do twenty seconds of one exercise, followed by a twenty-second rest. Another twenty-second exercise, followed by another twenty-second rest. We do this over and over again. When I go out onto the field on Sunday, I don't want my brain to think—or play—slowly. That's why I train fast. From the first play forward, every single one of my muscles is firing at 100 percent and is balanced, in its most optimal state.

In short, I train the way I want to play, based on the needs of my sport. That's why I'll end up playing the way I train. That's why I train all year in a holistic, integrated way.

FORM FIRST

At TB12, we emphasize the importance of proper form during workouts. You should always start in a biomechanically neutral position—knees over feet, hips over knees, shoulders over hips, a firm core—because if you're not in proper alignment, you're conditioning your body to be out of balance. Let's say that you're doing ten push-ups. After the seventh push-up, your chest is straining and you feel fatigued. You're having a hard time finishing the exercise. But your brain says, "Keep going! Fight hard!" It asks other muscles to step in to help you finish. It could be your lats, your triceps, or your butt—your brain calls on any muscle that will help you achieve your goal and finish what you set out to do.

But to me, form first means *engaging only the muscles you should be engaging for the movement you are attempting to do*. That's how you keep the proper balance.

Once I sense my form breaking down, I know I'm training my brain the wrong way. Other muscles are compensating for the muscle that *should* be working, and unless I stop, my brain will learn a new behavior—in this case, a negative one. Athletes often say, "I did ten reps!" But what if after the fourth or fifth rep, their form begins breaking down? *Form first.* Otherwise you'll begin activating muscles that shouldn't be activated, and you'll be training your brain to store bad behaviors. As a football team, why go out to the practice field and run fifty plays the wrong way? If you're going to practice, practice the right way. Therefore, if you are going to train, train the right way.

RESISTANCE BANDS: A PRIMER

At the TB12 Center we use three different kinds of resistance strengthening. The bands aren't necessarily unique to us. It's more how we use them that sets what we do apart from other training approaches.

SHEATHED BANDS. These bands have handles, which is why they're used primarily for exercises that emphasize the upper body, though you can use them to target other areas of your body, too. The bands are sheathed and handled and made from latex. They come with a strap that fits around a door or that can be anchored against any wall or solid surface at varying heights.

LOOPED RESISTANCE BANDS come in different thicknesses, which correspond to different intensity levels. These bands can go around your knees, ankles, or waist and allow you to do the same motions you would do with bars and free weights.

SHORTER-LOOPED RESISTANCE BANDS, which are smaller and thicker, also loop around your ankles and knees, and are a great way to add resistance and difficulty to agility skills or squats.

RANGE OF RESISTANCE

The band you should use depends on your size, strength, level of athleticism, and experience. But unless otherwise noted, the thirty-six exercises in the next three sections are suitable for beginner, intermediate, advanced, and elite athletes. If an exercise feels too easy, go up to the next color band, or adjust the distance that you're standing from the wall, door, or anchor point.

LOOPED BANDS

BEFORE YOU START

- The exercises ahead are not necessarily unique to TB12. What is different are the creative additions or variations we apply, and the pace at which the exercises are performed.

- The exercises combine cardio with strength training at the same time. If you do, say, a twenty-minute, high-intensity workout using resistance bands, you don't need much cardio before or after. Your heart rate will already be elevated, I promise.

- The category listed (upper body, core stability, lower body) indicates the part of the body where you will feel it most, though the exercises may activate multiple areas.

- To monitor your form, we recommend you exercise in front of a mirror, or alongside a partner who can give you feedback on your form, or even record yourself on your cell phone.

- Make sure you maintain the right biomechanically correct form—knees over feet, hips over knees, and your core engaged—before you start, and stop performing an exercise the moment your form starts to break down.

- In these exercises, our TB12 body coaches emphasize ground force production, which we define as the ability to transfer energy from the ground, through your body, and into the function you're asking your body to perform. For example, when I stand on the field with both feet planted, I'm generating force up through my legs into my torso, and then up into my shoulders and throwing arm. Without good core stability, I wouldn't have access to that level of strength and force.

- Do each exercise for twenty seconds, or until your form starts to break down. Over time, as you build up endurance and increase proficiency, you'll find yourself doing the exercise for the full twenty seconds.

SHEATHED BANDS

WHITE—Light   RED—Medium   BLUE—Heavy   BLACK—Extra-heavy

UPPER-BODY EXERCISES

We all need some degree of strength in our upper bodies, whether as athletes or simply as we carry out the acts of daily living—opening doors, reaching for something in the hardware store, gardening, moving furniture, pushing a baby carriage, carrying luggage, or mowing the lawn. Most upper-body exercises also call on our core and lower body, too. How often during the day do we use *only* our upper bodies, after all? The answer: Not often. What's great about these first twelve upper-body exercises is that they're explosive and quick-movement, but also low-tension. That reduced tension prevents overload and limits the risk of getting hurt. Like all the exercises in this book, they mimic many of the common movement patterns each one of us performs every day. Is there an order to them? To some degree, but switch them up now and then so that your brain and body are better able to adapt to new forces and stresses on command. For example, a typical workout is three sets times ten reps. If you do that same workout every day, at the same speed, with the same color band, you aren't creating any new neural priming. So try four reps, or change the level of resistance—it will keep your body guessing. Also, the exercises shouldn't be hard, and they shouldn't be easy. The goal is to create tolerable resistance and stress without overload.

1. SINGLE-ARM CHEST PRESS WITH VARIED LEG POSITIONS

EQUIPMENT: *RESISTANCE BANDS (SHEATHED OR LOOPED)*

RESISTANCE BAND POSITION: *ELBOW HEIGHT, OR SLIGHTLY ABOVE*

In this one, the goal is to activate your upper body while keeping your lower body stable. This exercise engages the chest through pushing and pulling and increased resistance in order to build strength. It becomes even more challenging when you switch stances.

Facing away from the wall, door, or anchor point, start with your legs together. Keep your posture upright and your core and glutes contracted. Hold one band underneath your elbow.

Step forward with your left foot. As you do, bring your right arm holding the band forward, making a continuous in-and-out motion. Continue this motion at a fluid pace for twenty seconds.

Switch to the other side and repeat.

2. SINGLE-ARM ROW WITH VARIED LEG POSITIONS

EQUIPMENT: *RESISTANCE BANDS (SHEATHED OR LOOPED)*

RESISTANCE BAND POSITION: *ELBOW HEIGHT, OR SLIGHTLY ABOVE*

When we pull ourselves out of bed or out of a chair, we're performing movements similar to the ones in this exercise. Again, just by varying your leg position, you'll make this one even harder.

Start in a split stance, facing the wall, door, or anchor point. Keep your posture upright and your core and glutes contracted.

Hold one band at elbow height with your arm extended, then bring your arm toward your body tight to your rib cage. Continue this motion at a fluid, continuous pace for twenty seconds.

Switch to the other side and repeat.

3. ALTERNATING ARM PUNCHES

EQUIPMENT: *RESISTANCE BANDS (SHEATHED OR LOOPED)*

This exercise gets your upper body moving, and moving fast. It focuses on explosiveness in your upper body, as you maintain stability in your lower body. It's a lot more challenging than it looks!

RESISTANCE BAND POSITION: *ELBOW HEIGHT, OR SLIGHTLY ABOVE*

Stand with your back facing the wall. Contract your core and straighten your spine.

With both hands gripping a band, and grasping the bands under your elbows, punch forward with alternating arms. Maintain full arm extension for each punch, and proceed at a fluid, continuous pace.

4. ALTERNATING ROWS

EQUIPMENT: *RESISTANCE BANDS (SHEATHED OR LOOPED)*

Similar to the previous exercise in explosiveness, this one calls on your back, biceps, and triceps to move your upper body with control.

RESISTANCE BAND POSITION: *ELBOW HEIGHT, OR SLIGHTLY ABOVE*

Crouching slightly, maintain a neutral stance, with your chest, neck, and head raised. Squeeze your glutes and your core.

Using alternating hands, pull each band toward you, then release. Continue this motion at a fluid, continuous pace for twenty seconds.

5. STANDING LATERAL EXTENSION

EQUIPMENT: *RESISTANCE BANDS (SHEATHED OR LOOPED)*   **RESISTANCE BAND POSITION:** *OVERHEAD*

This exercise will be familiar to anyone who's ever tried to pull themselves out of bed or who swims laps in a pool. Pull with your arms, bringing them from high to low, with both your core and glutes engaged.

With the band attached high on the wall, face the wall and maintain an athletic stance.

Grip the band with both hands. Pull the band down to your center and bring your arms back up to the starting position, with control. Pull the band back down to your center toward your right hip, and release. Now pull it down to your center toward your left hip, and release.

Continue this sequence at a rapid pace, with control.

6. CROSS-BODY STEP AND PRESS

EQUIPMENT: *RESISTANCE BANDS (SHEATHED OR LOOPED)*   **RESISTANCE BAND POSITION:** *ELBOW HEIGHT*

In this one, we use both our upper and lower body, while maintaining our stability. This is a great exercise for dealing with the forces and stresses of daily life!

Stand tall, with your stomach and glutes engaged. Using either a looped band or a handle band, grip the end in your right hand. As you extend the band straight away from your chest, step forward with your left leg.

The only moving parts should be your right arm and left leg. Your core and your glutes should remain stable.

Continue the step and press at a fluid, continuous pace for twenty seconds. Repeat, this time with your left arm and your right leg.

7. CROSS-BODY PULL

EQUIPMENT: *RESISTANCE BANDS (SHEATHED OR LOOPED)*

A beginner may struggle at first with this exercise—
but keep at it.

RESISTANCE BAND POSITION: *ELBOW HEIGHT,*
OR SLIGHTLY ABOVE

Stand with your side to the wall. Grip the handle or loop end of the band and pull it directly across your chest, keeping your elbow snug against your rib cage.

Accelerate the pace, remembering to keep your upper body straight at all times. There should be no rotation of your trunk.

Turn to face the other way, and repeat the sequence with the other arm.

8. BAND CORE ROTATION

EQUIPMENT: *RESISTANCE BANDS (SHEATHED OR LOOPED)*

RESISTANCE BAND POSITION: *ELBOW HEIGHT*

This is a great exercise for athletes whose sports require upper body rotation—golfers, tennis players—and quarterbacks! Even non-athletes rotate their torsos many times a day without realizing it.

Maintain a good athletic stance, with your hips back and your core engaged. With both hands gripping the handle or loop, bring your arms out in front of you and then—keeping your arms straight— pull the band across your chest as you rotate your torso, increasing your pace as you go.

Do this exercise for twenty seconds. Switch sides and repeat.

9. BAND-RESISTED PUSH-UP

EQUIPMENT: *RESISTANCE BANDS (SHEATHED OR LOOPED)*

Before attempting this exercise, make sure you can do a
simple push-up first. *Then* add the resistance band.

Loop a band behind your back, under the armpits. Hold both loop
ends under your palms as you assume a push-up position.

Do six or seven standard push-ups, as explosively as possible.

PLYOMETRIC VARIATION: As you come up from the push-up,
clap your hands.

NOTE: If you're using the sheathed bands, hold down part of the
sheathing to reduce slack.

10. BAND FRONT RAISE

EQUIPMENT: *RESISTANCE BANDS (SHEATHED OR LOOPED)*

This exercise typically requires a lighter band, but find the
one that suits you best.

Place a looped or sheathed band on the ground and step inside it with both feet.

Maintain a good athletic position, with your shoulders back and straight and your core engaged. Raise and lower the band, up and down, as fast as you can, maintaining good form.

The motion should come from your shoulders, and not from your hips, glutes, or trunk.

11. BAND PULL-APARTS

EQUIPMENT: *RESISTANCE BANDS (LOOPED)*

This exercise is similar to the movements we make when we swim or even throw a Frisbee in the backyard. You'll feel the effects afterward in your mid back and shoulders.

Place a looped band on the ground and step inside it with both feet.

Lift both hands to chest level. While maintaining an upright posture, stretch the band across your chest with both arms. Do this for twenty seconds.

VARIATION: Repeat the same motion at a faster pace.

12. FRONT-FACING CORE ANGEL

EQUIPMENT: *2 RESISTANCE BANDS (SHEATHED OR LOOPED)*   **RESISTANCE BAND POSITION:** *OVERHEAD*

A dynamic full-body exercise with lots of variables going on. You move your arms while you tap your feet, all while remaining stationary—and you do it fast, too.

With the bands attached high on the wall, face the wall and use both hands to grip both ends of the bands.

Begin shuffling your feet fast as you raise the bands overhead and lower to your sides. Do this for twenty seconds at an accelerated pace.

12

CORE STABILITY EXERCISES

Everything starts with the core, which encompasses several muscle groups, including your abdominals, your oblique muscles (they run down your sides), your low back, and your quads. With good core stability, we're able to use the core muscles designed to carry out the daily functions of life without putting stress or excess force on our knees, ankles, neck, shoulders, or low back. If someone bumps into you, with good core stability you won't ever get knocked down. In the end, your core needs to be able to take a lot of the stresses of life. For athletes who are absorbing a lot of external forces, a strong core is fundamental—but you really need to engage your core in *all* aspects of life *all* the time.

1. PALLOF SQUAT

EQUIPMENT: *RESISTANCE BANDS (SHEATHED OR LOOPED)*

RESISTANCE BAND POSITION: *ELBOW HEIGHT, OR SLIGHTLY ABOVE*

This exercise asks you to activate your upper body while resisting that same rotation—and to do it with control, too.

Stand with your side to the wall, with the band attached to the wall at elbow level, or slightly above.

Maintain a stable stance, holding the band at chest level.

Squat, while extending the band away from your chest, then back, in a continuous, in-and-out motion, never allowing the band to rotate.

Repeat on the other side.

2. PALLOF CORE SHUFFLE

EQUIPMENT: *RESISTANCE BANDS (SHEATHED OR LOOPED)*

RESISTANCE BAND POSITION: *ELBOW HEIGHT, OR SLIGHTLY ABOVE*

Another antirotation exercise, this one with a few more variables.

Stand with your side to the wall and your hips back. Squeeze your stomach and your glutes.

Using both hands, grip the band at chest level with your arms extended. Shuffle your feet from side to side while holding the band steady and taut.

To add resistance, raise and lower the band. Repeat on the other side.

VARIATION: Increase the pace of your shuffling.

3. CORE ANGEL

EQUIPMENT: *2 RESISTANCE BANDS (SHEATHED OR LOOPED)*   **RESISTANCE BAND POSITION:** *OVERHEAD*

In this one, you're being pulled backward as you move both your arms and legs fast—and maintain explosiveness.

Hold the bands overhead using both hands. Begin shuffling your feet.

Raise and lower the bands, maintaining a fast, fluid pace. Try to stay in one place, without moving forward or backward.

4. OVERHEAD CORE SHUFFLE

EQUIPMENT: *RESISTANCE BANDS (LOOPED)*

By keeping your body long as you stand as tall as possible,
this exercise is a great core activator.

Hold the looped band overhead, extending your arms until the band is taut.

Squeeze your stomach and your glutes and rock back and forth from one foot to the other, lifting your non-weight-bearing foot slightly as you rock. Your core should remain solid, and your arms should remain extended and fixed in place throughout the exercise.

Accelerate the pace, while maintaining your core stability.

5. OVERHEAD ARM FLUTTERS

EQUIPMENT: *2 RESISTANCE BANDS (SHEATHED OR LOOPED)*   **RESISTANCE BAND POSITION:** *OVERHEAD*

This one is harder than it looks—and you'll feel it afterward.

With bands attached high on the wall, stand straight with your back to the wall, keeping your core engaged. Hold the bands overhead, one in each hand.

Shuffle your feet in place as you move your arms subtly while keeping them extended for twenty seconds.

6. PLANK WITH A ROW

EQUIPMENT: *RESISTANCE BANDS (SHEATHED OR LOOPED)*　　　　**RESISTANCE BAND POSITION:** *KNEE HEIGHT*

Most people use a light band with this one. Also, make sure you can hold a plank before you add movement to it.

Assume a plank position, facing the wall, balancing on your arms or your elbows.

Hold a resistance band with your right hand. Continue to balance on your left hand as you pull the band toward your chest and stomach in a fluid, continuous motion, while maintaining the position.

Do this for twenty seconds. Switch hands and repeat on the other side.

7. X PLANK

EQUIPMENT: *NONE*

This exercise requires coordination of your arm and leg as you maintain stability. Again, make sure you can hold a simple plank before adding variations.

Assume a plank position, with both arms directly underneath
your shoulders. Keep your legs straight and your stance wide.

Engage your glutes and raise your left leg off the ground
while raising your right arm. Repeat, this time with your right leg
and left arm.

Go back and forth like this for twenty seconds.

8. LATERAL RESISTED BIRD DOG

EQUIPMENT: *RESISTANCE BANDS (LOOPED)*   **RESISTANCE BAND POSITION:** *KNEE HEIGHT*

A great exercise that uses your glutes and shoulders, while challenging your core stability.

Loop a band around your waist and attach it low to the wall.

Assume a tabletop position. Keep your back straight, your head down, and your core engaged.

Raise your left arm while simultaneously extending your right leg straight backward. Keep your back as flat as possible. Return to the starting position in a controlled manner, and repeat for twenty seconds.

Turn around and repeat, this time with your right arm and left leg.

9. SINGLE LEG BALANCE WITH HALO

EQUIPMENT: *RESISTANCE BANDS (SHEATHED OR LOOPED)*   **RESISTANCE BAND POSITION:** *OVERHEAD*

This one can challenge even very experienced athletes, but it is an excellent exercise for balance and core stability.

With your back to the wall and your core stable, hold the band over your head.

Raise your right knee to 90 degrees and lower the band to your right shoulder, then back overhead, then to your left shoulder.

Next, raise your left knee and repeat the exercise.

10. HIGH TO LOW/LOW TO HIGH ROTATION

EQUIPMENT: *RESISTANCE BANDS (SHEATHED OR LOOPED)*

Any golfer—or hockey player—will find this diagonal movement familiar.

RESISTANCE BAND POSITION: *OVERHEAD AND KNEE HEIGHT*

Begin with the band up high on the wall, door, or anchor point.
Grasp the handle or loop end. Keeping your lower body stable,
bring the band across your body in a diagonal from high to low,
back and forth, for twenty seconds.

Reattach the band to a low point on the wall. Repeat the exercise, this time going from low to high.

Switch sides and repeat.

11. FOUR-WAY OVERHEAD RESISTED FOOT FIRE

EQUIPMENT: *RESISTANCE BANDS (SHEATHED OR LOOPED)*   **RESISTANCE BAND POSITION:** *OVERHEAD*

Unlike Overhead Arm Flutters, this exercise keeps your upper body static.

With the band up high, stand facing the wall. Grip one handle overhead with both hands. Keep your posture upright.

As you hold the band taut, shuffle your feet in place for twenty seconds.

Adjust your stance so you are facing away from the anchor point. Repeat the exercise, again for twenty seconds.

12. RESISTED WALKING PLANK

EQUIPMENT: *RESISTANCE BANDS (LOOPED)*

RESISTANCE BAND POSITION: *KNEE HEIGHT*

This exercise is a very challenging variation of
the conventional plank.

With the band at a low point on the wall, loop it around your waist. Assume a plank position.

Keeping your hips level, move as far away from the wall as you can, using your legs and your arms, and maintaining control at all times.

Switch sides and repeat.

LOWER-BODY EXERCISES

Many gym trainers tell athletes to target their upper bodies on Mondays and Wednesdays and their lower bodies on Tuesdays and Thursdays. At TB12, we advise athletes to do upper body, core, and lower body in the same workout. By engaging your entire body at once, you activate every muscle group, are holistically stronger and more balanced, and also move better. Why do we at TB12 emphasize explosive movements? Because in the course of our daily lives, our bodies—especially our lower bodies—need to move quickly and efficiently, whether we're walking, standing, running, getting up out of a chair, or climbing stairs. Our legs are involved in lots of movements, and it's important to stress their muscles beyond just our body weight, but always in a tolerable way. It shouldn't be like climbing Mount Everest! Vary these exercises, and add heavier resistance bands as you go. As with all of these exercises, focus on the amount of strength that's appropriate for your life.

1. SQUAT

EQUIPMENT: *NONE*

This exercise mimics the motions—standing, sitting, getting up again—we do every day. The goal is to use your glutes while keeping pressure off your knees.

Assume an upright posture, with your feet hip-width apart.

Stick your butt out and gradually lower yourself into a squat. Keep your knees directly over your toes, and don't allow them to collapse inward. As you come back up, remember to squeeze your glutes.

Rise and lower for twenty seconds. As with all these exercises, focus on the amount of strength that's appropriate to your life.
As we said earlier, think fast and move fast—*that's* why we train fast.

VARIATION: Adding a short looped band around your knees is a good way to add challenge to the exercise.

2. LATERAL RESISTED SQUAT

EQUIPMENT: *RESISTANCE BANDS (LOOPED)*   **RESISTANCE BAND POSITION:** *WAIST HEIGHT*

A squat, but with the variation of side resistance.

Loop the band around your waist so it's taut.

With your posture upright and your feet hip-width apart, lower yourself into a squat. Keep your knees directly over your toes, and don't allow them to collapse inward.

Do this for twenty seconds. Turn, face the other way, and repeat on the other side.

3. LEG-ASSISTED SIDE PLANK

EQUIPMENT: *NONE*

This exercise activates your body's lateral stability as you push up from one side and then the other.

Assume a short side-plank position, with your knees bent and pressed slightly forward. Brace your weight on your right arm.

Raise your top leg so that it's parallel with the ground and extend your left arm straight over your shoulder so it's perpendicular to the ground. Maintain this position for five seconds, then begin fanning your leg up and down, using short motions.

Do this for twenty seconds, then repeat on the other side.

4. FORWARD LUNGE WITH HIGH HOLD

EQUIPMENT: *RESISTANCE BANDS (SHEATHED OR LOOPED)*

RESISTANCE BAND POSITION: *OVERHEAD*

Whether we're climbing the stairs or stepping down off a porch, a lunge is a fairly common, everyday movement. In this exercise, overhead resistance bands add challenge.

With the band attached high on the wall, face away from the wall, door, or anchor point and grip the handle or loop with your right arm.

Drop down into a lunge position, while keeping your right arm overhead in a locked position.

Switch arms and repeat on the other side.

5. FOUR-WAY BAND RUNNING IN PLACE

EQUIPMENT: *RESISTANCE BANDS (LOOPED)*

By running in place as fast as you can while maintaining stability, you train your brain and body to do these same movements, only slower, in the course of daily living.

RESISTANCE BAND POSITION: *WAIST HEIGHT*

Attach a band around your waist.

Move away from the wall until the band grows taut. With your stomach and glutes engaged, begin running in place at a comfortable speed for twenty seconds. Keep your knees up at all times.

Turn so your side is to the wall. Begin running in place.

Now turn and face the wall. With the band taut, run in place for another twenty seconds. Turn sideways and do the same, then turn in the other direction and repeat.

6. RESISTED SHUFFLE

EQUIPMENT: *RESISTANCE BANDS (LOOPED)*

The challenge in this exercise is to stay stable, level, and relaxed at all times. It's not easy.

RESISTANCE BAND POSITION: *WAIST HEIGHT*

With the band looped around your waist, crouch low, engaging your glutes, with your feet hip-width apart.

Now shuffle-leap from one side to the other, making quick explosive motions as you go.

Turn, face the other direction, and repeat.

7. HEIDEN HOP

EQUIPMENT: *NONE*

A great knee-stability exercise that we use a lot at TB12. Start
with small jumps, then work your way up.

The goal of this exercise is to jump from one leg to the other.

Keeping your knee directly over your toes, jump up and land on the other side. Hold for two seconds. Jump again, switching directions.

Do this for twenty seconds. The goal is height, not distance.

8. SINGLE-LEG CLOCK JUMPS

EQUIPMENT: *NONE*

Jump, land on one foot, and turn. This exercise seems
tailor-made for wide receivers.

Sit backward slightly, with your knees directly over your toes. Engage your core and glutes. Now raise one leg and jump in place. Rotate 90 degrees and repeat, then another 90 degrees, until you're back to where you started. Don't let your raised leg touch the ground.

Do the exercise for twenty seconds. Repeat, this time counter-clockwise.

ALTERNATIVE: If the single-leg clock jump is too difficult, do the same exercise on two feet (without raising one leg).

9. SQUAT JUMP

EQUIPMENT: *NONE*

If you've ever jumped down off a stone wall, this exercise will
remind you of the importance of landing on both feet.

Keep your knees directly over your toes. Raise your arms in front of you at chest level.

Assume a squat for a 1–2 count. Jump up, and then return to the squat position. Hold again for a 1–2 count. Repeat.

Go faster to increase the cadence. The emphasis is on height, not distance. Keep your knees directly over your toes at all times.

Do the exercise for twenty seconds.

10. SQUAT TO PRESS

EQUIPMENT: *RESISTANCE BANDS (LOOPED)*

In this exercise, you explode upward while lifting your arms
high up over your head.

Step inside the band with both feet and assume a squat position, with the band at shoulder level.

As you straighten up, raise the band overhead. Return to your squat and repeat the motion. Keep your knees directly over your toes, making sure they don't collapse inward.

Do this for twenty seconds, gradually increasing the pace.

11. HIP THRUSTERS

EQUIPMENT: *RESISTANCE BANDS (LOOPED)*   **RESISTANCE BAND POSITION:** *KNEE HEIGHT*

Imagine doing a squat while being pulled backward.
This one can take a little time to master.

Attach the band to a low point on the wall, door, or anchor point and loop it around your waist. With your back to the wall, walk out a few steps until the band is taut.

Assume a squat position, keeping the band taut. Rise up in an explosive movement, then lower back down to your squat position. Repeat for twenty seconds.

12. BAND DEAD LIFT

EQUIPMENT: *RESISTANCE BANDS (SHEATHED OR LOOPED)*

A much better way to do a dead lift, since a resistance band is more forgiving than weights.

Place both feet over a sheathed or looped band. Hold both sides of the band (or the handles) with your hands and manipulate the slack in the band until it is taut. Assume a squat, keeping your back as flat as possible.

Pull up with the bands, pushing your hips forward.

By manipulating the slack in the band, you can make this exercise easier or harder.

Making sure I get proper hydration is critical to my performance on and off the field.

CHAPTER 7

HYDRATION

ACHIEVING SUSTAINED PEAK PERFORMANCE MEANS BUILDING UP AND MAINTAINING YOUR BODY'S ABILITY TO DO WHAT IT NEEDS TO DO AT ITS HIGHEST LEVELS. TO ACCOMPLISH THAT, ONE TOOL ISN'T ENOUGH. WE NEED A SET OF TOOLS WE CAN USE AT THE SAME TIME, THE GOAL BEING THE HEALTH AND CONSTANT REGENERATION OF OUR MUSCLES—IN OTHER WORDS, OUR INNER ENVIRONMENT. AS WE GET OLDER, WE ALL HAVE TO DEAL WITH SOME DEGREE OF SLOWDOWN, BUT BY BRINGING TOGETHER THE RIGHT VARIETY OF TOOLS IN A HOLISTIC MANNER, WE CAN DECELERATE THAT AGING PROCESS AS MOST PEOPLE EXPERIENCE IT TODAY. AT TB12, WE DO THAT THROUGH PLIABILITY AND AMPLIFIERS THAT MAXIMIZE OUR DAILY VITALITY.

Of these tools, the first—proper hydration—is, to me, by far the most important. The body's lymphatic system—which helps vacuum out damaged cells and fight infection—can flush out many of the effects of poor nutrition, but if we don't drink enough water, the lymphatic system can't flush out much at all. The lymphatic system is more than 95 percent water, and we need to keep it clean and flowing constantly so it can rid our bodies of toxins that build up. That's one reason why keeping well hydrated is key to our overall health. Not only that, but it increases our chances for optimal pliability.

Twenty years ago, when I was playing at Michigan, I didn't drink nearly as much water as I do today. On top of that, I drank a lot of other things—alcohol, juice, soda—that I later found out can be *dehydrating*. I definitely experienced a lot more fatigue in my twenties than I do today, and I got more headaches, too. Today I rarely get fatigued, I never get headaches, and I never cramp. I credit this to the amount of water and electrolytes I drink.

Electrolytes are chemicals and nutrients that are already present in our bodies in the form of potassium, sodium, magnesium, and others. They create an electric charge, either positive or negative, whenever they dissolve in the blood, urine, or body fluids. Electrolytes are essential for maintaining blood chemistry, proper nerve and muscle function, and acid-alkaline balance. They help our muscles expand and contract and our lymphatic system circulate water and fluids inside the body. That's why electrolytes are so critical to proper hydration—which maintains our levels of pliability.

On any given day, I easily drink more than 150 ounces of water with TB12 Electrolytes, and on active days I drink close to twice that. To help you visualize, a can of soda or a normal bottle of water is twelve ounces. I drink the equivalent of twelve to twenty-five of those every day, and always with TB12 Electrolytes. Basically you'll never see me without a bottle of water in my hand, and I add electrolytes to virtually everything I drink—and that's been true for the past twelve years. Even if I'm drinking lemonade, I'll add electrolytes to it. Otherwise I feel like I'm doing myself a disservice. For anyone who exercises regularly and who's committed to sustained peak performance, the rule of thumb at

TB12 is simple: *Drink at least one-half of your body weight in ounces of water every day.* That's the minimum. Ideally, you'll drink more than that, and with added electrolytes, too.

This makes sense, considering the composition of our bodies. As is well known, our bodies are made up of anywhere from 60 to 80 percent water, and our muscles alone are 75 percent water. Water aids in brain function; ensures healthy metabolism, digestion, and kidney function; helps circulate oxygen into the bloodstream; lubricates joints; and ensures proper muscle function. If we don't drink enough water, we risk decreasing the supply of oxygen in our bloodstream and depriving our muscles and organs of the proper nutrients. That means we build up more toxins in our cells, tissues, and organs. Let me repeat: *That means we build up more toxins in our cells—which creates an unhealthy inner environment.* Our metabolism slows down, which makes us more vulnerable to infection and inflammation. For athletes especially, drinking enough water decreases joint pain by softening and hydrating cartilage and increasing how much water gets absorbed.

That's why proper hydration is linked to pliability. Our body coaches can often predict how sore clients who come to the TB12 Sports Therapy Center may be based on their discomfort level after their first pliability session. Pain and soreness are normal responses to pliability if an athlete's muscles are dehydrated from poor hydration or nutrition. A trained body coach can literally feel the difference between someone who's eating well and is properly hydrated and another person who doesn't drink enough water and eats poorly. How fast or slowly we're able to develop pliable muscles, and optimal strength, depends to a large extent on how hydrated we are.

That's why the first and most critical amplifier of the TB12 Method, and of pliability, centers on making sure you drink enough water, ideally with electrolytes.

WATER BASICS

Dehydration is a chronic problem, and is more common than most people realize. I'm not just talking about for athletes, either. I'm talking about everybody. A lot of people I've met through the TB12 Sports Therapy Center believe that they're properly hydrated, or at least hydrated *enough*. They might drink one or two glasses of water in the morning, bottled water at lunch, tap water at dinner, and keep a glass by their bedside at night. But when you add up the totals, they're getting only about three or four cups of water daily, which doesn't come close to how we at TB12 define proper hydration. Most athletes don't realize they're sweating and breathing out anywhere from eight to ten cups of water a day, especially in warm temperatures. That water needs to be replenished—and ideally with electrolytes, too.

When people ask whether other beverages count in their daily hydration, I remind them that coffee, tea, alcohol, and soda can be dehydrating, and that the sugar content in alcohol and soda makes them even worse. Put another way, water adds to pliability, and diuretic drinks containing sugar, caffeine, or alcohol take away from pliability. Dehydration is also a compounding issue, meaning that you need to drink more fluid ounces of water to make up for each fluid ounce of a dehydrating liquid you drink. This is why I try to limit caffeine and my intake of alcohol, as they go against all my efforts to stay as hydrated as possible.

If there's one simple thing everyone can do to enhance their own muscle pliability, it's to drink enough water regularly and continuously. Also, it's not enough to drink one-half of your body weight or more in ounces of water on Monday, thinking your body will be properly hydrated one or two days later. Reaching a baseline of proper hydration takes at least fourteen days.

When I explain hydration to people, I use the analogy of going into a butcher shop. Imagine the difference when you look behind the counter at a beautiful, fresh piece of tenderloin and right next to it you see a dried-up piece of beef jerky. The tenderloin is healthy and supple, whereas the beef jerky is shriveled and dried out. That beef jerky is what dehydrated muscles look like. No, it's not a perfect or exact analogy, but the next time you consider drinking a cup of coffee or a glass of wine without rebalancing their dehydrating effects with water and electrolytes, you need to picture that image!

Consider that when you drink a single cup of coffee or glass of wine, it can create a "dehydrating factor" of as much as 2 to 1 per cup or glass. In other words, to offset the effects of a single serving of coffee or beer, you may need to drink two glasses of water with electrolytes on top of the water you already drink.

It's also important to recognize that not all waters are created equal. Here are some of the varieties out there.

A REMINDER

Remember that the only way our brains and bodies store positive and intentional trauma is via nervous-system stimulation during a pliability session. When we contract and relax our muscles as they're being lengthened and softened, we're re-educating our brains to train those muscles to stay long, soft, and primed. And how quickly or slowly we're able to develop pliable muscles, and optimal strength, depends to a large extent on how hydrated we are.

TAP WATER

Tap water is water that comes from a municipal source. Depending on where you live, most sources of tap water contain fluoride, chlorine, and, in some cases, lead. Excessive amounts of both fluoride and chlorine have now been linked to a number of health risks. Drink tap water only if you filter it first, which gets rid of many impurities. Even when you use tap water for steaming vegetables, it's better to filter it first.

DISTILLED OR FILTERED WATER

Distilled water is water purified of any contaminants or pollutants. Unfortunately, it's also been stripped of its mineral content, which means it doesn't give our bodies the nutrients they need. If I were drinking distilled water, I would always add electrolytes.

SPRING WATER

Most bottled waters start off as spring water, which may or may not have gone through a treating or purification process. That said, many bottled waters contain bacteria and chemicals. In addition, as a result of their popularity and demand, more than half of all bottled waters whose labels claim to be "spring water" are nothing more than treated tap water, drawn from multiple sources.

MINERAL WATER

Many brands of mineral water contain alkalizing minerals, and therefore have an alkalizing effect on the body, which is optimal (I'll talk about alkalinity in the next chapter). Some mineral waters claim to be "naturally alkaline," but always check the label to make sure. Mineral water is always a great option.

CARBONATED WATER

Carbonated water—such as seltzer water, sparkling water, and, in cases where sodium is added, club soda—is water pressurized using carbon dioxide gas. Carbonated water has less oxygen than regular water, is slightly more acidic, and can also be dehydrating. I avoid it.

PURIFIED WATER

Purified water has the fewest number of impurities, since chemicals and pathogens have been eliminated to a degree exceeding what the US Environmental Protection Agency requires for everyday tap water. As the name says, purified water, which is identified on the label, is the purest water out there. It's my recommendation for what to drink, though I add electrolytes to it first to replenish the electrolyte and mineral content I lose each day.

When I was growing up, and playing outside in the sun, I got sunburned a lot. I was a fair-skinned Irish boy, after all. These days, even if I get an adequate amount of sun, I won't get a sunburn, which I credit to the amount of water I drink. I always hydrate afterward, too, to keep my skin from peeling. When I once told that to my sister, she said, "You mean I don't have to use all those moisturizers and facial products to keep my skin looking good? I should just drink as much water as you do? I think you should market your TB12 Electrolytes as a beauty product." I just laughed.

SIGNS OF DEHYDRATION

Water helps our bodies carry out their normal functions—and dehydration means only that we've lost water in our bodies without replacing it. The more we exercise, the more water we lose. Even nonathletes are vulnerable to dehydration. Dry lips, dry skin, dry eyes, headaches, nosebleeds, and waking up in the middle of the night with a dry throat are all symptoms of dehydration. Personally, I've always noticed that the more hydrated I am, the less likely I am to get sunburns! (I'm in the sun a lot, especially on the practice field.) I credit that to my hydration levels.

Electrolytes replace the minerals our bodies lose through working out. I go through a bottle of TB12 Electrolytes every day.

WHY THE RIGHT ELECTROLYTES MATTER

During and after exercising, athletes lose a lot of water and electrolytes via breathing and sweating, which can lead to faintness and dizziness. That's why I go through a bottle of electrolytes every day. In 2013, we at TB12 developed what we believe are the purest, highest-quality electrolytes available. TB12 Electrolytes, which are enriched with seventy-two trace minerals and contain no added preservatives, flavors, or sweeteners, are a natural mineral concentrate that allows athletes to turn any liquid into a hydrating sports drink.

To recap, electrolytes are chemicals and nutrients that are already present in our bodies in the form of potassium, sodium, magnesium, and others. Alex has explained it to me this way: Our muscle cells can either resemble soft soap bubbles or hard glass bubbles. When you're dehydrated, your muscle cells are more likely to take on the look and consistency of hard glass bubbles. You can drink a gallon of water, but unless it has electrolytes in it, the water molecules won't be able to pass into and out of the fluid compartments in your body. They run off and never permeate the cell. Imagine a rain jacket doing its job by resisting rain. We don't ever want to prevent water molecules from penetrating our cells. By contrast, water that's been enhanced with electrolytes passes into and out of your muscle cells easily and efficiently. The more electrolytes your body has, the more easily water is able to penetrate your muscles, and the more likely your cells are to take on the qualities of soap bubbles. Imagine a sponge that absorbs maximum amounts of water. During a workout, if you're drinking only plain water to replace the natural salts your body loses through perspiration, you're not replacing them with the minerals your body needs. The goal of electrolytes is to make the water you drink "wetter" and more likely to be absorbed by your body's cells. It's the best way to hydrate.

In my belief, not all electrolytes are the same. Some electrolytes have a positive charge, and others have a negative charge, and it's possible for these negative and positive ions to cancel each other out.

Every day we deal with an excess of positive ions coming from our cell phones, TVs, microwave ovens, lightbulbs, and indoor environmental pollution. It may sound counterintuitive, but in my belief, *negative* ions have the greatest benefit on our physica and mental health. They increase our bodies' alkalinity and serotonin levels and accelerate healing and recovery, while amplifying our levels of pliability.

CAN YOU OVERHYDRATE?

Alex and I both believe there's an optimal point of hydration, and theoretically you can overhydrate in the same way you can overdo anything. You can also reach a point where your body has taken in so much water in so short a period that it can't metabolize it. But in reality this happens to people so rarely that it shouldn't be a top concern. The larger issue is that most people are underhydrated relative to the optimal pliability levels we recommend at TB12.

DEVELOPING A WATER ROUTINE: STEP-BY-STEP BASICS

Where hydration is concerned, balance and pacing are important. As usual, don't do everything at once. Work toward proper hydration step-by-step, line by line, precept by precept. Drinking at least one-half of your body weight in ounces of water every day is a great place to start. Drinking those ounces of water enhanced with electrolytes is even better. It has taken me many years to get into a great routine—but I know I will have great hydration for the rest of my life.

DRINK ONE OR TWO GLASSES OF WATER WHEN YOU FIRST WAKE UP

Drink a glass or two of water with electrolytes when you wake up, but be sure to wait half an hour before you eat breakfast, and don't drink water while you're eating (see below). It gets in the way of optimally digesting foods and absorbing their nutrients.

SPREAD OUT YOUR HYDRATION DURING THE DAY

Try not to drink all your water at the same time. Space out your water drinking over the course of the day. In general, it's not good to drink more than four eight-ounce glasses during a one-hour period. If you weigh 160 pounds, via our rule of thumb you should be drinking at least 80 ounces of water per day. Assuming you're up by 8:00 a.m. and in bed by 10:30 p.m., that's a glass of water every couple of hours. I carry a water bottle with me wherever I go, and I make sure I'm always properly hydrated.

LIMIT DRINKING WATER DURING MEALS

Try not to drink too much water during a meal, as it can interfere with digestion. Wait an hour or so after you're done eating before you drink water, since water washes away the body's natural enzymes, which break down your food. Rule of thumb: Drink more water before and after meals than during meals.

TB12 ACTION STEPS

- Hydrate, hydrate, hydrate. Drink at least one-half of your body weight in ounces every day, and more if you can.

- Add electrolytes to your water as often as possible.

- Reduce or eliminate your intake of caffeine, soda, and alcohol. All three can be dehydrating. If you drink coffee, soda, or alcohol, rebalance your hydration by drinking two glasses of water for every one of those beverages you consume.

- Remember that if we don't drink enough water, our lymphatic system can't flush out the built-up toxins in our bodies. That's one reason why keeping well hydrated is key to our overall health.

- Hydration and pliability are interdependent. How fast or slowly you develop pliable muscles depends to a large extent on how well hydrated you are.

WATER IN OUR BODIES

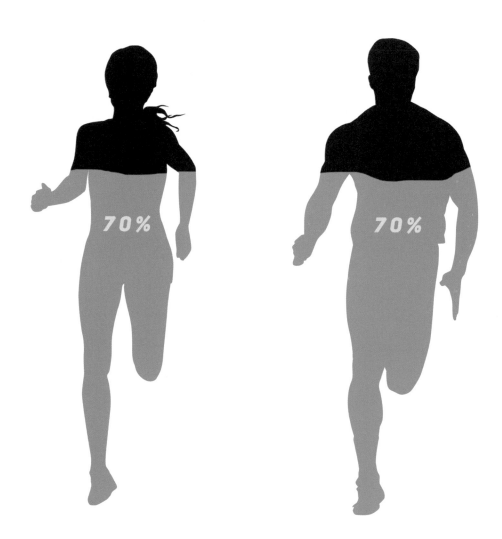

WHY HYDRATION MATTERS

Our bodies are made up of anywhere from 60 to 80 percent water, and our muscles alone are 75 percent water. Water aids in brain function; ensures healthy metabolism, digestion, and kidney function; helps circulate oxygen in the bloodstream; lubricates joints; and ensures proper muscle function. Proper hydration helps restore the body's natural percentage of water while creating optimal pliability.

CHAPTER 8

NUTRITION

This is what a healthy diet looks like to me.

BY NOW, HOPEFULLY YOU REALIZE THAT PLIABILITY DOESN'T REFER ONLY TO TARGETED, DEEP-FORCE MUSCLE WORK. YOU CAN DO PLIABILITY TREATMENTS AND WORK OUT EVERY DAY, BUT IF YOU DON'T PAY ATTENTION TO WHAT YOU PUT INSIDE YOUR BODY, OR IF YOU IGNORE THE CONNECTION BETWEEN GOOD NUTRITION AND HEALTHY MUSCLES, THEN YOU'RE NOT GIVING YOURSELF THE OPPORTUNITY TO ACHIEVE YOUR PEAK PERFORMANCE. IT REALLY DOESN'T MATTER HOW MUCH EXERCISE YOU DO IF YOU'RE NOT EATING THE RIGHT FOOD AND PROVIDING YOUR BODY THE RIGHT NUTRIENTS.

One important point to remember goes back to one of the principles of the TB12 Method—balance. You need to optimize and maintain your pliability even when you're not in the gym or on the field. To do that, proper nutrition is critical. What's more, the type of nutritional regimen you choose will either promote or reduce inflammation. That's why after pliability training and making sure I drink enough water every day, the next most important choice I make as an athlete centers on nutrition.

During the season, I know I'll be hit hard every Sunday—and I will be dealing with negative-unintentional traumas that lead to inflammation responses in my body. I also know my body will generate trauma responses to deal with the line-of-duty soreness and pain I feel. On and off the field, my goal is to avoid additional inflammation on top of the inflammation I get from playing football. Every Monday after a game, for example, the whole team comes into the weight room to bench-press, squat, and do other weight-bearing activities. The way I see it, they are creating more trauma in addition to the "car crash" our bodies were experiencing less than twenty-four hours earlier. Knowing my body needs to recover after a game, I'm careful about how I train on Mondays. I do enough to keep my strength optimal and my muscles firing at 100 percent, but I stop

short of generating additional inflammation. Younger athletes may be able to get away with this routine because of their natural pliability. But as a forty-year-old athlete, I have to think differently about my time allocation, as discussed previously.

That extends to my nutritional regimen. After Monday practice, and with Tuesdays off, a lot of players will go home and not think much about their nutritional choices. I was that way myself in my early twenties. If I was going to work out and play hard, I told myself, I could be as undisciplined with my nutrition as I wanted. Back then I didn't give much thought to what I ate, so long as I stayed in the 220–30 pound weight range. Of course, not all calories are created equal. The calories you get from an apple are different from the ones you get from an apple pie. It's the nutrients in that apple that can help accelerate recovery and reduce inflammation, and a big reason why I can recover from Sunday's game significantly faster than players who may be ten or fifteen years younger than me.

Some younger players don't give too much thought to nutrition. They think they can eat anything they want, and their bodies will burn off the damage. The problem is that by eating inflammatory foods, they're eating things that create inflammation on top of the weight lifting they've done on top of the football game they just played on Sunday. That's an inflammation response times three. As I said, if I know my body will experience inflammation every Sunday during the season, the last thing I want to do is stack on more inflammation on top of it—not if I want to feel great every time I take the field.

That's why for the past ten years I've followed a pretty disciplined nutritional regimen. It's based on eating fresh, seasonal, organic foods from authentic and, ideally, local sources. I also subscribe to the philosophy and principle of eating 80 percent alkaline-forming and 20 percent acid-causing foods. What that means in practical terms is that, while I'm not a vegetarian by any means, I do subscribe to a commonsensical, mostly plant-based/plant-heavy and seasonal nutritional regimen. What we're learning from the slow-food and farm-to-table movements is that if the food we eat is grown naturally and locally, and we avoid processed foods, we're already doing our bodies and minds a big favor. For these reasons, I try to eat only "real food"—food that comes from nature rather than from industrial sources. A lot of what we buy and eat today is sold to us as "natural" when it isn't, or else it's so watered-down or pumped full of additives, chemicals, and preservatives that it has almost nothing in common with the real thing.

The regimen I follow is a mix of Eastern and Western philosophies. Some of these principles have been around for thousands of years. My nutritional regimen may seem restrictive to some people, but to me it feels unnatural to eat any other way. Many people have conditioned their bodies to a nutritional regimen made up of lots of white or pale-looking foods—french fries, potato chips, white bread, chicken nuggets—that don't exist in nature. A friend once told me that when his young son was asked in school where ketchup came from, he said, "A bottle." He had no idea that the source of ketchup is supposed to be tomatoes. Still, it's never too late to teach children how to eat right. If children learn nothing else but the principle of eating more real food and fewer processed or refined foods, it won't just benefit their pliability, it will also help reduce obesity levels and help them feel healthier and more energetic.

The principles behind my nutritional regimen have nothing to do with fads or trends. As you go over them and, more important, the specifics of what I eat, remember that this is what works for me in my life and my job. Everybody is different. Changing a nutritional regimen isn't easy—I know that. Modify things at your own pace. As always, try cutting out or adding something here, something there. Halfway measures are better than no measures at all. Try to figure out what works best for you, and if it gives you more energy or improves your performance, you're on the right path.

Vegetables are obviously a very important—and alkalizing—part of my diet.

GENERAL GUIDELINES

THE DOS

EAT AS MUCH REAL, ORGANIC, AND LOCAL FOOD AS YOU CAN

I eat foods that are as fresh as possible, and most of the time that means I choose to eat organic foods. Their nutrient content is much higher than the foods you find in the supermarket, and organic foods don't have any of the pesticides, preservatives, stabilizers, growth hormones, and other chemicals the commercial food industry uses to grow and preserve food. Even if you eat only a small percentage of organic foods, you'll have more energy and you'll feel more satisfied. Why? Because the chemicals in some industrial foods stimulate natural chemicals in our brains that block leptin, a protein that governs our metabolism and that creates a feeling of "fullness" during meals. Basically, the chemicals that food companies put in our foods increase food cravings. Our brains never turn off. They're always hungry. Nutrient-dense, high-fiber foods, on the other hand, not only give us more energy but also, thanks to their natural fiber content, make us feel fuller faster, and with smaller servings.

If eating 100 percent organic food isn't an option, focus instead on eating real food, whether you buy it at a supermarket, a farm stand, or through a farm share program. Most food sold locally is real food, and most of the time close enough to organic—the difference being that local farmers may not have devoted the time, expense, and paperwork needed to get official US Department of Agriculture Organic Certification. Real food is also local and seasonal. Unlike industrial processed food, which puts old things or ingredients in new products or packages, real food never changes, and eating real food

makes the most sense—humans have been eating vegetables, fruits, meat, and fish for centuries. It may go without saying, but whether you buy fruits and vegetables in the supermarket or at a local health-food store, always wash them before eating them.

EAT MOSTLY VEGETABLES

Vegetables are high in nutrients, fiber, and enzymes. I try to eat as many as I can at every meal. I also try to eat some percentage of vegetables either raw or lightly steamed. Very high cooking temperatures can strip away the nutrient and enzyme content of vegetables, and raw foods also have an alkalizing effect on the body. I'll be talking more about alkalizing foods later in this chapter, but as I've gotten smarter about eating, I've moved toward adopting an alkalizing diet—and most vegetables are alkalizing. The benefits of vegetables and their alkalizing effects is that they promote less inflammation than other foods do—and create healthier muscles, which leads to optimal pliability and helps maintain great vitality and peak performance.

A mostly whole-food, plant-based nutritional regimen is one centered on vegetables, fruits, whole grains, and legumes. It limits meat and fish, dairy products, and any refined, processed foods, including flours, sugars, and oils. When people ask if I'm a vegan or a vegetarian, I tell them no, decidedly not. I may be plant- and vegetable-focused, but I also eat meat, chicken, and fish in limited amounts. If anything, I subscribe to balance. In grade school, we all learned to eat in a balanced way—the difference being that we now have a better idea about how to achieve that balance and are smarter about the differences between real foods and processed or refined ones.

Let food be thy medicine.
—HIPPOCRATES

Leafy greens are packed with vitamins and antioxidants—
I try to eat as many of them as I can.

EAT LOCAL FOODS WHENEVER POSSIBLE

In general, the more local your food is, the better. The fruits and vegetables you see in the supermarket have been shipped anywhere from 1,500 to 2,000 miles on average to get there. They've been packed in Styrofoam in trucks and on planes, and by the time you see them on the shelves, they're a week to ten days old—and the average apple for sale in a US grocery store was picked up to ten months ago. Most have likely been frozen and thawed out at least once. With national soil levels nutrient deprived to begin with, the vitamins and minerals in the fruits and vegetables we buy have degraded even more. When food travels, it begins a long, slow death. This slow death depletes the nutrients of the food we eat, so our bodies are never really being nourished with what we need for optimum health.

The principle behind my eating habits is simple: I want to eat food in ways that maximize its nutritional value. The more concentrated my nutrition, the fresher it is, and the more local and organic, the better it is for me. I know that local and organic food often costs more, but the way I see it, I'm making up those savings in decreased health-care costs in the long run—and, most important, I feel better and have performed better as I've eaten healthier. It's impossible to eat the cheapest foods while also eating the best foods. Eating healthy is an investment I make in myself. We all have one body and one life. I've made it a priority to treat that body and life as respectfully as possible.

EAT SEASONALLY

In my experience, my body needs and responds to different foods depending on the climate where I live, and also on what season it is. I know, for example, that following a mostly plant-based nutritional regimen is good for my health, but that's because I live in New England most of the year. If I were living in a place like Alaska, where the climate is colder and darker for a longer period of the year, my diet would need to shift to incorporate a higher percentage of fat and protein, which counteract the cold temperatures outside. It's all about balance. That's why your environment, and what you ask your body to do in it, is a big part of determining what nutritional regimen best suits you.

In some medical traditions, there are certain "warm property" foods that are higher in fat and protein, while other foods, known as "cold property" foods, are lower in fat. On hot summer days, it feels more natural to cook or eat foods that are light or "cool," like salad or fruit. On colder days, our cravings naturally skew toward stews or soups. A few warm-weather foods that cool the body include cucumbers, asparagus, avocados, broccoli, and celery. On the list of cold-weather foods are root vegetables, fennel, oats, quinoa, and rutabaga. Some foods fall in the middle. They're neither warm-weather nor cold-weather, and are considered neutral: apricots, beets, grapes, green beans, lentils, pineapples, potatoes, and raspberries. These principles are thousands of years old, and they make intuitive sense.

A good rule of thumb is to observe the seasons and eat whatever foods are locally available in the climate you inhabit. Spring vegetables in the spring. Fall vegetables in the fall. If one food feels more "summery" and another feels more "wintery," they probably are. Once I understood this concept, I became more aware of what I ate and when I ate it, and why I was better off eating more meat in the winter than during the summer. When I could feel the difference in my body, the habit stuck. The bottom line is, I try to eat as seasonally as possible. This nutritional regimen works for me, and I would expect it to give you the same results. But again, take your time. Making changes in your nutrition is challenging, so start slowly and build on your positive results.

CONSUME ESSENTIAL FATTY ACIDS

Many believe the best sources of dietary fat are essential fatty acids, especially omega-3 and omega-6 fats. These can be found in sardines, wild game, flaxseed and flaxseed oil, walnuts, pumpkin seeds, and canola oil. The media and most high-profile diets would have us believe that fat is the enemy, but the truth is our bodies require a certain daily percentage of fats. Fats create insulation in our bodies, stabilize our body temperatures, give us more energy, transport oxygen, and help us absorb fat-soluble vitamins. Best of all, they act as natural anti-inflammatories. Omega-3 fatty acids, which are concentrated in the brain, have been shown to enhance both memory and performance.

EAT FOODS HIGH IN FIBER

Along with essential fatty acids, I also make sure my diet has lots of fiber in it. The best fiber sources out there are fruits, vegetables, bran, rolled oats, brown rice, and various other complex carbohydrates. High-fiber diets are associated with a reduced incidence of heart disease, high blood pressure, and of certain kinds of cancer and GI conditions.

EAT A VARIETY OF FOODS

I try to eat as wide an assortment of foods as I can every day. Different foods contain different nutrients and minerals, and no single food can give your body exactly what it needs. Even if you eat spinach three

You can be creative with what you eat.

Fruit is a core ingredient of my morning smoothies.
I also snack on fruit throughout the day.

meals a day, you're missing out on dozens of other nutrients your body needs to achieve optimal health. Just as you shouldn't get all your greens from spinach, you shouldn't get all your protein from a piece of beef. By varying the foods you eat, you also avoid boredom. As part of the TB12 Method, I've also created a line of healthy snacks and protein bars that help me refuel in between meals. They're raw, nutrient-rich, and alkalizing, and a regular part of my diet.

We at TB12 also work with a great meal-delivery service that aligns with the goals of TB12 to provide meals that make the type of eating we subscribe to at TB12 available for everybody. Their food is nutrient-rich and tastes great. I've been eating it all year on a weekly basis, and I feel great results. If you're lacking for time, this could be a great solution for you.

FOODS TO LIMIT OR AVOID: THE DON'TS

AVOID REFINED CARBOHYDRATES

The negative effects of eating too many refined carbohydrates, which are in junk foods and fast foods, include excessive insulin production, excessive fat storage, and elevated blood sugar levels. I try to keep my insulin levels balanced, since the more stable they are, the lower my inflammation rates will be. For that reason I try to avoid eating anything that comes in a box or a bag, as well as foods containing white flour or added sugars. That means I try to limit cereal, white bread, white rice, pasta, cakes, and cookies. Less inflammation is the key for me.

AVOID UNHEALTHY FATS

Trans-fatty acids and saturated fats are both found in hydrogenated oils, which are used in the commercial production of cookies, crackers, peanut butter, and breakfast cereals. Hydrogenation is the process of turning healthy oils into solids to keep them from going bad. Basically, trans fats are the worst kind of fat out there. If hydrogenated or partially hydrogenated oils appear on the label's ingredients list, try to avoid that product. (If a food has fewer than 0.5 grams of trans fat in it per serving, by law its label is allowed to say "0 grams of trans fat." So always read the label.) Trans fats not only create inflammation but are also linked to heart disease, diabetes, and stroke. Saturated fats, which are found in red meat, milk, butter, cheese, palm oil, and coconut oil, also increase the risk of heart disease. Of the two, saturated fats are "better" than trans fats, but try to limit your consumption of foods containing either. I will very rarely eat anything with these types of fats.

LIMIT DAIRY

The protein in dairy products—cow's milk, cheese, ice cream, yogurt—increases inflammation in both the digestive tract and the thyroid gland, which means your body is less able to absorb the right nutrients. When I was a kid, the dairy industry rolled out lots of campaigns urging people to drink lots of milk. Remember milk mustaches? I actually did that campaign back in 2002! But research today is pretty clear that we should consume dairy in more limited amounts. Our belief at TB12 is that dairy products are high in calories and lower in nutritional value than other foods, and milk shakes, cheeseburgers, and ice cream every night isn't going to make for a healthy diet, certainly not when you expect your body to perform at the highest levels.

LIMIT SALT

Our bodies need salt, but too much of it elevates blood pressure and interferes with our ability to eliminate toxins and waste from our cells. If you use salt, at least taste your food first, or use just a small pinch of salt

THE FOOD INDUSTRY

The way we eat has changed more in the past fifty years than it had in the previous ten thousand. There are around forty thousand products for sale in a supermarket. Most are manufactured by one of the ten or so multinationals that control our country's trillion-dollar industrial food system.

Most people define "food" as any substance we eat that provides proteins, fats, carbohydrates, vitamins, and minerals. Our body's cells absorb and metabolize these nutrients, which in turn give us energy and ensure continuing growth in our bones and muscles. But most of what we buy in the supermarket are food-like products or compounds marketed and sold to us as "food." They're not food. They're refinements or inventions that someone made up. Consider what the industry does to fruits and vegetables, too. Green apples, bananas, and tomatoes ripened by ethylene gas are available all year round, but are those real? Moreover, a lot of studies show that the mineral content of our soil has declined steadily since the 1950s, along with the nutritional value of the fruits and vegetables that grow in that soil.

The way I see it, food companies are more like chemical companies than anything else. But we keep eating what they sell us and then wondering why the rates of disease and obesity are so high. Our bodies become toxic when we ingest toxic chemicals. Just go into the grocery store and scan the ingredients on a can of soup or a jar of peanut butter. Ascorbic acid. High-fructose corn syrup. Potassium chloride. Citric acid. Sodium caseinate. Silicon dioxide. Xanthan gum. Turmeric sodium carbonate. Monopotassium phosphate. Fully hydrogenated vegetable oils. Then of course there's genetic engineering. Does that sound like something you'd want to eat? It sounds like a chemistry experiment to me.

When I think about "food," I picture an avocado, a banana, a salad, a handful of nuts, or a piece of fish. I don't picture a box of cereal, a tub of margarine, a box of doughnuts, a bag of potato chips, or anything else manufactured using salt, sugar, fat, additives, stabilizers, and chemicals. Food should look like, smell like, and taste like food. I'm not saying to never eat the foods I just mentioned, as I know they taste good (and are marketed well). But try to limit them and eat more real, organic, local food.

rather than overdoing it. There's a big difference between seasoning your food and flavoring it so completely that you can barely taste it. One of the problems I have with food that isn't "real" is that most of the time our palates are responding to one of three ingredients: salt, sugar, or fat. Whenever the media claims that some of the dietary methods I pursue are new-agey or even quackery, I tell them that some of the biggest advertisers on television and in the stadiums I've played in are marketing all the wrong things. Which message seems more sensible? It's common to see soda or alcohol commercials infiltrating every part of popular culture. I advocate for seeing more types of healthy food choices in advertising to help balance these out.

LIMIT NIGHTSHADES

Nightshades are a family of darker plants and foods that include mushrooms, eggplants, potatoes, strawberries, and bell peppers. Nightshades are a really great source of antioxidants. Now, eating vegetables like tomatoes and eggplant won't affect most people's performance levels, but, again, as an NFL quarterback, I need to do everything possible to maximize

225

my pliability and minimize even small amounts of inflammation. For that reason, I rarely eat dark-shaded vegetables. Again, my diet is engineered and matched to the job I need my body to do. As long as I play pro football, I'll be as disciplined as possible. At some point in my life, this may relax, but my diet has become so natural and ingrained that I can't really imagine any large changes in the future. Put another way, I enjoy how I eat, and what I eat, and I never feel I'm missing out—which brings me to the two things many adults indulge in: caffeine and alcohol.

LIMIT CAFFEINE

Roughly half of all Americans are addicted to coffee, tea, or soda. Drinking moderate amounts of coffee (200 milligrams of caffeine a day, which is about two cups of coffee) is harmless, but too much caffeine can lead to a wide range of health problems, not to mention edginess and stress. More to the point, caffeine can be dehydrating. I steer clear. If you're going to drink caffeine, you'd better stick to the 2-to-1 rule of thumb I mentioned earlier.

LIMIT ALCOHOL

If you drink alcohol, do so only in moderation. Too much alcohol is linked to hypertension, diabetes, obesity, and impaired liver function, but, again, the biggest problem for me is that alcohol is a diuretic and therefore is dehydrating. Alcohol is full of sugar, too, and for that reason alone it creates inflammation. From time to time I'll have a beer, and when I'm in a social setting, maybe a few drinks. But in general, I don't drink alcohol with my meals or as a stand-alone drink. In fact, at this point in my life, I rarely drink alcohol at all. If I do, I make sure I compensate for the loss in hydration by drinking twice that amount in water the next day.

ALKALINE VERSUS ACIDIC FOODS

In addition to eating as much real food as possible, I also follow a nutritional regimen that's made up of 80 percent alkaline and 20 percent acidic foods. In general, foods that are acidic cause inflammation, and alkaline-forming foods reduce inflammation.

To explain, every food we eat mixes with the oxygen in our body's cells to create energy. Whenever we digest and metabolize a food, it forms a signature inside the body. That ash is either acidic, alkaline, or neutral. The body's optimal pH range—pH is a measurement of the hydrogen ion concentration in our bodies—is around 7. A pH range below 7 means the body is too acidic. When we maintain good pH levels, the body is properly oxygenated, which accelerates recovery and healing.

Alkaline or neutral ash helps the body thrive, whereas eating too many acidifying foods leads to a condition called acidosis, which makes us more prone to infections, colds, flu, low energy, fatigue, sore muscles, joint pain, hip fractures, bone spurs, poor concentration, and mood swings. All of these things are opposite to what I need as an athlete. Strongly acidifying foods include white rice, bread, butter, cheese, yogurt, and beef. The optimal goal is an 80/20 balance between alkalizing and acidifying foods, and a pH balance of 7. By decreasing the percentage of acidifying foods in your diet, your body is better able to neutralize whatever acids it produces during digestion and protect itself from further acidity.

The foundation of an alkalizing meal is vegetables. All vegetables have lots of vitamins, alkalizing minerals, salts, enzymes, nutrients, and fiber. Again, try to eat as many green vegetables as you can—they're rich in chlorophyll, which gives them their green color—along with beets, green cabbage, carrots, cauliflower, garlic, onions, radishes, bell peppers, and squash. Still, don't eliminate acidifying foods altogether. No matter how acidic your pH levels are, your body still needs some acidic, protein-rich foods to work properly. We all need some percentage of acidifying protein to establish alkaline minerals in our muscles in the first place, and protein in turn helps our muscles retain alkaline minerals.

By following a nutritional regimen of around 80 percent alkaline or alkalizing foods and the remaining balance of 20 percent more acidifying foods, I try to keep my body in a naturally alkaline state. I try to eat alkalizing foods at every meal, and I spread them out during the day, too. A healthy diet means less inflammation, more energy, and faster recovery. These things align with TB12's philosophies, and they work great for me.

IF YOU CAN'T EAT RIGHT

Sometimes I'm in a situation where it's not possible to eat the things I want. When that happens, I do the best I can and focus on enjoying my night out. If the only options on a menu are pasta, pizza, or even cheeseburgers, I'll order a cheeseburger. I just won't order two or three of them. Or I'll eat half. I may love the taste, but I know that eating cheeseburgers or pizza won't help me accomplish my athletic goals. To me, it's about prioritizing. My regimen works for what I'm asking my body to do. In the end, it's balance in all things.

THE SHORT LIST

STRONGLY ALKALIZING FOODS

Artichokes	Lettuce (except for
Beets	iceberg)
Broccoli	Potatoes
Brussels sprouts	Red cabbage
Cabbage	Spinach
Carrots	Squash
Cauliflower	Sweet peppers
Chicory	Sweet potatoes
Cucumbers	Vegetable juice made in
Dandelion greens	a juicer
Escarole	Yams
Green beans	Zucchini

STRONGLY ACIDIFYING FOODS

Beef	Pecans
Black currants	Pineapples
Butter	Pistachio nuts
Cheese	Pork
Chickpeas	Pumpkin seeds
Cold cuts	Raspberries
Crayfish	Red currants
Hazelnuts	Salmon
Herring	Soybeans
Kiwis	Strawberries
Lobster	Sunflower seeds
Mackerel	Walnuts
Mandarin oranges	White bread
Millet	White rice
Nectarines	White wheat
Oranges	Yogurt
Peanuts	

PORTION SIZES

The cut of meat, chicken, or fish you eat shouldn't be any bigger than the size of your palm. It should be accompanied by at least two palms' worth of vegetables. As a general rule, it's good to leave the table feeling 75 percent full. That way your body can digest and absorb the food you've eaten more easily.

Here's a tip: If I'm in a restaurant and I order something savory, like fish or a steak, I make sure to order a lot of vegetables on the side. I eat them first, so by the time I get to the steak, I'm already pretty full. If I ate the steak first, I would have less room for the vegetables. In general, I try to eat what's good for me first, like the nutrient-rich vegetables, and save the stuff that's less good for me for last.

HOW MUCH ADDED SUGAR SHOULD YOU BE EATING EVERY DAY?

We get a lot of sugar naturally from the fruits and vegetables we eat. Athletes who burn a lot of calories can get away with eating up to 50 grams of added sugar a day, but for most people I wouldn't recommend more than 25 grams per day. Again, I try to limit sugar, as it raises insulin and creates inflammation. As you know by now, inflammation is the enemy for an athlete.

TIMING BETWEEN EATING AND REST

Try to give yourself around three hours from when you finish dinner to the time you go to bed. The body's metabolic burn rate starts slowing down at night, and sleep is when our bodies should be recovering from the day's activities. That's why eating late at night isn't a great idea. Your body can't prepare for recovery when it's digesting the food you've just eaten.

SNACKING

Snacking is normal, especially in the late morning and midafternoon. But if you experience food cravings throughout the day, your body is telling you it's nutrient deprived. If you're eating real food, your body should be metabolizing the nutrients you've taken in. You're better off modifying your diet and adding more nutrient-dense meals over the course of the day. Still, try to snack throughout the day. It curbs your appetite, helps you retain energy, and lowers your chance of overeating during meals. I snack quite a bit throughout the day myself, and at TB12 we created an assortment of snacks so I know I have healthy choices available that I also love to eat.

COMBINING FOODS

The foods we eat—fruits, vegetables, grains, meat—each belong to specific food groups. We digest each one more easily or with more difficulty, depending on what other foods we pair with them. When we digest, say, protein-rich foods like beef or chicken, our bodies require an acidic environment. When we digest carbohydrates, our bodies require a more alkaline environment. In this case, opposites don't attract.

Here are four principles to keep in mind:

1. Try to avoid eating proteins like meat, poultry, fish, or dairy with carbohydrates like potatoes, breads, wheat, or grain products.

2. Mixing vegetables—cooked or raw—with either proteins or carbohydrates is ideal and won't interfere with good digestion.

3. Eat fruits alone. They digest quickly. Other foods don't.

4. Drinking water with your meals can interfere with good digestion. Drink water half an hour before a meal, and then wait an hour before you have your next glass. If you're going to drink with your meals, I recommend only a little bit of water in order to ensure proper digestion.

I always make sure I have great sources of vitamin C.

SUPPLEMENTATION

Even if you eat fresh, organically grown food at every meal, it can be tricky to meet your nutritional needs. Various other factors may be working against you—noise and air pollution, food pesticides, even your own stress levels. A lot of people don't have access to locally grown or organic food, and even if they do manage to eat real food, a lot of times it's flown cross-country and shipped frozen from warehouses along the way.

Would I love it if everyone started following a mostly plant-based, real-food nutritional regimen? Absolutely. But not everyone can do that. At TB12 we use the word *supplement* as it's intended to be used—as a supplementation to the foods we eat. The right supplements won't replace a proper nutritional regimen, but they can ensure you get what your body might be lacking.

I'm a big believer in the smart use of certain supplements—they've been a regular part of my daily routine since 2000. As I said earlier, along with daily doses of electrolytes and trace mineral drops, I also take a daily multivitamin, vitamin D, vitamin B complex, an antioxidant, essential fish oils, protein powder, and a probiotic. The TB12 Method is about *quality* of life, and the supplements I take help me sustain peak performance and promote muscle regeneration. Whenever I read news articles casting doubt on supplements or saying they don't work, I take them at face value. All I can do is look back on my own experience and track record. I do less strength training today than ever before, and my muscles are healthier than ever.

MULTIVITAMIN

A multivitamin is a good supplement for average people as well as for athletes. It supplements the basic vitamins and minerals we get from our food.

VITAMIN D

Vitamin D helps our bodies absorb calcium by regulating how we metabolize both calcium and phosphorus. It helps our bones and our teeth, and aids in the regulation of our nervous system, cardiovascular health, and blood clot function. Vitamin D is found in egg yolks, liver, milk, and in oily fish like salmon, herring, mackerel, and sardines. If you have a vitamin D deficiency, you risk bone softening, osteoporosis, and muscle spasms, which is why I take the daily recommended dose. I suggest taking vitamin D_2 *and* D_3.

VITAMIN B COMPLEX

B complex, which is made up of a group of eight distinct B vitamins, increases our energy by helping to convert food into glucose and metabolizes the health of our nervous and immune systems.

TRACE MINERALS

Even if we eat real food every day of our lives, thanks to commercial farming we don't get the minerals from the soil our bodies need. Trace minerals work alongside the vitamins and nutrients in our bodies to regulate biological functions, ranging from proper blood formation to energy production to nerve transmission. They also help our bodies regulate the balance between acidity and alkalinity. The most important trace minerals are calcium, copper, magnesium, boron, phosphorus, potassium, silica, and zinc. I get all of these in my TB12 Electrolytes, which are critical in replacing the minerals I lose in my sweat when I work out.

ANTIOXIDANTS

I get most of my antioxidants from fruits and vegetables—exept for nightshades!—and I need the extra insurance that antioxidants provide. They protect the body from the damage caused by free radicals, which can lead to atherosclerosis and various other arthritis-related conditions. Again, it's all about reducing inflammation.

I love eating pomegranates in the morning—they're another great source of antioxidants and vitamins, and help me reduce inflammation.

ESSENTIAL FATTY ACIDS

Our bodies need certain kinds of fat to carry out the daily acts of living. Most people don't get enough of these, because the word *fat* scares them. Our bodies don't naturally produce essential fatty acids, which means we need to get them from our diets or from supplementation. Essential fatty acids, especially DHA and DEPA, help with energy, musculoskeletal function, and calcium metabolism, as well as hormone, nerve, and brain function. They also help reduce the risks of heart attack, hypertension, and stroke, as well as overall inflammation. I have found these to be a great benefit in my life.

PROTEIN POWDER

Our bodies require a certain amount of daily protein. At TB12 we only use the purest protein possible and avoid the use of sugar, fat, binders, or stabilizers. It has greatly improved my ability to maintain muscle mass while strength training less than half of what I used to in my twenties. I can add one to two scoops of protein powder to anything I eat, from pancakes to smoothies.

PROBIOTICS

Probiotics are live microorganisms that naturally produce digestive enzymes that help your body digest food and absorb the nutrients from that food. Seventy to eighty percent of your immune system resides in your gut bacteria. Antibiotics destroy your inner stomach environment, and over a long period of time can affect your digestion. That's why probiotics are so important to me.

PROTEIN POWDER AND THE TWENTY-MINUTE RULE

When athletes work out, they break down their muscles. Two of the best sources of protein and carbs are either a protein bar or 20 grams of protein powder mixed into a protein shake. Protein is easily and quickly digestible, and goes immediately toward rebuilding and repairing muscles. To facilitate muscle repair and generate muscle protein synthesis, you should ingest protein within twenty minutes of finishing your workout. Wait any longer and your body will begin seeking its own protein sources and start tearing down the muscles you've just been building up. I am committed to the twenty-minute rule, and rarely will I break down my muscles without having a protein shake immediately following intense workouts.

Our bodies require a certain amount of daily protein. Our TB12 Protein Powder is the purest whey protein on the market today. It has greatly improved my ability to maintain muscle mass while strength training less than half of what I used to in my twenties. I can add one to two scoops of protein powder to anything I eat, from pancakes to smoothies.

HOW TO READ A LABEL

Everyone who's been in a supermarket knows that *supplement* is a pretty broad category that includes vitamins, minerals, herbs, "green drinks," essential fatty acids, and other nutrients that are either derived or synthesized from food sources. According to the Dietary Supplement Health and Education Act of 1994, supplements aren't considered drugs, which means they can go to market without the US Food and Drug Administration reviewing them beforehand.

To choose the right supplements, it's important to choose a brand whose ingredients are made of food-grade concentrates—meaning that its ingredients come from natural foods and herbs—since the body also metabolizes them more easily than it does synthetic components. Try to avoid supplements that contain fillers, dyes, binders, or any other unnecessary ingredients. The reason those are used is because they're cheaper, and there are bigger profits and more marketing dollars, which create more influence. It can be a vicious cycle.

The product label on a supplement consists of a statement of identity, a structure/function claim, the form the product takes (gel, liquid, capsule), directions on how to take it, a supplement fact panel, a list of other ingredients, and the name and address of the manufacturer. We'll take them one by one.

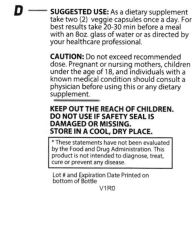

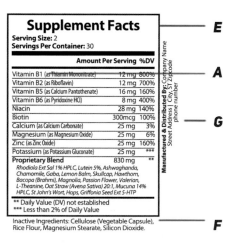

D — **SUGGESTED USE:** As a dietary supplement take two (2) veggie capsules once a day. For best results take 20-30 min before a meal with an 8oz. glass of water or as directed by your healthcare professional.

CAUTION: Do not exceed recommended dose. Pregnant or nursing mothers, children under the age of 18, and individuals with a known medical condition should consult a physician before using this or any dietary supplement.

KEEP OUT THE REACH OF CHILDREN. DO NOT USE IF SAFETY SEAL IS DAMAGED OR MISSING. STORE IN A COOL, DRY PLACE.

* These statements have not been evaluated by the Food and Drug Administration. This product is not intended to diagnose, treat, cure or prevent any disease.

Lot # and Expiration Date Printed on bottom of Bottle
V1R0

NUTRIBRAND

MULTI VIT

*HELPS MEET NUTRITIONAL NEEDS

30 CAPSULES
DIETARY SUPPLEMENTS

C   **B**

Supplement Facts		
Serving Size: 2		
Servings Per Container: 30		
Amount Per Serving		**%DV**
Vitamin B1 (as Thiamin Mononitrate)	12 mg	800%
Vitamin B2 (as Riboflavin)	12 mg	700%
Vitamin B5 (as Calcium Pantothenate)	16 mg	160%
Vitamin B6 (as Pyridoxine HCl)	8 mg	400%
Niacin	28 mg	140%
Biotin	300mcg	100%
Calcium (as Calcium Carbonate)	25 mg	3%
Magnesium (as Magnesium Oxide)	25 mg	6%
Zinc (as Zinc Oxide)	25 mg	160%
Potassium (as Potassium Gluconate)	25 mg	***
Proprietary Blend	830 mg	**
Rhodiola Ext Sal 1% HPLC, Lutein 5%, Ashwaghanda, Chamomile, Gaba, Lemon Balm, Skullcap, Hawthorn, Bacopa (Brahmi), Magnolia, Passion Flower, Valerian, L-Theanine, Oat Straw (Avena Sativa) 20:1, Mucuna 14% HPLC, St John's Wort, Hops, Griffonia Seed Ext 5-HTP		
** Daily Value (DV) not established		
*** Less than 2% of Daily Value		

Inactive Ingredients: Cellulose (Vegetable Capsule), Rice Flour, Magnesium Stearate, Silicon Dioxide.

Manufactured & Distributed By: Company Name | Street Address | City, ST Zipcode phone number

E

A

G

F

A. STATEMENT OF IDENTITY

The *statement of identity* tells you the name of the supplement, or what it is—e.g., vitamin D, B complex, or melatonin—and identifies it as a vitamin, a mineral, a dietary supplement, etc.

B. STRUCTURE/FUNCTION CLAIM

The structure/function claim tells what the supplement does or what its health benefits are. By law, the structure/function claim can't say that a supplement treats or cures a disease, but it can set out what role or function the supplement will play in your body.

C. FORM OF PRODUCT AND NET CONTENTS

This identifies whether the supplement is a capsule, a gel, a liquid, or a powder, and how much or how many the bottle contains.

D. DIRECTIONS FOR USE

This tells you how you're supposed to take the product—once a day, twice daily, once a week, and so on.

E. SUPPLEMENT FACTS PANEL

Here you'll find the serving size—a capsule, two tablets—along with a list of active ingredients and the total percentage of the recommended daily intake the supplement provides for each ingredient. If there's an asterisk in the daily value column for any ingredient, it means the manufacturer hasn't determined a daily value.

F. OTHER INGREDIENTS

This list tells you what inactive ingredients were used to create and manufacture the supplement. On this list you'll find ingredients like binders, fillers, coatings, water, and gelatin. Again, try to avoid supplements with too many inactive ingredients in them.

G. PRODUCT MANUFACTURER

What it says—the name and address of the manufacturer.

HOW TO TAKE SUPPLEMENTS

CHECK WITH YOUR DOCTOR BEFORE TAKING SUPPLEMENTS

As with all issues pertaining to diet, nutrition, and health, make sure your doctor knows if you are taking a high dose of any nutritional supplement. Also, remind your doctor of any prescribed medications you take, as some supplements can interfere with dosages or cause side effects.

TAKE SUPPLEMENTS WITH MEALS

Try not to take supplements on an empty stomach. Take them with meals, as this helps your body absorb them more easily. If you supplement your diet with vitamins A and E, beta-carotene, or essential fatty acids, try to take them with whatever foods you eat that have the highest fat content. Divide the doses up so that you parcel your intake over the course of the day. If you take them all at once, your body might not know how to respond.

AVOID TAKING MINERAL SUPPLEMENTS WITH HIGH-FIBER MEALS

Fiber can interfere with your body's ability to absorb minerals.

AVOID TAKING SUPPLEMENTS WITH TOO MANY INACTIVE INGREDIENTS

This means reading the label carefully and avoiding supplements that contain sweeteners, binders, coatings, fillers, preservatives, or added sugars.

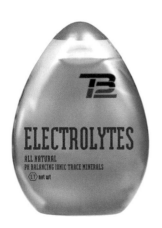

EATING AND WORKING OUT: AN AVERAGE DAY

BREAKFAST	*6:00 a.m.* *7:00 a.m.*	I wake up and immediately drink twenty ounces of water with electrolytes. I shower, then go downstairs and make some variation of a smoothie. Typically it contains blueberries, bananas, seeds, and nuts. It's nutrient dense, high in fat, high in protein, and high in calories.
WORKOUT SNACKS	*8:00 a.m.* *9:00 a.m.* *10:00 a.m.*	I work out. In between, I continue drinking a lot of water with electrolytes. As soon as I'm done (and always within twenty minutes), I'll drink a protein shake—one scoop of TB12 Protein Powder in a glass of almond milk, along with my TB12 Electrolytes.
ALL-DAY ENERGY BOOSTERS	*11:00 a.m.*	If I feel the urge, before lunch I'll have some TB12 Snacks, which are raw, vegan, organic, gluten-free, and dairy-free.
LUNCH	*12:00 p.m.* *1:00 p.m.*	Lunch is often a piece of fish, but always with lots of vegetables. I make sure most of what I eat is alkalizing.
AFTERNOON ENERGY BOOSTERS	*2:00 p.m.* *3:00 p.m.* *4:00 p.m.* *5:00 p.m.*	I might have another protein drink, a protein bar, or fruit. I never go that long without snacking—whether it's chips and guacamole, hummus, raw vegetables, nuts, homemade crackers, TB12 Snacks, or fruit—grapes, a banana, an apple. Throughout the day I keep drinking as much water as I can, always with electrolytes. If I've worked out really hard, I might have an extra protein shake. I'm never lacking for protein, and some days I'll have up to three or four scoops of protein powder.
DINNER	*6:00 p.m.* *7:00 p.m.*	Dinner is another nutrient-dense meal that includes a lot of vegetables. I don't really drink tea, but I might drink a cup of bone broth. Sometimes I'll have another protein shake at night if I know I'm working out hard the next morning.

THE TB12 GROCERY LIST

FISH, MEAT, AND POULTRY

At TB12, we recommend you eat meats and poultry that are organic, grass-fed, free-range, hormone-free, and antibiotic-free. The fish you eat should be wild, hormone-free, and antibiotic-free. As I said earlier, more important than eating organic food is eating *real food*, washed carefully before you prepare it.

Clams/Mussels

Halibut

Herring

Mackerel

Mahi mahi

Shrimp

Tuna, fresh

Wild salmon, fresh

Wild tuna and salmon, canned

Beef

Lamb

Eggs—organic, cage free, omega-3 enriched

Skinless chicken

Skinless turkey

AVOID

Commercially raised beef and poultry

Cured meat and ham

Farm-raised fish

Processed lunch meats

Processed meat such as bacon, sausage, pepperoni, hot dogs

Choose among fresh, preferably organic vegetables such as:

Artichokes

Asparagus

Bean sprouts

Bell peppers

Bok choy

Broccoli

Brussels sprouts

Butter lettuce

Cabbage

Cauliflower

Celery

Chard

Cucumbers

Endive

Ginger

Green beans

Kale

Leeks

Onions: green, red, white, yellow

Radishes

Romaine lettuce

Salad mix, organic

Shallots

Snow peas

Spinach

Squash: green, yellow, summer, spaghetti

Sweet potatoes

Watercress

Zucchini

FRUIT

Apples: green, red

Avocados

Bananas

Berries: blueberries, raspberries, blackberries

Cherries

Coconut

Grapefruit

Grapes: green, red

Lemons

Limes

Mango

Oranges

Papayas

Peaches

Pears

Pomegranate seeds

FRESH HERBS

Basil

Chives

Cilantro

Dill

Marjoram

Mint

Oregano

Parsley

Rosemary

Sage

Thyme

CANNED/JARRED FOODS

Artichoke hearts

Cacao butter

Capers

Chicken broth, low sodium

Coconut butter

Nut butter: almond, cashew, macadamia (sugar-free)

Pasta sauce (sugar free)

Pumpkin, organic

Tomato paste

Tomatoes: crushed, stewed, whole

Vegetable broth, low sodium

NUTS AND SEEDS

Raw nuts: almonds, cashews, macadamia nuts, pine nuts—no peanuts!

Seeds: chia, flax, hemp, pumpkin, sunflower

NOODLES/GRAINS/PACKAGED FOODS

Beans: black, kidney, pinto, white, garbanzo

Lentils

Quinoa

Quinoa pasta

Split peas

Steel-cut oats

FLOUR/BAKING

All-purpose gluten-free flour

Almond meal

Baking soda

Baking powder

Chia flour

Coconut flour

Flax meal

Oat flour

Rice flour

SUPERFOODS

Acai powder

Cacao: powder and nibs

Camu camu powder

Freeze-dried greens powder

Goji berries

Goji powder

Lucuma powder

Maca root

Maqui powder

Pomegranate powder

OILS

Almond oil

Coconut oil

Macadamia nut oil

Olive oil, extra virgin

Sesame oil

Walnut oil

CONDIMENTS

Balsamic vinegar

Guacamole

Horseradish sauce

Hummus

Dijon mustard (gluten-free)

Salsa

Tamari sauce

Vegan mayonnaise

MILK AND CREAM

Almond

Coconut

Rice

Hemp

Hazelnut

SWEETENERS

Coconut sugar

Honey, raw unfiltered

Maple syrup, pure

Stevia—plain, chocolate, berry, vanilla crème, cinnamon

WATER AND DRINKS

Coconut water	Organic coffee
Green tea	Mineral water

SPICES (KEEP THESE ON HAND)

Basil	Maple extract
Black pepper	Marjoram
Cayenne pepper	Mint
Chili powder	Oregano
Cilantro	Nutmeg
Cinnamon	Parsley
Cloves	Rosemary
Coriander	Saffron
Curry	Sage
Dill	Thyme
Garlic	Vanilla extract
Ginger	

FOODS TO LIMIT OR AVOID

Alcohol	Grain-based foods (cereal, rice, instant oatmeal, wheat, barley, rye, and corn)
Bread, pasta, tortillas, and other foods that contain gluten	Jams, jellies, pancake syrup
Breakfast cereals	Most cooking oils (corn, safflower, canola, soy)
Condiments like ketchup, soy sauce, and barbecue sauce containing sugar, artificial ingredients, excessive salt or gluten	Processed frozen dinners
	Processed meats such as lunch meats
Corn (including popcorn, corn bread, and popped-corn chips)	Salty processed snacks (potato chips, popcorn, pretzels, nacho chips, crackers, etc.)
Dairy foods such as milk, cheese, cream, yogurt, and ice cream	Soy-based foods such as powders, oils, and snack foods
Foods that contain genetically modified ingredients	Sugary processed snacks (cakes, cookies, cupcakes, candy)
Foods that contain high-fructose corn syrup or trans (hydrogenated) fats	Sweetened drinks (lemonade, soda, fruit punch)
Foods that contain sugar, artificial sweeteners, or soy	White potatoes
Fruit juice (even 100 percent fresh!)	

When I was younger, I had a horrible diet! I ate processed meats, peanut butter and jelly sandwiches on white bread, muffins, doughnuts, hot dogs, nachos with cheese out of a tin can, breakfast cereal—you name it. I rarely drank water; I mostly drank milk, juice, and soda. I've talked a lot in this book about my improvement over the years, and I believe a big reason is the changes I've made in my nutrition. Looking back, why wasn't I as good as I could have been in high school? Why was I a late bloomer? Why couldn't I compete with those other guys? I really didn't give myself a chance, based on the diet I was following. One reason I've improved over the years is that the foods I eat today are nutrient-dense and good for me, and I limit anything that could cause inflammation.

Coconuts taste great, especially when they're fresh off the tree. Coconut water is a great form of hydration, and a natural source of electrolytes.

12 FITNESS AND NUTRITION MYTHS

1. THE STRENGTH AND CONDITIONING MODEL WORKS

The strength and conditioning model—that is, elevate your heart rate and lift weights—is necessary, but it can injure millions of athletes every year. **Pliability** is the crucial missing leg that will complete and complement your workouts. That's what sustained peak performance means to us at TB12.

2. IF YOU EXERCISE REGULARLY, YOU CAN EAT WHATEVER YOU WANT

A diet high in sugar, salt, fat, gluten, processed, refined, and fast foods undoes many of the benefits of working out.

3. IF IT'S IN THE SUPERMARKET, IT MUST BE FOOD

The commercial food industry is in the business of marketing and selling chemicals. Try to eat as much real, organic food as you can—local, fresh foods that reduce inflammation—and limit your intake of toxic chemicals.

4. ORGANIC FOOD COSTS MORE THAN ANYONE SHOULD PAY

You have only one body, and one life. Take care of it by eating real food. You'll see the benefits in greater health and vitality, as well as in reduced medical costs down the line.

5. THE ONLY SOURCE OF CALCIUM IS DAIRY

Calcium is a mineral naturally found in the soil. A whole food, mostly plant-based diet can supply your daily calcium needs.

6. CAFFEINE BENEFITS SPORTS PERFORMANCE

Caffeine can be dehydrating, and its cumulative effects can work against the maintenance of healthy muscles. Limiting caffeine will benefit overall performance.

The strength and conditioning model is necessary—but incomplete, as it can injure millions of athletes every year. Pliability is the missing leg—but remember that a diet high in sugar, salt, fat, gluten, processed, refined and fast foods undoes many of the benefits of working out. You have only one body, and one life. By hydrating properly, and eating real food, you'll see the benefits in greater health and vitality, as well as in reduced medical costs down the line.

7. RESISTANCE BANDS CAN'T DO WHAT WEIGHTS DO

Resistance bands work your body functionally better than weights do in terms of elasticity, resistance, versatility, and efficiency. They also allow for a bigger, more fluid range of motion. Better yet, they will reduce your chances of injury because they limit the chances of overload. Plus they're portable!

8. EVERYONE NEEDS TO DO THIRTY MINUTES OF CARDIO, FOLLOWED BY THIRTY MINUTES OF WEIGHT TRAINING

Using resistance bands, it takes only twenty to thirty minutes a day to elevate your heart rate while increasing muscle mass. Working smarter, and reallocating your time, will provide great benefits

9. DRINKING 3–4 GLASSES OF WATER EVERY DAY IS PLENTY

Most of us are dehydrated and don't know it. You should drink at least one-half of your body weight in ounces of water daily, with electrolytes, and ideally more than that.

10. INFLAMMATION IS THE RESULT OF INJURY

Besides injury, inflammation results from the foods we eat, inadequate hydration, high stress levels, and negative attitudes, among other things.

11. YOU SHOULD DRINK SPORTS DRINKS WITH ELECTROLYTES

The high sugar content in many commercially sold sports drinks can make them counterproductive.

12. YOU GET EVERYTHING YOU NEED FROM YOUR DIET

It's possible, but unlikely, based on our busy lives. The right supplements won't replace a good diet, but they can help your body by supplementing your diet with what it may be lacking.

Time is an asset for all of us— and most of us lead busy lives. That's why in addition to eating as much real food as possible, I recommend the smart use of supplements. They won't replace a good diet, but they can fill in what might be lacking.

RECIPES

SEASONAL SALAD WITH SAVORY VINAIGRETTE

The crunchy, creamy, salty, and savory mix in this salad is delicious, and a showcase for a variety of plant foods that provide valuable macronutrients. It's great for reducing inflammation, and is perfect for the spring and fall.

MAKING MUSTARD CAPER VINAIGRETTE

1 tbsp. ground mustard seed

1 tbsp. capers (with juice)

¼ cup lemon juice

2 tbsp. walnut oil

4 tbsp. extra-virgin olive oil

Salt and pepper to taste

Blend all ingredients (except for salt and pepper) in a high-powered blender until smooth. Season with salt and pepper.

PREPARING SALAD

1 cup salad greens

1 cup baby vegetables

½ cup cooked grains (of your choice)

1 tbsp. crunchy grains (of your choice)

1 tbsp. sprouted beans

1 tbsp. pistachios (raw or toasted)

½ tbsp. seeds (mixed)

¼ avocado

Handful of alfalfa sprouts

2 tbsp. mustard caper vinaigrette

Place greens in a salad bowl and arrange remaining ingredients around them. Finish with vinaigrette.

POTATO AND BROCCOLI FRITTATA

To prevent fresh artichokes from browning, place artichoke quarters in cold water with lemon after removing outer leaves and inner fibers. This is one of my favorite things to eat for breakfast.

MAKING FRITTATA

1 medium potato

1 whole egg

1 egg white

½ tbsp. water

1 to 2 tbsp. coconut oil

½ to 1 tbsp. garlic

¼ cup broccoli
(small florets)

¼ cup brown or red rice
(soaked or cooked)

Handful of collard greens
(chopped)

1 tbsp. basil (picked)

Salt and pepper to taste

Preheat oven to 375°F. Scrub potato under cold water, dry, and bake for 25–35 minutes. Remove potato from oven, let cool, and then dice small.

In a small bowl, whisk egg and egg white with ½ tbsp. of water.

In a nonstick pan, sauté ¼ cup potato in coconut oil over medium heat until crispy. Add garlic and broccoli and cook for 1–2 minutes. Add rice and collards and cover for 10 seconds, or until collards are wilted.

Pour egg mixture evenly over vegetables in the pan, then sprinkle basil on top. Season with salt and pepper.

With a rubber spatula, lift the edges of the frittata as it cooks, allowing the runny egg mixture to seep below until it becomes firm enough to flip (about 2–3 minutes). Using the spatula, flip the frittata over and finish cooking for 1 additional minute. Move frittata to a cutting board and slice into wedges.

POACHING ARTICHOKES

¾ cup artichokes

Juice of ½ lemon

1 tsp. garlic (minced)

1 tsp. extra-virgin olive oil

Salt and pepper to taste

Poach artichokes for 16–20 minutes, until tender. Note: If using fresh artichokes, use enough water to cover the artichokes and half a lemon.

Cut artichokes into quarters.

Toss artichokes with lemon juice, garlic, and extra-virgin olive oil. Season with salt and pepper.

FRESH VEGGIE LASAGNA

This vegetable-based dish has many of the same great flavors as conventional lasagna, and can even be prepared in less time.

MAKING "CHEESE"

½ cup raw cashews

⅓ cup water

½ tbsp. lemon juice

2 tsp. smoked salt

Put all ingredients into a blender and blend on high until smooth.

MAKING WALNUT MEAT

½ cup raw walnut pieces

1 tbsp. tamari

½ tbsp. thyme (picked)

1 tsp. extra-virgin olive oil

Put all ingredients into a food processor and pulse until coarsely ground.

MAKING TOMATO SAUCE

1 cup sun-dried tomatoes

½ cup water

2 tsp. red wine vinegar

1 tbsp. extra-virgin olive oil

Pinch of red pepper flakes (optional)

Salt and pepper to taste

Soak tomatoes in water for 2–6 hours (until soft), then put tomatoes and other ingredients into a blender and blend on high until smooth. Season with salt and pepper.

CREATING LASAGNA AND ASSEMBLING DISH

Vegetables shaved into thin ribbons using mandolin:

2 medium zucchini

2 medium summer squash

1 medium carrot

Handful of basil leaves

¼ cup lemon juice

½ tbsp. extra-virgin olive oil

1 tsp. salt

1 tsp. pepper

Lay shaved vegetables in a casserole dish and soak at room temperature in a mixture of lemon juice, extra-virgin olive oil, salt, and pepper for 30 minutes (until softened).

On a cutting board, stack a ribbon of zucchini, squash, and carrot (first removing the excess liquid from each ribbon). Spread "cheese" across top, then sprinkle ¼ of the walnut meat and ⅛ of the sauce. Repeat for four more (three-vegetable) layers, adding basil leaves every other layer. Square lasagna edges with sharp knife, then serve with remaining sauce on the side.

This vegetable-based dish has many of the same great flavors as conventional lasagna, and can even be prepared in less time! As I said earlier, as an NFL quarterback, I do everything I can to maximize my pliability and minimize inflammation, which is why I mostly abstain from nightshades, including mushrooms and tomatoes. But even for athletes who play professional sports, an occasional tomato or mushroom won't harm you.

GREEN RISOTTO WITH LEMON CREAM

Leftover risotto makes for great rice cakes. Just blend leftover rice in a food processor until it's sticky, and then shape into cakes.

MAKING SPICY LEMON CREAM

½ cup raw cashews

½ cup water

1½ tbsp. lemon juice

¼ tsp. red pepper flakes (optional)

Salt to taste

Blend all ingredients in a high-powered blender until smooth. Season with salt.

MAKING SPINACH RISOTTO AND ASSEMBLING DISH

1½ cups brown rice (soaked and cooked)

½ pound spinach

8 basil leaves

1 tbsp. onion (minced)

1 tbsp. garlic (minced)

1 tbsp. coconut oil

2 tbsp. extra-virgin olive oil

Handful of pea greens

Salt and pepper to taste

1 tbsp. spicy lemon cream

Put spinach and olive oil into a mini (3-cup) food processor and pulse until smooth (similar to the consistency of pesto).

In a sauté pan over medium heat, toast onion and garlic in coconut oil until golden brown.

Add rice to pan and cover on low heat until rice is warm, then remove pan from heat. Fold spinach "pesto" into rice mixture and season with salt and pepper.

Fold pea greens into mixture, then place in a deep bowl.

Drizzle 1 tbsp. of spicy lemon cream on top.

CHICKEN BURGERS WITH RADISHES

These burgers are always a family favorite. You can use any type of radish—or any other vegetable—in the marinade.

MAKING SPICY TOMATOES

1/3 cup cherry tomatoes (whole)

2 dried chilies

1/2 tbsp. coconut oil

Salt to taste

In a small sauté pan over high heat, bring coconut oil to the sizzling point.

Add tomatoes and chilies, turn off heat, and cover. Let sit for 2 minutes.

Remove when ready to serve. Season with salt.

MARINATING RADISHES

1/4 cup daikon (sliced thin)

1/4 cup red radish (sliced thin)

1 tbsp. rice wine vinegar

1/2 tbsp. lime juice

1/4 tsp. garlic (grated)

1/2 avocado (cut into chunks)

1/4 cup cucumber (diced large)

Bed of lettuce

Combine all ingredients except avocado, cucumber, and lettuce, and let marinate for at least 20 minutes (or up to 4 hours, if time allows).

MAKING CHICKEN BURGERS AND ASSEMBLING DISH

5 oz ground dark meat chicken

1/3 cup almond meal

1/2 tbsp. onion (minced)

1/2 tbsp. garlic (minced)

1 1/2 tbsp. coconut oil

Salt and pepper to taste

In a sauté pan over medium heat, toast onion and garlic in 1/2 tbsp. coconut oil until dark brown, then let cool.

Combine with remaining ingredients in a bowl. Season with salt and pepper.

Shape into two burgers. In a sauté pan over medium-high heat, sear burgers in 1 tbsp. coconut oil for 4–5 minutes on each side (until dark brown and cooked through).

Serve with spicy tomatoes, marinated radishes, diced cucumber, and avocado chunks on top of a bed of lettuce.

ROAST CHICKEN WITH PUMPKIN AND BRUSSELS SPROUTS

This roasting method works for any whole bird or meat roast. The flavor and texture of this natural reduction is unlike any starch-thickened sauce.

PREPARING CHICKEN AND REDUCTION

1 whole chicken
(2–2.5 pounds)

4 garlic cloves

½ lemon
(cut into two pieces)

1 sprig of rosemary

½ tbsp. coconut oil

4 quarts of water

Salt and pepper to taste

Preheat oven to 475°F. Rinse chicken and pat dry. Stuff garlic, lemon, and rosemary into cavity, then seal cavity (truss chicken or fold back wings and put a wooden skewer through ankles). Rub coconut oil over chicken and season with salt and pepper. Place chicken on a rack in a roasting pan and place in oven. Brown for 16–20 minutes, then decrease heat to 300°F. Finish cooking to internal temperature of 160°F, then remove and let rest for 30 minutes. (Follow brussels sprouts method now.)

Unseal cavity and discard lemon. Remove legs/thighs and breasts/wings, leaving meatless carcass. Cut into pieces and place in saucepan over medium heat. Sear bones for 15 minutes (until deep golden brown). Add garlic and rosemary from cavity and 4 quarts of water, and bring to a simmer. Reduce to thick sauce (will take about 45 minutes and yield about ¾ cups of flavorful sauce). Skim off fat and impurities and strain through fine mesh strainer. Add salt only if needed.

COOKING BRUSSELS SPROUTS

1½ cups brussels
sprouts (cut in half)

½ tbsp. garlic (minced)

Salt to taste

Toss sprouts with garlic in a bowl until evenly coated. Immediately after removing chicken from roasting pan, turn oven up to 375°F, add sprouts to pan of drippings, and place in oven for 6–8 minutes.

PREPARING PUMPKIN PURÉE

1 cup raw pumpkin meat

1 tbsp. onion (chopped)

2 garlic cloves

1 cup water

½ tbsp. coconut oil

Salt to taste

In a small saucepan over medium heat, caramelize onion and garlic in coconut oil until light brown. Add pumpkin meat and water and simmer for 14–16 minutes (until tender), then put into a high-powered blender and blend until smooth. Season with salt.

ASSEMBLING DISH

Spread pumpkin purée across half of a plate and put sprouts on the other half. Slice a 5-oz piece of chicken breast (or one leg and thigh) and layer over the middle on top. Finish with broth reduction.

SALMON BURGER WITH AVOCADO SALAD

These fries are a great, kid-friendly option in the cooler months. Using white yams cut into strips, they're hard to tell apart from French fries.

BAKING FRIES

1 medium yam

½ tbsp. coconut oil

Salt to taste

Scrub yam under cold water, dry, and bake at 375°F for 25 minutes.

Let cool and cut into wedges, then toss with coconut oil and salt.

Lay wedges cut side up on perforated sheet pan lined with parchment paper and bake at 375°F for 35 minutes (until crispy).

MAKING BURGER

4 oz salmon (skinless)

½ tbsp. shallots (minced)

1 tbsp. scallions (sliced thin)

1 tbsp. dill (chopped)

1 tsp. paprika

Pinch of cayenne (optional)

1 tbsp. coconut oil

Salt to taste

Cut salmon into chunks. Put into a food processor and pulse until ground.

Transfer ground salmon to a mixing bowl and combine with remaining ingredients. Season with salt. Shape into burger.

In a sauté pan over medium heat, sear burger on both sides until golden brown and cooked through (or cooked to your liking).

PREPARING AVOCADO SALAD

1 cup kale (chopped)

½ avocado (cut into chunks)

2 tsp. lime juice

1 tsp. extra-virgin olive oil

1 tsp. raw pumpkin seeds

1 tsp. hemp seeds

Salt and pepper to taste

In a small mixing bowl, gently combine all ingredients (except kale). Season with salt and pepper.

Make a bed of kale on half of a plate and serve the avocado mixture on top, with burgers and fries on the side.

PASTA WITH CREAMY SAUCE

Using a pasta that is 100 percent brown rice flour and rice bran is a great way to turn a guilty pleasure into a nutritious meal. Personally, I don't eat this often, for reasons I described earlier— but again, it's always about balance.

MAKING PASTA AND CREAM

6 oz brown rice pasta (cooked)

1 medium-size red pepper

Dab of coconut oil

¼ cup raw cashews

1 tbsp. lemon juice

½ cup water

1 tsp. thyme (picked)

Pinch of red pepper flakes (optional)

Salt and pepper to taste

Rub red pepper with coconut oil. Roast the pepper over an open flame, turning periodically, until the entire surface is blackened.

Place blackened pepper in a mixing bowl and cover for 15 minutes (allowing it to soften and absorb flavor from roasting).

Peel pepper, but leave a few small flecks of burnt skin (discarding the rest). Cut pepper open to discard seeds, but do not run pepper under water.

Place pepper in a high-powered blender with cashews, water, lemon, and red pepper flakes (if desired) and blend until smooth.

Season with salt and pepper. Fold sauce into cooked pasta. Sprinkle thyme on top.

COOKING ASPARAGUS

¼ pound asparagus

1 tsp. garlic (minced)

½ tbsp. coconut oil

Salt and pepper to taste

In a sauté pan over medium heat, toast garlic lightly in coconut oil.

Turn heat to medium-low, add asparagus, and cover for 4–6 minutes (until asparagus is slightly tender).

Season with salt and pepper.

BRADY BOWL

This recipe is quick and easy to prepare, but still combines a variety of delicious flavors and interesting textures.

MAKING LEMONGRASS CURRY SAUCE

4-inch lemongrass stalk (smashed)

2 cups water

¼ cup raw cashews

¼ cup raw Brazil nuts

½ tbsp. lime juice

1 tsp. rice wine vinegar

1 tbsp. curry powder

Salt to taste

In a saucepan over medium heat, bring lemongrass and water to a boil, and simmer down to about ¾ cup of total liquid.

Strain and put into a high-powered blender with nuts, lime juice, vinegar, and curry powder and blend until smooth. Season with salt.

PREPARING SWEET POTATOES, BROCCOLI, AND KALE AND ASSEMBLING BOWL

¾ cup quinoa (soaked and cooked)

1 cup kale (chopped)

½ cup broccoli (small florets)

1 medium sweet potato

1 tbsp. shredded carrot

½ tbsp. garlic (minced)

1 tbsp. tamari almonds (chopped)

1 tbsp. coconut oil

Salt to taste

2 tbsp. water

2 tbsp. lemongrass curry sauce

FOR SWEET POTATOES: Scrub sweet potato under cold water, dry, and bake at 375°F for 25 minutes. Let cool and cut into wedges, then toss with ½ tbsp. coconut oil and salt. Lay wedges cut side up on a perforated sheet pan lined with parchment paper and bake at 375°F for 35 minutes (until crispy).

FOR BROCCOLI: In a small sauté pan over medium heat, add 2 tbsp. water and broccoli. Cover and steam for 1 minute. Remove broccoli and wipe pan dry.

FOR KALE: In a small sauté pan over medium heat, toast garlic in ½ tbsp. coconut oil until golden brown. Turn off heat, add kale, and cover for 1 minute (until kale is wilted).

Arrange all components side by side in a bowl. Serve 2 tbsp. of lemongrass curry sauce and almonds on the side.

GREEN JUICE

This alkalizing green juice is a great way to start the day.

1 bunch broccoli stems	2 stalks celery
1 cucumber	½ lemon (peeled)
½ pound kale	2 inches fresh turmeric
1 green apple (optional)	1 inch fresh ginger

Put all ingredients in juicer and extract juice. Drink within
15 minutes (on an empty stomach) for best results.

SMOOTHIES

These smoothies are ideal for refueling after a workout.

BLACKBERRY ACAI SMOOTHIE

1 cup blackberries

1 acai pack (3.5 oz)

1 medium banana

⅓ cup raw coconut water

1 large medjool date (pitted)

½ tbsp. raw cacao powder

Blend all ingredients in a high-powered blender for 1–2 minutes (until smooth).

NOTE: Frozen raw coconut meat can be purchased online, or can be extracted from fresh Thai coconuts using proper tools (which are also available online). Alternately, an additional banana or ⅓ cup cashews can work as a substitute (just be sure to blend fully if using cashews).

BLUEBERRY BANANA SMOOTHIE

¾ cup blueberries

¾ cup almond milk

1 medium banana

½ tbsp. flaxseed (ground)

1 tbsp. chia seeds

1 tbsp. hemp seeds

Blend all ingredients in a high-powered blender for 1–2 minutes (until smooth).

ORANGE COCONUT SMOOTHIE

⅔ cup fresh orange chunks (peeled)

⅔ cup raw coconut water

⅓ cup coconut meat (from young coconuts)

1 medium banana

1 inch fresh turmeric

1 lemon wedge (peeled)

Blend all ingredients in a high-powered blender for 1–2 minutes (until smooth).

GREEN APPLE SMOOTHIE

¾ cup apple (chunks)

½ cup raw coconut water

⅓ pound fresh spinach

1 medium banana

Handful of wheatgrass (fresh)

1 lemon wedge (peeled)

Blend all ingredients in a high-powered blender for 1–2 minutes (until smooth).

AVOCADO ICE CREAM

This modern interpretation of ice cream is just as delicious but much healthier. Try topping with coconut flakes, cacao nibs, or toasted almonds.

MAKING AVOCADO ICE CREAM

1 avocado (ripe and soft)   1½ cups dates (pitted)

½ cup raw cashews   1 cup raw cacao powder

½ cup coconut meat   1¼ cups water
(from young coconuts)

Blend all ingredients in a high-powered blender until smooth.

Put mixture in freezer until ice cream reaches desired thickness. (For quicker ice cream, freeze half of the water into ice cubes before blending.)

Scoop ice cream into 4 dishes and serve with your choice of topping.

TB12 ACTION STEPS:

- Focus on eating real food, preferably organic and mostly plant based.

- Eat some percentage of your vegetables raw—that is, uncooked.

- Shop and eat locally as much as possible. Most supermarket foods have traveled long distances and been frozen and thawed before reaching the shelves.

- Try to eliminate or cut back on foods that cause chronic inflammation, including fast foods, processed foods, and the five W's: white bread, white pasta, white potatoes, white milk, and excess white salt.

- Supplement your dietary regimen by taking, at minimum, a multivitamin and a B complex.

TB/ **CHAPTER 9**

BRAIN TRAINING, REST, AND RECOVERY

A good night's rest is critical to my on- and off-field performance.

BY NOW IT'S CLEAR THAT MY METHOD FOR SUSTAINED PEAK PERFORMANCE FOCUSES ON PLIABILITY, HYDRATION, NUTRITION, AND SUPPLEMENTATION. THE GOAL IS TO STRENGTHEN THROUGH WORKOUTS AND LENGTHEN AND SOFTEN THROUGH PLIABILITY SESSIONS, WHICH EXERCISE MY MUSCLES BUT PREVENT ANY ADDED INFLAMMATION IN MY BODY. BUT JUST AS IMPORTANT TO CREATING A HEALTHY INNER ENVIRONMENT ARE OUR THOUGHTS, EMOTIONS, AND ATTITUDES. ARE THEY POSITIVE OR NEGATIVE? DOES IT MATTER WHETHER YOU EAT AND DRINK WELL IF YOUR THOUGHTS ARE ANGRY OR YOU GO AROUND FEELING LIKE A VICTIM? WHAT IF YOU HAVE A POSITIVE ATTITUDE BUT YOU EAT POORLY? THE BOTTOM LINE IS THAT UNLESS YOU CREATE A HEALTHY INNER ENVIRONMENT AND A HEALTHY OUTER ENVIRONMENT, YOU WON'T ACHIEVE OVERALL HEALTH AND WELL-BEING.

That's why another amplifier of pliability is brain fitness, starting with maintaining the right mind-set and attitude, whether it's during a game or in life, and doing actual exercises to train and develop your cognitive focus.

IT BEGINS WITH THE RIGHT MIND-SET

During the season, one of my biggest priorities is making sure I have the right mental toughness and attitude. As I said earlier, much of the success I've been lucky enough to have in my career I owe to a lifelong "will-over-skill" mind-set. Maybe you've noticed that my competitive drive on the field extends to everything I do. When I'm asked about what motivates me, it always comes down to the *coulda/shoulda* question. If I don't

play my best, why am I disappointed? Because I coulda, shoulda *played* better, *done* better, *worked* harder, *prepared* more. It could be my effort, my execution, or my mind-set—it doesn't matter. In the end, for me it's less about the outcome than it is about whether I put in the best effort relative to our team's potential. Some games we may win by a big margin, and in others we may be outscored, but the ones I remember best are the closely fought games in which, no matter what the scoreboard says, our team put in our best effort.

Regardless of the outcome, I always ask myself whether we did the best we were capable of, and what we could do differently and better next time. To me, that's a big part of creating the right mind-set. Mental toughness is an attitude centered on doing the best you can in the present, while believing you can do even better in the future. For example, during a game my process may have been right, but the outcome wasn't. So what changes do I need to make in my process to create a better outcome? My motivation has never been connected to externals such as individual accolades or breaking records. Those things have honestly never mattered to me. If I leave practice knowing my throwing mechanics were off, I will refocus my energy to work on the corrections I need to make to sharpen those mechanics. I *always* want to do better. As I mentioned earlier, I love what John Wooden said—that "Success is peace of mind which is a direct result of self-satisfaction in knowing you did your best to become the best you are capable of becoming." For me, it's always about what I can do better in the future. That journey is never-ending. In many ways I don't think I'll ever be satisfied.

At the same time, I consider mental toughness a learned behavior. When I look back on my career, I have always given my best effort, and never accepted the place I was at—not at Serra High School, not at Michigan, and certainly not in the pros. At certain points, I could have chosen *not* to keep trying to reach my goals, but I never backed down, and I had a lot of people who supported and encouraged me when I faced my own personal doubts. Together those experiences and people honed my mental toughness in ways they never could have if I hadn't faced those challenges in the first place. In so many ways, the worst experiences I've had in my life have been my best experiences, because I learned the most—and learning turns everything into a positive.

Earlier I said I've never thought of myself as a naturally blessed athlete (and neither did anyone else!). The thing is, though, if you're naturally the best at something, you're never challenged, and you lose the opportunity to develop the right mental toughness. In general, that's how things have gone in my life. It may *look* easy to some people, but it's never *been* easy. And because I found that challenges bring out the best in me, today I think back on them as gifts. I fought hard to get to where I am today, which means I know what

it *means* to fight hard. When you're in a Super Bowl game and your team is three touchdowns down and the clock is running, mental toughness is what makes the difference in the end. In turn, the right mind-set and attitude give us opportunities to do the best we can and to realize the potential that's in every one of us.

KEEPING POSITIVE

Each day when I wake up, I can choose what I want my outlook to be. I'm naturally a very positive person, and in regard to my health and everything else, I realize I'm an active participant in my decision to feel as healthy as possible at all times. I really don't like leaving much up to fate—certainly with regard to my football career. If, like me, you're serious about your peak performance, you need to work hard at the things that are within your control: your work ethic, how you treat your body, and your attitude. Especially your attitude. Things happen sometimes that I don't welcome or want, but I make the choice to remain positive. That is something *within* my control. I don't like to focus on negatives or to make excuses. I am never a victim. I gain nothing if I get angry or frustrated. You can make life a lot harder for yourself by focusing on negative things in your path or making excuses for why things didn't go your way. Or, you can refuse to take things personally, let them go, learn from them, and become the best version of yourself. It's a *choice*. It's actually *your choice*. If I throw an interception or have a bad day or make a bad business decision, by staying in that place I will just make things worse. Wisdom, someone said, is about knowing the difference between the things you can control and the things you can't.

Today, if things go my way, great; and if they don't,

that's okay, too, since I always have the chance to overcome them in the future. Whenever my team loses a game, it's an opportunity to learn something. A game is always an experiment. You walk onto the field armed with various strategies, ideas, and hypotheses about how the game will play out, based on things you've studied. But in the end, you don't know what's going to happen. If we've lost but I've learned something, the game turns into a positive experiment. Sometimes in the moment it doesn't feel that way, because the emotions are running so high—but you try to learn and move on. I'm not a robot. In fact, I'm actually a very emotional person. But I've learned to use losses in games as ways to be better the next time I take the field.

In all my years playing football with Patriots coach Bill Belichick, he and I have almost always believed we could do better. Sometimes by a little, sometimes by a lot. Other times we knew our team didn't give our best effort. Usually what I learn afterward, through reviewing game tapes or thinking back on how I felt and what I did on the field, is a greater positive than whatever benefits might have come from winning.

Of course, I'm not naïve, and I know that terrible things can happen in people's lives. As a public personality, it's been my privilege over the years to help serve large numbers of people. Sometimes I get the chance to meet with men, women, and children who are going through difficult situations in their lives, whether they've been in an accident or are dealing with disease. Almost always I'm the one who comes away feeling inspired, especially when I meet people who've been dealt a tough hand and are still facing their challenges with resilience and a positive outlook.

It's not always possible, but again, if you can learn from experiences that don't work out, they become positive events. When your team is losing in the third quarter, there's not a whole lot to be positive about. That's

when I think, *If we can manage to come back from this, imagine how incredible a story this is going to be for our fans, for our team, for our families, for our kids, and for our grandkids.* Sometimes—not always, but sometimes—a story like that has a happy ending. Look no further than the last quarter of Super Bowl LI. One of my main thoughts during the second half was how much sweeter the victory would be after we came back and won.

CENTERING YOURSELF AND GOING INTO THE ZONE

Cultivating the right mind-set and attitude also means making the time to center yourself, which will give you a better chance of getting "into the zone" during competition. At TB12, our body coaches recommend that every client set apart some time every day—five minutes, ten minutes, half an hour—to bring themselves back to center. For some people, this takes the form of meditation. My wife has been meditating for years and has developed the ability to take a moment to free herself from distraction. Other people find different ways to recenter themselves in order to help get into the zone.

A good way to recenter yourself is by letting your brain get lost in a task or hobby. It might be gardening, painting, drawing, doing crosswords, or taking a walk. Spending sixty seconds doing something you love is better than spending no time at all. I know a businessman who's on his phone pretty much all the time who insists on hand-washing his family's dishes most nights after dinner. It's one of the few times he lets himself zone out. For me, reading magazines, listening to music, driving in my car, lying down in my bed, or working in my garden are the things that help me recenter.

Don't ever forget that attitude and mind-set are within your control. When I run out before a game for the first time to warm up, a lot of times I'm pumped up. To get into the game mind-set, I might let out a scream. Other times, if I don't scream, it's maybe because I'm *too* pumped up, and I want to balance that energy out. But no matter what I do, I'm always trying to rebalance whatever energy or emotion I feel. If I'm too up, I want to rebalance and settle down. If I need more energy, I will scream, yell, or work myself into a lather to create room for my best performance.

THE THREE-PART TB12 BRAIN TRAINING AND FITNESS PROGRAM

We've discussed mind-set, so now let's talk about the other ways we can train the brain. We focus a lot on our physical fitness, but most of us don't pay nearly as much attention to the fitness of our minds. The only time we go to a neurologist, after all, is when we get a head injury or a headache that won't quit, and even during our annual physical, doctors almost never test to see if our brains are working properly. But building and strengthening our brain functioning, and making sure

we give our brains the right daily workout, is another critical component of sustaining peak performance.

The TB12 Method has three ways of training the brain. The first is through the neural priming that takes place during pliability. Remember that by creating a physical stimulus—what we call "positive and intentional trauma"—before and after a workout or game, my brain and body learn how I want my muscles to function during practice or game competitions. Muscles naturally tighten when they contract or when they take a hit, but if I train my brain, and by extension my muscles, to remain in a long, soft, primed state, they'll perform more optimally, with lower risks of injury, by absorbing those forces.

The second way of training the brain is through the learned behaviors of mind-set and attitude—remembering to maintain the right mental toughness, and also that it's a choice we make every day to be and stay positive.

The third way to train the brain is by doing daily brain exercises that improve speed, focus, and mental agility. Train yourself to learn something new every day. Your body needs to stay pliable—but it's important to keep your mind pliable, too.

Your body needs to stay pliable, but it's good to keep your mind pliable, too. The equivalent of nonpliable muscles is a brain that's rigid in its opinions, or that believes what it wants to believe, or that's unwilling to change, expand, or grow. Me, I love learning new things.

BRAIN EXERCISES FOR FOCUS, MENTAL AGILITY, AND PATTERN RECOGNITION

Football is a strategic, tactical game, more like chess than checkers. In chess, a player has a choice of strategic moves he can make, with his goal being to stay one or two steps ahead of his opponent. Both teams take the field with the same number of players, but the focus is on matchups, and those can change from play to play. For example, your opponent can double-team your tight end, leaving your wide receiver open—which will affect what decisions you make as a quarterback. There are other variables, too. A pass rush. Visibility. Wind. Rain. When I go to the line, information is coming in from the offense and the defense, moment by moment. During the snap, a defensive tackle pushes through the center. Do I step up or roll out? Our brains can process only so many variables at the same time, but on the field I need to be able to handle a bunch of elements and unknowns simultaneously.

That's why I spend time every day doing brain exercises. I can do them on my computer, my tablet, or even my phone. Since a big part of my job as quarterback depends on optimal pattern recognition, the more focus, attention, quickness, clarity, navigation, and retention I can bring to patterns and plays, the better my performance on and off the field will be. When people ask, I just tell them I'm "training my brain."

In 2013, we at TB12 sought out the world's leading experts in brain plasticity—the brain's lifelong ability to change in response to sensory and other inputs. You can think of plasticity as your brain's pliability. Our search brought us to the scientists behind BrainHQ, and they worked with us to develop my brain fitness regimen, which you can find out about at http://tb12.brainhq.com. There are other brain training programs out there, but studies have repeatedly shown that only these exercises

translate to real-world activities. The exercises increase the speed and accuracy with which I take in sensory information and improve my ability to process, store, and retrieve that information. People say, "You've got to exercise your brain just like your muscles," and we shouldn't wait for a trauma or a disease to appear to start training. It's all about getting ahead and staying ahead. One of the reasons I keep my muscles—and my brain—pliable, especially during the off-season, is to get ahead and stay ahead when the season starts.

The brain exercises I do start with the most basic building blocks of cognition—speed and attention—and move from there to higher brain function—for example, memory and decision-making. Even if at times they seem instinctual, most movements in sports are based on split-second decisions. For the best results, you need to quickly process the most complete and accurate information available. Faster brain speed lets me process and evaluate more information—and more accurate information is easier to store, manipulate, and retrieve, and also leads to better decision-making. As a result of using BrainHQ exercises, I can see more of what's happening more accurately, and therefore make better decisions faster. Regardless of your age or condition, your brain will stay healthier and function better if you regularly do brain exercises.

To give some sense of what BrainHQ training involves, one exercise might have me searching for a series of things that flash on the screen for a split second. As I correctly identify those series, the items get faster and more difficult, pushing my abilities and improving my recognition and reaction time. Although a lot of my brain training focuses on visual processing, there are also auditory exercises that target my speech and language processing, which includes remembering plays and play names and processing what I hear on the field (including through the speaker in my helmet). It's hard to imagine any movement that isn't helped by processing information more accurately and split seconds faster—whether I'm scanning the field for a receiver or an opening, reading the defense as I pass through the line of scrimmage, seeing defenders rush me, or taking the right step at the right time. Even if you're not a football player, these exercises can help you improve your reflexes or your brain agility and power. I strongly recommend them.

These exercises have been extremely helpful to me over the past five years. TB12 has partnered with experts and organizations with great reputations that confirm their efficacy, and many peer-reviewed studies in scientific journals have validated them, too. Studies show that, after doing these exercises regularly, an average user improves his or her processing speed, reaction time, visual acuity, visual search, multiple object tracking, useful field of view, peripheral vision, attention, memory, executive function, balance, and gait. Those kinds of abilities improve my performance in sports and in life.

Here are some of the exercises we've incorporated into TB12 BrainHQ:

TARGET TRACKER

This game focuses on divided visual attention as I try to track several objects that are moving around the screen. In the game, various target objects appear on the screen, followed by additional moving objects that are designed to distract or interrupt my focus. As the game goes on, the target objects move faster, and over a larger area, and the contrast between the objects and the background gets dimmer, making the objects harder to track.

MIXED SIGNALS

If our brains took in all the information we saw, heard, felt, or thought, it would be impossible to know where to focus our attention. This game asks me to focus on a number, letter, color, or symbol while ignoring competing numbers, letters, symbols, or words. The goal is to help me distinguish between my visual and auditory attention and narrow my focus quickly as other distractions compete for my attention.

FREEZE FRAME

Alertness helps athletes with skills like higher-order reasoning, problem solving, learning, and memory. At its best it means performing in a state of readiness, relaxation, productivity, and full engagement. This exercise targets inhibition response (withholding the wrong movement), a key component of mental control on and off the field.

DOUBLE DECISION

What athletes see in a glance, from their center of gaze to the periphery, is called their "useful field of view." The slower my processing speed, the longer it takes my brain to see what's at the periphery. Improved processing speed means that I see more, and I see what I see faster. By having me identify the right object (from a pair) in the center of my gaze as I track the location of another target (among distractors) at the periphery, this exercise sharpens and speeds up my visual processing while expanding the scope of accuracy within my useful field of view.

DIVIDED ATTENTION

With information coming in left and right, I need to focus on what really matters. In this exercise, two shapes appear on the screen, and I'm asked to note the similarities between the shapes without getting confused when the two shapes match up in some ways but not in others. Over time, the images move more quickly and the rules change, which requires my brain to adjust quickly to changing conditions.

These and other brain exercises, along with recovery and rest, are essential for making sure my brain remains in the same optimal state of pliability as my body.

REST AND RECOVERY: SLEEP

Breaking down my body as regularly as I do through negative and unintentional traumas and muscle contractions (especially imbalanced muscle contractions) through the daily acts of living, I have worked hard to find ways to rebuild my body to its optimal state through proper rest and recovery. My general discipline and pattern is to sleep from 9:00 p.m. to 6:00 a.m. The greatest benefit of sleep is that it's uninterrupted therapy and natural regeneration. Sleep is an opportunity to relax every part of your body, and is critical for all of us to recover for the next day's activities. If we don't get the right amount of it, our mental and physical acuity is lowered. We also need proper sleep to develop healthy neuroplasticity. In addition, over time the stress that builds up from not getting enough sleep takes a toll on our bodies. We don't recover well, and it affects our energy and overall performance.

Sleep has several stages, but the ones that we pass through every night are light sleep and deep sleep. During the deep sleep phase, your body can recover and repair itself. During the REM, or rapid eye movement, stage of light sleep, dreaming helps our brains eliminate any stored stress and tension. If you're having trouble sleeping, here are some recommendations.

CHANGE YOUR DIET

Don't eat right before bedtime. Too much alcohol and caffeine can also cause sleep problems, so be careful about their role in your life. The last thing I eat at night is dinner—and if I ever eat dessert, I try to do it after lunch, so the excess sugar won't keep me up at night.

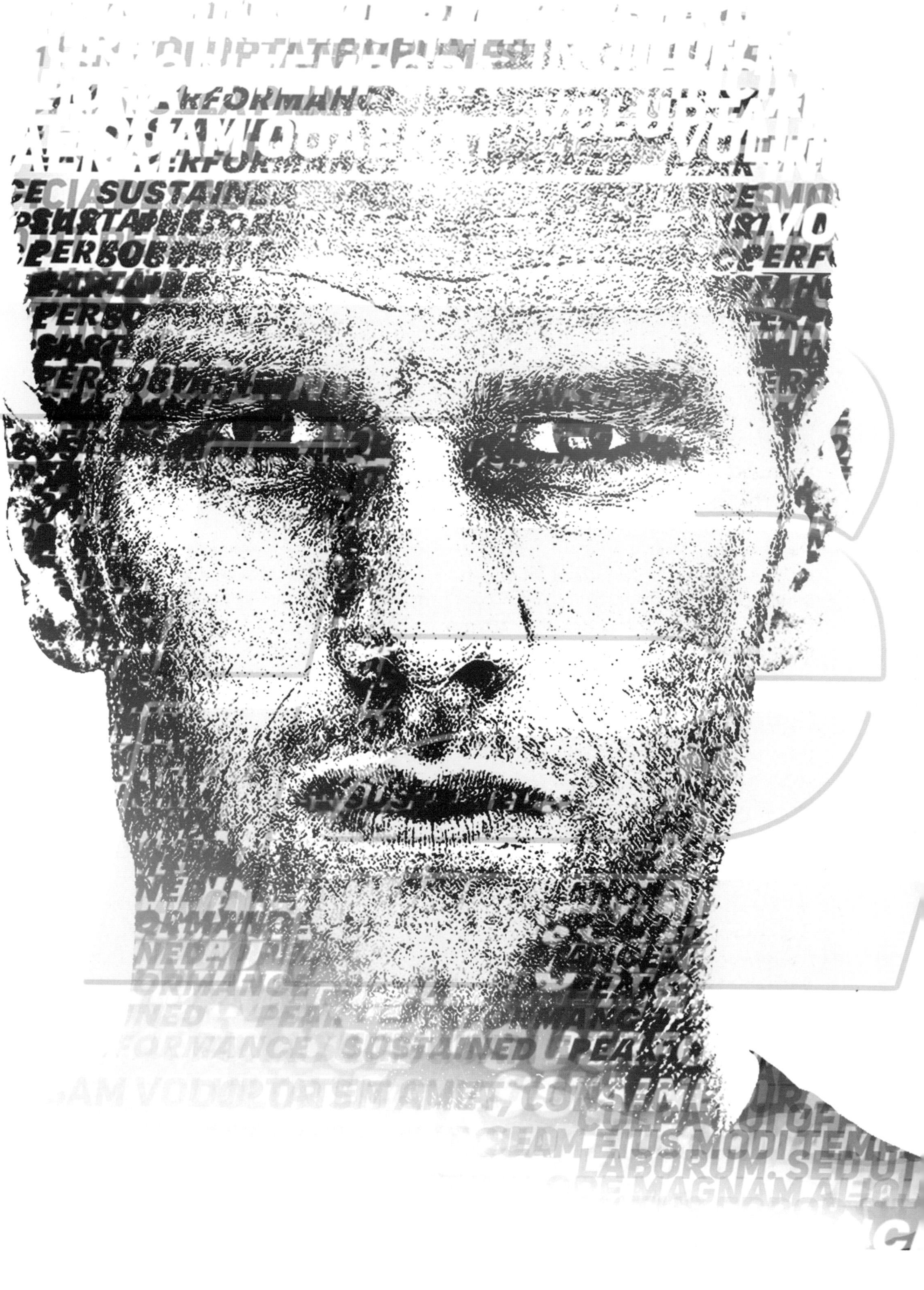
SUSTAINED
LABORUM.

TIME YOUR EXERCISE RIGHT

Insomnia is often the result of not getting enough exercise. If you exercise at night, make sure it's two to three hours before you go to sleep, since you don't want to overstimulate your body and brain. If it's night and you're feeling awake, try drinking herbal tea anywhere from forty-five minutes to an hour before going to bed. I usually don't have much of a problem going to sleep at night, as I'm pretty tired from that day's activities.

PAY ATTENTION TO YOUR SLEEP ENVIRONMENT

Create a good pre-sleep routine to relax. Train your body to get into a rhythm by going to bed at a regular time, and turn off all your electronic devices a half hour before you go to sleep. If there's a TV in your bedroom, consider putting it somewhere else. It's a bedroom, not a tech cave. My wife doesn't even allow cell phones near the bed when we sleep.

TEMPERATURE MATTERS

Stay cool—the ideal temperature in your room should be around 65 degrees Fahrenheit, or 18.5 degrees Celsius. I like my room cool, dark, and as quiet as possible to make sure I get a great night's sleep.

SO DOES CLEANLINESS

Keep your bedroom clean, and make sure it gets enough fresh air. Contaminants like animal dander and dust can interfere with proper breathing and sleep. Consider putting a plant in your bedroom, as plants create moisture, filter out carbon monoxide and other chemicals, and pump more oxygen into the environment. You might also invest in a negative ion generator. Negative ion generators, which produce air molecules supercharged with electrons, enhance respiratory function, filter out indoor air pollutants, and guard against mold and bacteria. If the air in your bedroom is too dry, a warm mist humidifier is a smart idea, since it doesn't need a filter and uses tap water.

KEEP THE NOISE DOWN

Create the quietest environment you can, or use a sound machine. Eliminating noise keeps your sleep uninterrupted—the quieter the better.

DON'T SKIMP ON YOUR MATTRESS OR YOUR BEDDING

Invest in a good mattress. If you can, avoid synthetic materials in your sheets, pillowcases, blankets, or duvets. When I was younger, I didn't care what I slept on. But realizing one-third of my life is spent sleeping, I decided to invest more in my mattress, and I've realized the benefits from a better night's sleep. Now a good mattress is important wherever I go, as I'm always trying to find something that's comfortable and allows me to sleep as well as I possibly can.

FUNCTIONAL APPAREL AND SLEEPWEAR

Sleeping well helps our brains rest and rejuvenate, but I also want to make sure my body remains in a state of recovery even at night. I accomplish this through functional apparel and sleepwear. I've been wearing functional apparel for the past three years. It's a very easy part of my routine. There's no sacrifice involved, since I know I'm getting great recovery. This is a no-brainer.

There's no standard regimen for how players recover in the NFL. Everyone is different. Before I discovered functional apparel and sleepwear, Alex lengthened and softened my muscles before and after practices and games, and then I went home, rested, and made sure not to overexert myself. Minus the pliability sessions, most NFL players do pretty much the same thing. After the game on Sunday—assuming our team won!—players celebrate, hang out with friends and family, or hit the town. On Mondays, the whole team comes in for a workout. Everyone is still pretty sore from the day before. We do a strength training workout, followed by a conditioning run to get our muscles pumping and blood circulating in order to flush out waste. Tuesdays are a day off, and practice starts up again on Wednesday. By Thursday, everyone's body has pretty much bounced back. Practice on Friday is rhythmic and fluid, and Saturday is a day to recover and get ready for the next day's game. Throw in a massage or two during the week for some players, and by Sunday afternoon, everyone is ready to take the field. Then it starts all over again.

A few years ago, we at TB12 began looking into the role of bioenergetic apparel and sleepwear, with the goal of reducing the amount of time it takes my body to recover during the season. I started experimenting with clothing infused with bioceramics, which give off far infrared rays, or FIRs, which stimulate

and heat muscles, bones, and tendons. It didn't take long to realize bioceramic apparel not only worked but also worked fast. Alex could feel the difference when he did pliability training on me from one day to the next. Because he and I have worked together for so many years and are so in sync with what we're trying to accomplish, we knew it worked and how effective it could be. It's really a no-brainer—regeneration all night long.

Alex and I spent a couple of years researching the best materials and results of high-tech apparel, and in early 2017, in conjunction with bioceramic sources, we partnered with Under Armour to launch a line of bioceramic recovery sleepwear.

It works like this: Up to twenty different ceramics—calcium, magnesium, and others—are combined with mineral oxides and heated to around three thousand degrees. The resulting powder is known as a *bioceramic*, which is imprinted directly onto the interior of our TB12 recovery apparel. Think of the result as a cutting-edge form of tech-enabled functional apparel.

Like I said, bioceramics have a vibration frequency and give off a form of energy known as far infrared rays. These FIRs are able to penetrate the skin up to 1.5 inches, stimulating muscles, bones, and tendons. Studies show that FIRs help relieve chronic pain, increase rates of muscle repair and cell oxygenation, and—not least—reduce muscle inflammation, as well as increase overall energy.

One of the biggest benefits of using bioceramic-infused recovery and sleepwear is better oxygenation. When I wear my recovery clothes during the day or at night, the increased oxygen flow they generate helps eliminate the by-products and toxins caused by exercise, including lactic acid. This allows nutrient-rich blood to circulate more efficiently throughout my body. FIRs also stimulate the production of adenosine triphosphate, or ATP, the energy source for our muscle cells. Without ATP, muscles simply can't work, and finding ways to accelerate and store my body's own ATP production amplifies my ability to perform at the highest possible level. ATP is also the key to having enhanced, oxygen-rich blood and better circulation. I admit, I like the idea of my body working for me—both creating and banking energy—during the night! I think of functional apparel and sleepwear as a mobile, 24/7 hyperbaric chamber. If my opponents aren't wearing what I am, I'm getting the edge on them even when I'm sleeping.

The improvements I've experienced since I started wearing functional apparel and sleepwear are hugely important to my recovery. Percentage points can make the difference between success and failure, when there's so little margin for error in professional sports. Since wearing the sleepwear, the overall soreness I feel after games has decreased, and my inflammation levels are low. My dream is to someday have bedding as well, giving you bioceramic coverage all night long, from your head to your toes. After eight hours of sleep in my recovery wear, I wake up feeling alert and energized. During the day I wear recovery pants under my uniform at practice and when I work out. If your goal is oxygen-rich blood, why not oxygenate any chance you get? Teammates of mine who were skeptical at first but who tried recovery wear now love it. They can feel the difference. I can, too. In fact, over the past three years, I can count on one hand the number of times I *haven't* worn recovery sleepwear. It requires no effort

> I like the idea of my body working for me during the night. If my opponents aren't wearing what I am, I'm getting the edge on them even when I'm sleeping.

or discipline, too; you just put it on at night.

Best of all, with functional apparel and sleepwear helping to stabilize my levels of blood oxygenation, my muscles are always in a state of regeneration. That's one reason why at age forty, I run faster and am still as strong as I was when I was twenty-five.

Along with pliability, hydration, nutrition, and other amplifiers, recovery wear contributes to why I'm able to *recover* faster than a lot of other athletes. In the future, it's easy to imagine even more technology embedded in apparel and gear, from biometric sensors that measure activity to fabrics and materials geared toward preventing injury and amplifying performance—and I'm proud to say TB12 is at the forefront of this movement. If I could, I'd wear recovery apparel every hour of the day—which, in fact, is close to what I do.

To sum up, we need to give our brains the same focus and attention we give to our bodies. The first part of the TB12 train-your-brain program begins when we reeducate our brains during pliability sessions to make connections between our minds and our muscles. Part two involves developing and maintaining the right mind-set and attitude on and off the field. Part three consists of daily brain exercises. As I said earlier, the TB12 Method is a holistic and integrative regimen—by which I mean that no real healing takes place in our bodies unless we focus on our brains, too.

TB12 ACTION STEPS

- Mental toughness is a learned behavior. Focus on learning from experiences that don't work out. Often they become positive events.

- Choose to remain positive. It's within your control.

- Take time to recenter yourself every day, whether it's through meditation or just by doing something you love—mindless or mindful restorative rest.

- Practice brain exercises to maintain brain fitness.

- Get the appropriate cognitive rest by sticking to a regular bedtime and getting at least eight hours of sleep every night. To ensure your body is working for you day and night, use TB12 functional apparel and sleepwear, with the latter increasing your body's oxygenation while you're sleeping. In my opinion, again, a no-brainer.

As we reeducate our brains during pliability to create a mind–body connection, we also need to develop and maintain the right mind-set and attitude on and off the field, and to practice the right daily brain exercises. Proper sleep, along with functional apparel and sleepwear, also reduces the amount of time it takes your body to recover. Bottom line: no real healing takes place in the body unless we also focus on the brain.

⊓2 / **CHAPTER 10**

CONCLUSION

Thinking about all the years I've been privileged to play—and how happy I am to be able to share the TB12 Method with you.

EVERY YEAR PEOPLE LIKE TO REMIND ME THAT ANOTHER TWELVE MONTHS HAVE GONE BY, AND THAT FATHER TIME IS UNDEFEATED. THAT SAYING HAS BEEN AROUND FOR A LONG TIME. IT'S PROBABLY TRUE—AND REALIZING THAT HAS MADE ME CONTINUALLY RETHINK MY APPROACH TO MY CAREER AND MY HOLISTIC, INTEGRATIVE TRAINING REGIMEN. IN MANY WAYS, MY ROUTINE IS BETTER THAN IT HAS EVER BEEN, AND I FEEL BETTER THAN I DID WHEN I WAS IN MY TWENTIES. OF COURSE, AS I'VE SAID, I'M NOT NAÏVE. WE ALL NATURALLY AGE. BUT HERE'S THE QUESTION: WHAT DOES IT MEAN TO NATURALLY AGE? THERE ARE SO MANY THINGS PEOPLE DO TO ACCELERATE THEIR OWN AGING PROCESS THAT WE'VE CREATED ASSUMPTIONS AROUND WHAT WE EXPECT OUR BODIES TO LOOK LIKE YEAR AFTER YEAR. WHEN A PERSON SAYS TO ME, "I'M NOT TWENTY-TWO ANYMORE" OR "I CAN'T RECOVER THE WAY I USED TO," IT'S HARD FOR ME TO ACCEPT. TO MY MIND, PEOPLE IN THEIR THIRTIES, FORTIES, FIFTIES, AND BEYOND CAN FEEL AS VITAL AS THEY DID IN THEIR TWENTIES, WITH THE SAME POTENTIAL FOR PEAK PERFORMANCE AND OPTIMAL HEALTH.

To me, getting older has been a positive experience athletically. It means I have another year of experience and pliability at my disposal. I discovered pliability at age twenty-seven, but I wish I could have started it even earlier. When I was in my teens, I distinctly remember having growing pains. My knees would always hurt. My elbow and shoulder were always in pain. My nutrition choices were terrible—and I was poorly hydrated. Looking back, my solution would have been the lengthening and softening of my muscles through pliability treatments to keep the tension off my growing bones and body, as well as better hydration and nutrition. As I said in the introduction, if I'd begun what we now call the TB12 Method when I started strengthening at sixteen years old, I know I could have avoided many years of unnecessary pain, as many athletes suffer.

To me, the TB12 Method is more than a new way to think about peak performance. My perspective may be that of a pro quarterback, but Alex and I have worked hard over the years to ensure that the TB12 principles are applicable to anyone who is committed to a healthy, holistic lifestyle. (At the conclusion of this book you can read some testimonials from people whose lives have been changed by coming to the TB12 Sports Therapy Center.) I'm proud of playing football and of our team, and I'm also excited to educate people and inspire a movement that can change the lives of people from many walks and stages of life. I believe we can and should rethink not just the way we train but the way we live. As I said earlier, it's a natural human bias to focus on instant gratification. Amateur and professional athletes face pressure to get back out on the field. Younger players may put off the right nutritional regimen today, believing they'll start eating better next week, next month, or next year. When I was a younger athlete, I didn't know any better myself. But a core part of the TB12 Method is developing the mind-set and discipline of thinking long-term. Put simply, your health and lifestyle choices will eventually catch up with you in ways either negative or positive. The habits and behaviors you adopt right now will determine whether you'll face a headwind or a tail-wind in the years and decades to come.

Ask yourself: What does sustained peak performance mean to *me*? Every person who comes into the TB12 Sports Therapy Center gets asked this same question. It's not surprising that most of the answers have to do with sports. A sixteen-year-old high school baseball player wants to play his best during the upcoming season. A twenty-year-old cross-country runner wants to make the college team. A thirty-year-old pro athlete wants to play for the next three years without injury. A forty-five-year-old working mother wants to feel as great during her morning run as she did when she was in her twenties, and still be able to play competitive tennis on the weekends with her high-school-aged son and daughter. A sixty-year-old businessman wants to continue playing pickup basketball every Sunday and be back behind his desk on Monday morning, pain-free and full of energy. A sixty-five-year-old physician wants to be able to ski with her grandchildren without worrying that her knees might hurt.

Sustained peak performance brings up a second question: *What does it mean to be the best at what you do?* Being the best at anything requires discipline, focus, and hard work. Whether you're a high school, college, or pro athlete, a coach, a farmer, an executive, a teacher, a doctor, a student, a parent, a graphic designer, or anything else, sustained peak performance asks you to commit to being the best you can be every day of your life. Your

life doesn't end when you leave practice or drive home at night or shut off your laptop—so why should your commitment to peak performance? We all want, or should want, to play and live to our fullest potential.

As for me, I envision every high school, college, and professional team creating pliability programs in the same way they've made a commitment to strength and conditioning. I envision parents doing pliability on their kids, coaches doing pliability on their players, and athletes around the world doing self-pliability before and after workouts. I envision TB12 Sports Therapy Centers all around the world, where everyone who's invested in their own peak performance and optimal health can come—and I also envision health insurance companies stepping forward to realize that pliability is key to *preventing* injuries before they happen. More to the point, coaches, trainers, and parents need to get started on incorporating these methods to the best of their abilities.

It's worth saying again: Pliability isn't only for elite athletes. It's for anyone who wants to live a vital life as long as possible. It doesn't just benefit our bodies, either. Life can be hard, and challenges come up out of nowhere. What would it mean to meet those challenges in a pliable way—without tension or rigidity but with readiness, openness, and receptivity? On and off the field, pliability is a metaphor for the way I try to live my life.

In many ways, I feel it's my responsibility—and even my calling—to bring attention to what I've learned for the purpose of helping others. I'm aware some people may respond cynically or skeptically. But to anyone who says, "Why should I do what *he* says?" my response is: Please don't take my word for it. Try it. See for yourself. Experience the difference the TB12 Method will make in the quality of your life. Even if you start with only a thirty-day commitment, you'll begin to feel the difference. From there, try sixty days. Then 120 days. Before you know it, the TB12 Method will become second nature.

We all have choices, and our lives are what we make of them. I believe we need to be proactive participants in our own health and well-being. *We* have to take responsibility for them. We are not victims. Hold *yourself*—not your doctor or your coach—accountable. Good health and a good life don't just happen. When you incorporate pliability into your strength and conditioning regimen, along with hydration, nutrition, supplementation, rest, and recovery, I promise you'll be on your way to living the best, healthiest, most productive, most durable life possible. I do not believe we are entirely victims of fate or destiny in our approach to peak performance. We have a choice in how our lives play out.

1. Incorporate pliability as the missing leg of your strength and conditioning regimen. Balance your inner environment to absorb and disperse the forces in your life.

2. Hydrate, hydrate, hydrate. Drink at least one-half of your body weight in ounces of water with electrolytes every day, and more if you can. Optimal pliability cannot be achieved without proper hydration.

3. Reduce or eliminate your intake of caffeine, soda, and alcohol. All three can be dehydrating. If you drink coffee, soda, or alcohol, rebalance your hydration by drinking two glasses of water with electrolytes for every one of these beverages you consume.

4. Focus on eating real food, preferably organic and mostly plant based.

5. Eat some daily percentage of your vegetables raw—that is, uncooked.

6. Shop and eat locally as much as possible. Most supermarket foods have traveled long distances and been frozen and thawed before reaching the shelves.

7. Try to limit and possibly eliminate foods that cause chronic inflammation, including fast foods, processed foods, and the five W's: white bread, white pasta, white potatoes, white milk, and excess white salt.

8. Supplement your dietary regimen by taking at minimum a multivitamin and a B complex.

9. Supplement with protein powder or a protein bar to help your body rebuild and rejuvenate, especially after workouts—and snack when hungry throughout the day.

10. Take time to recenter yourself every day, whether it's through meditation or just by doing something you love. This is an important part of rebalancing your inner environment.

11. Our brains are our control centers. Never lose track of the importance of brain fitness. Practice plasticity-based brain exercises to keep your brain in optimal condition.

12. Get the appropriate cognitive rest by sticking to a regular bedtime and getting at least eight hours of sleep every night. To ensure your body is working for you day and night, use TB12 functional apparel and sleepwear, with the latter increasing your body's oxygenation while you sleep.

I practice and live the TB12 Method in my job and in my life, and I want you to experience the same results I have in *your* job and *your* life. What if a month from today you felt better doing everything you love to do? And even better six months after that? What would it feel like to *only get better* with time, to feel better than everyone else you know, and to sustain your own peak performance for longer than you ever believed possible?

The answer is in your hands. Our goal isn't just better training, it's better living. Let's change ourselves—and the world—for the better. I wish you the best of luck on your journey as you become the very best version of yourself.

TESTIMONIALS

I STARTED TRAINING AT TB12 ALMOST TWO YEARS AGO, DOING one to two sessions per week. I have torn both ACLs (only one of which I chose to surgically repair), and I was limited in doing the activities I enjoyed the most—skiing and playing basketball. When I met with Alex and told him I thought I would never be back on the slopes again, he simply laughed. Alex assured me that I would be skiing all winter long if I followed the training regimen. The rest is history. I have been skiing almost every weekend for two years now, and I play basketball regularly.

[ALEX] IS QUITE AMAZING. I DID THREE DAYS OF INTENSE therapy with him for my neck and hand pain. I'm really happy and relieved to say that after ten years of increasing pain, and a surgery that didn't do anything . . . I feel like I have a new life without pain. All I can say is, Alex is amazing and brilliant at finding these solutions, and has made a huge difference to me.

I ENJOYED THE EXPERIENCE [AT TB12] IMMENSELY. THE treatments and short workouts were focused and professional. A week was the perfect amount of time—and now the rest is up to me until the next visit. I had minimal but hopeful expectations, and [TB12] didn't let me down—in fact, you far exceeded my goals. I now have the confidence to get back in the gym and manage my workouts without worrying about injury.

I WANT TO THANK YOU FROM THE BOTTOM OF MY HEART FOR YOUR expert, kind, encouraging attention toward my son, who suffered an ACL injury and had to miss his [college] lacrosse finals. As we walked to the car, he kept saying, "Mom, that was amazing! He knew exactly how I move and how I did it." He added, "That was life-changing." Tearing and repairing an ACL a second time was a bullet he dodged. We are so blessed to be where we are, as my son moves through his final summer at home and toward his goals. He is extremely grateful for you and for all he has. Thank you for being a powerful part of my son's life at a seminal time.

FROM MY INITIAL PHONE CALL TO THE LAST TIME I WALKED OUT the door, [TB12] was an absolutely positive experience. I had heard firsthand about great results for athletes under twenty-five—which is what I am not. After a thorough intake, [the TB12 body coach] worked on my shoulder, determining the damage. He was able to pinpoint what he could rectify with deep manipulation and pressure. He was patient and optimistic about where I could be when he was done. Within an hour and a half, he had my bum shoulder returned to a normal range of motion, without pain. Seriously, I have been pain-free since he worked on it. I left with instructions and demonstrations for upkeep exercises, foods that would help me (it is TB12, after all), and an understanding of why hydration is important. Highly recommended.

SIX MONTHS AGO, I WAS IN A TAXICAB ACCIDENT WHILE ON business in Phoenix. The two-car collision left my dominant arm broken in three places, and I suffered vertebral misalignment, dislocation of the jaw, and a severe concussion. However, despite my obvious facial abrasions, the ER doctors did not give me a CAT scan, and a traumatic brain injury went undiagnosed for some time. In fact, to compound the injury, the ER doctor suggested I fly back home to Boston to see an arm surgeon immediately—less than twenty-four hours after the accident. Needless to say, I was compliant. Whether it was shock, the unrelenting arm and neck pain, or my willingness to believe that the physician knew best, I don't know.

Landing in Boston, I was in agony. I envisioned putting my head in a vise and tightening it until my head exploded to relieve the intense pressure and pain. I saw various physicians and specialists, but no one seemed to hear me. My TBI wasn't diagnosed until ten days after my accident, at which point I was ordered to be on "pure rest" for two weeks at minimum. No work, email, text, TV, exercise. Just sit in a dark room and meditate. This extended to four weeks, and then six weeks. No narcotic or analgesic alleviated my head pain. I was unable to think clearly, read, work, or walk down a flight of stairs without holding on for dear life. Under medical "house arrest," feeling helpless and hopeless, I began to deteriorate emotionally and physically. More important, my cognition was not improving, and my pain would not relent.

Two friends suggested I see Alex Guerrero at TB12. I'm in no way a professional athlete, and thus was unsure whether he would take me as a patient. But after a twenty-minute conversation, I was set up for an evaluation at TB12 the very next morning. I don't remember much about my first visit due to the concussion haze I was in—only that my life as I knew

it had changed for the better. Not only was I relieved of the intense pressure and excruciating pain but also, for the first time in two months, I had hope. Alex understood what I was experiencing even when my brain was unable to articulate the words to describe my ailments. He calmed my fears and gave me a plan (and homework) and the motivation to succeed. Not only have Alex's recommended nutrition plan and body and "brain training" exercises helped my recovery without conventional pharmaceuticals but his proactive treatments have also improved residual issues from my TBI: balance, memory, gait, depth perception, and strength building. Alex lifted the "fog" that has surrounded me ever since the accident.

After nearly eighteen weeks working with TB12, I have almost fully recovered from my injuries. I still struggle with some cognitive issues, but I am in better overall health than I have ever been in my life. Alex's unwavering support (at all hours), concern, and insight have helped me get through a very rocky period.

ON JUNE 28, 2015, I FELL OFF A LADDER TRYING TO REFILL MY BIRD feeders. The ground was wet, and the foot of the ladder sank into the ground. I started to fall, so I tried to break the fall by turning toward my left side. Unfortunately, my foot got stuck under the handle of the ladder, and my leg twisted—and I heard a loud pop from my right knee as I fell.

My husband took me to the emergency room, and the doctor I saw put me in an immovable brace. The MRI results showed that I had a severed ACL and Grade 3 MCL and Grade 1 PCL tears, along with a small Baker's cyst. After eight months of physical therapy, I still did not have the quality of life I wanted. I had difficulty squatting, I had difficulty getting my knee to bend, and I was walking with a limp. Then a good friend referred me to TB12. My body coach's knowledge and expertise gave me back my quality of life. Within a very short time, I was walking down the stairs without difficulty.

I can't thank the [TB12] staff enough for all that they have done for me in restoring my body to its previous state of health. The facility is outstanding—and I highly recommend TB12 to all my friends.

OUR SON, AGE TWELVE, WAS EXPERIENCING HIP, LEG, AND JOINT pain, which ultimately sidelined him from playing fall sports. We came to TB12 unsure of what the future would look like for sports with our son—and were immediately put at ease by Alex.

I listened as they explained to him that things would get better. They taught him about the importance of diet and hydration and the effort it would take to heal. I watched as they began working on my son's recovery. Almost a year later, our son is not only able to compete again but even has the ability to push himself further as an athlete. Watching him be able to play the sports he loves is a gift to us and is something we do not take for granted.

I RANDOMLY FOUND TB12 AFTER A GOOGLE SEARCH AND HAD NO idea of the scope of the organization, or even what "TB" meant!

I made an appointment because my recovery from hip replacement had gone awry. I felt I was running out of options. It was difficult to walk without pain, and I was putting on weight after the surgery. [My TB12 body coach] began a program for me to correct the surrounding muscle and devised brief workouts and a quick manipulation to store the corrections in muscle memory.

I lost twenty-four pounds, and have kept it off. My vertical leap is 32", which is pretty good for a sixty-five-year-old, and I adopted the TB12 diet and resistance-band program. I would say I gained back about ten years. I now play extremely strenuous tennis with top club pros and stay in there quite well, especially on the forehand side, for hours on end.

TB12 SAVED MY SHOULDER—AND MY SANITY. AS A SENIOR partner at my company, I work long hours and travel often. Exercise is my outlet, and a torn bicep and partially torn tendons in my rotator cuff prevented me from doing my usual Pilates and HIIT. Once my orthopedist recommended surgery, I called TB12. [The TB12 body coach] has helped me regain range of motion, reduce pain, and begin to get back to the exercises that keep me mentally and physically at my best.

AS A PROFESSIONAL BASEBALL PLAYER IN JAPAN, I WENT TO TB12 three years ago in search of the best massage techniques, diet, and workouts. I have to say TB12 has been a big part of my evolution as a person and an athlete. My first visit influenced me to be at my best every day, eating clean, which resulted in my losing ten pounds and getting into the best shape of my life. The approach to training and lifestyle is a perfect fit for me, as I have tried every type of training, diet, etc. I truly believe this is the way of the future in training and recovery. The confidence and knowledge of everyone, and the results I achieved, made the visit very comfortable, fun, and easy. I can't say enough great things about the TB12 center, the people who work there, and my own experience.

YOU GUYS AT TB12 WORK MAGIC. IT'S AS SIMPLE AS THAT. MY SON had an injury that local physical therapists did nothing to correct or improve. After a single visit to TB12, my son was ready to play in his football game that weekend. You also did the same for another one of my sons the previous season: one visit, and he felt great and could play.

THE REALITY IS THAT TB12 DRAWS THE BEST THERAPISTS FROM across New England and employs the latest techniques and physical therapies in sports. The connection with Tom Brady may add to the allure of TB12, but the simple fact that you are the best is why I bring my children to you, and why I recommend you to every parent I know.

LAST YEAR MY ACTIVE SPORTS AND WORKOUT ROUTINE WAS INterrupted by a painful low back spasm and sciatica nerve pain that made simple tasks very challenging. I am a "mature" athlete and an active golfer, and to not be able to freely involve myself in these activities was depressing.

I immediately started searching my database for sports massage, chiropractic clinics, etc., but after a few months with no success I was introduced to TB12 by a friend. After the very first treatment, I actually felt relief. The facility and staff were top-notch. I am now back to my "old" self, actively pursuing my favorite activities, free of pain and enjoying myself. Thanks, TB12.

I HAVE BEEN PLAYING SOCCER SINCE I WAS EIGHT YEARS OLD. AS little kids do, I had lots of dreams of playing someday in college or beyond, but these thoughts started to get farther away from me because of the pain in my legs, which I'd experienced since I was five. As I started playing at a higher level in my middle school and high school years, I was told it was shin splints—but I knew it was something else. Over the years, I've had knee pain, hamstring pulls, quad strains, patella issues, and severe pain in my calf muscles that would remove me from the field.

Then, randomly, a high school teacher told me I should look into TB12. It was like someone was finally speaking to me directly. TB12 has helped me in more ways than just recovery. I have gained new confidence and now move my body with full mobility and strength. I don't fear injury anymore. I have learned so much about my body and mind, and have been well informed and educated about hydration, nutrition, recovery, and, of course, pliability! Today I no longer feel like the injured kid. I was blessed to receive this gift, and I do not take it for granted. I have the utmost respect for all of you, and all you do! Thank you from the bottom of my heart!

I AM A FIFTY-SEVEN-YEAR-OLD MALE WHO HAS ALWAYS TRIED TO maintain good health. I played three sports during high school and went on to play Division I football in college. After college I continued to be active by running marathons, lifting weights, taking yoga classes, snowboarding on family vacations, and working out with my three children in the various sports they played. After years of hard physical activity, I learned I had put an incredible strain on my hips and would need both replaced. In 2009, after my second surgery, I set out on a mission to get back in shape as fast as I could. I worked very hard at getting back to my previous physical condition and active lifestyle. I thought I was doing all the right things until three years ago, when I had the honor of meeting Alex Guerrero. After learning about the TB12 method and their beliefs, I knew I had to adopt that kind of lifestyle. I had always thought I was doing the right things, but after talking with Alex, I realized that by doing things a little differently, I could be even better. With TB12's guidance I changed the way I ate, slept, and trained—essentially I was training the same way Tom Brady does. The physical, mental, and spiritual changes that have resulted from going to the TB12 Sports Therapy Center have been magic for me.

FAQ

1. What is the TB12 Method?

The TB12 Method is a performance training approach and lifestyle that Alex and I developed over the past twelve years, with the goal of maximizing my potential both on and off the field. It can enable active individuals to sustain their peak performance by preventing injury and promoting faster recovery through holistic, whole-body wellness programs.

The TB12 Method incorporates exercise, nutrition, hydration, brain exercises, rest, and recovery, and—at its core—targeted, deep-force muscle work techniques to help maximize what we define as *muscle pliability*.

I believe this approach is optimal for long-term results—and I credit the TB12 Method for my sustained peak performance in professional football, and for the health and vitality I enjoy every day.

2. What is pliability?

Pliability refers to the state of muscles that stay long, soft, and primed through the acts of daily living and activity—in contrast to muscles that are tight, dense, and stiff, and less able to adapt to the stresses placed on them. When our muscles are pliable, they recover faster, are less susceptible to injury, and are better able to absorb loads and forces. The TB12 Method incorporates a range of techniques to increase and maintain pliability, including pliability exercises using assisted devices, self-pliability, partner pliability, and, in its highest form—the one I recommend—a certified TB12 body coach who applies manual deep-force pressure to muscles as they functionally contract and

relax through movement. A key principle at TB12 is integrating pliability treatments both *before* and *after* workouts or activities. Our primary long-term objective is to help athletes develop a brain–body connection that allows their muscles to remain long, soft, and primed during workouts, practices, or games. Muscle pliability optimizes oxygen-rich blood circulation while substantially decreasing microtearing and scarring, thereby reducing the risk of injury and accelerating recovery from injury if and when it happens.

3. How is pliability different from flexibility?

Pliability is all about lengthening and softening the muscles. Flexibility, which often comes as the result of stretching, may *lengthen* the muscles to some degree—but it doesn't *soften* them. Lengthening and softening the muscles removes tension from them. Stretching doesn't. Another difference between pliability and stretching is that pliability training requires some level of positive and intentional trauma to stimulate the muscle and "train the brain" to contract and relax the muscle through its longest, softest state. If you stretch, I recommend you incorporate pliability treatment *before* and *after*. For more explanation of the differences between flexibility and pliability, see page 73.

4. How can I get started with the TB12 Method?

The best way to get pliability training is through an experienced and certified TB12 body coach. There is no real substitute for in-person pliability sessions at the TB12 Sports Therapy Center, but as I explained earlier, there are other ways to incorporate lifestyle and training choices that will put you on the path to peak performance. It begins with a commitment to incorporate pliability and its amplifiers into your daily routine to whatever degree possible. Hydration comes first. Drinking half your body weight in ounces of water every day is an easy lifestyle change to make, and the positive results may surprise you! It's also important to make the right nutrition choices (complemented by smart supplementation) in order to keep your body's inflammation rates low and to maintain a healthy, positive attitude. Look for ways to recenter yourself, too—understanding that brain exercises, the proper mind-set, rest, and regular sleep go a very long way and have a cumulative effect on your long-term health.

5. What are TB12's most important nutritional recommendations?

Our nutritional recommendations are tailored specifically for each TB12 client based upon his or her unique situation and goals—but overall, our diet program emphasizes a balanced, seasonal, mostly plant-based diet of real and organic foods, and adequate intake of foods with alkalizing properties. Review chapters 7 and 8 for more detail. Above all, remember that exercise alone will never make you healthy if you're not eating well. Good nutrition will improve overall vitality in your life.

6. Why all the focus on resistance bands?

Muscles aren't for show. They serve to protect our bone structure and to carry out the jobs we ask them to do, whether playing sports or lifting heavy boxes.

Since the core of the TB12 Method is muscle pliability, we focus on functional exercises that keep muscles long, soft, and primed. Resistance bands allow for a bigger, more fluid range of motion than weights do, and help build strength and power without shortening or damaging muscles, creating inflammation, or overloading any one muscle. By targeting accelerating and decelerating muscle groups at the same time without overloading our joints, resistance bands also mirror the body's normal, everyday movements. Review chapter 6 to see our TB12 exercises incorporating resistance bands.

7. Does the TB12 Sports Therapy Center in Foxborough focus on post-injury recovery or injury prevention and performance optimization?

Both! TB12 body coaches work with injured athletes to accelerate their recovery, and also with non-injured athletes to enhance their overall performance and minimize their likelihood of experiencing non-contact injuries in the future. For clients who come to the TB12 Sports Therapy Center for post-injury recovery, we recommend continuing with a training program geared toward preventing potential injuries before they happen.

8. Can I visit, or get an appointment at, the TB12 Sports Therapy Center?

We don't offer tours of the TB12 Sports Therapy Center, since it's a fully operational performance training and therapy center. But appointments are available to the general public! We work with athletes of all ages and all levels—whether they're seeking a healthier lifestyle or recovering from injury (see our testimonials section). Each session is tailored to the individual's needs. Please note that due to high demand, there is currently a waiting list for appointments. Call 508-543-4900 or email info@TB12sports.com for more information about scheduling an appointment. In the near future, we look forward to having more certified TB12 body coaches and TB12 facilities in other parts of the country.

9. What happens during a typical session at the TB12 Sports Therapy Center?

All our sessions at the TB12 Center are one-on-one, and most last at least an hour. To begin, one of our certified TB12 body coaches will analyze a client's complete biomechanics and review his or her unique goals. We then combine pliability sessions in private rooms with functional movement on our turf area, where clients learn exercises that further promote pliability, including working with resistance bands. Each client receives a comprehensive, customized, sports- and (if applicable) position-specific program that integrates cutting-edge concepts in athletic preparation, hydration, nutrition, brain fitness, rest, and recovery.

10. Does the TB12 Sports Therapy Center offer group programs?

Our approach at the TB12 Sports Therapy Center is focused on developing comprehensive and highly tailored solutions that require individual attention from our body coaches. This is why we offer only a limited array of programming for groups or teams (e.g., the TB12 ACL Injury Prevention Program, which we offer to schools and coaches of youth sports teams). Please email info@TB12sports.com for more information about these programs.

11. Why do you suggest a vibrating foam roller or sphere? Where can I buy one (and other TB12 products)?

We recommend the use of a vibrating foam roller or vibrating sphere because they create neural stimulation. Neural stimulation is critical in forging the brain–body connection and helping train our muscles to understand that they need to stay long, soft, and primed through muscle contraction. Our belief is that no real healing can take place unless the brain is involved. In our facility, we exclusively use vibrating rollers or spheres to assist with pliability (see pages 80–100 for pliability exercises that use the vibrating foam roller and/or the vibrating sphere). Our vibrating foam roller, vibrating sphere, and other TB12 products are available exclusively through our online store at www.TB12store.com.

12. I want to be a body coach at TB12. Who should I contact?

We're always interested in speaking with qualified and motivated individuals who are interested in training as body coaches. Please note that all our body coaches are certified athletic trainers and/or licensed physical therapists. We will be expanding our body coach certification program in the near future. For more information, please email bodycoach @TB12sports.com.

ACKNOWLEDGMENTS

WRITING A BOOK IS A LONG, INVOLVED PROCESS. IT'S A lot like what I've experienced in my own professional career, in fact. It requires great teamwork, focus, determination— and everyone doing their job at the highest possible levels. First, of course, I want to thank one of my dearest friends, and my body coach, Alex, who developed the TB12 Method ideas with me not just in this book but over the last twelve years, and whose genius, friendship, and ongoing support have enabled my own sustained peak performance. We have an unbreakable bond—and it has been so much fun sharing in our success on and off the field. Thank you. None of this would have been possible without you.

Of course, I also want to thank the New England Patriots and especially Robert Kraft for believing in me and giving me the opportunity to lead and play my sport with the best ownership, coaching, staff, and fans anyone could hope for. I can never adequately express the gratitude I feel to all the friends, teammates, former teammates, and coaches and mentors past and present who've inspired me to learn and grow and to get where I am today. It's the highest privilege to have had the shared experiences and collective success we've enjoyed together, and I look forward to accomplishing even more. I also want to thank all my competitors past and present, who always push me to work harder and dig deeper—as well as all the people who've come to the TB12 Sports Therapy Center over the years, whose stories continue to inspire *me.*

I also want to thank all my friends for the support they have given me from high school to college to today. My friends have been instrumental in supporting me and teaching me what love and friendship mean over the course of my life. Thank you for always pushing me to be my best, from elementary school to my eighteenth professional year. There are too many of you to mention, but you know who you are, and I love you all.

Thank you to all the people at TB12—our board, our staff, our body coaches, and all the clients we've been privileged to serve over the years. My friend and TB12 board member Tony Tjan was key in bringing this book from concept to reality, including coordinating the process and content development. It was Tony who introduced me to my writing collaborator, Peter Smith, who was instrumental in shaping, organizing, and bringing clarity to my ideas. Peter has a unique gift with words while always staying true to voice, story, and meaning. I also want to thank Hilario Bango for his creative direction, Shubhani Sarkar for her incredible design work, Kevin O'Brien for many of the photographs throughout the book, and literary agent James Levine. From the outset of this book project, I knew I had the right publishing partner in Simon & Schuster. Thank you to my dear friend Les Moonves, and to the president of Simon & Schuster, Jon Karp, and to my editor, Jofie Ferrari-Adler, for all your support, commitment, and hard work on behalf of this book.

Finally, I dedicate this book to my incredible family. Thank you to my mom, dad, sisters, and extended family for all the love and support you've always given me. I've always wanted to represent our family in a positive way. You have all been my role models, and I couldn't accomplish anything without you. I also want to thank my wife, Gisele. Your love and support for me and all that you do for our family makes it possible for me to live my dream, and I am beyond blessed to have you as my partner. I love you more than you will ever know. You are the light of my life. And to my three children, Jack, Benny, and Vivian—Daddy loves you.

INDEX

A

ACL injuries, 18, 23, 25–26, 56, 287–88, 295
adductors
  diagram, 78, 79
  See also inner thigh/groin
Aguirre, David, 3
alcohol, 40, 69, 206–7, 212, 224–25, 238, 276, 286
alkaline
  acid-alkaline balance, 206, 217
  alkaline *vs.* acidic foods, 217, 225–26
  carbohydrates and, 228
  electrolytes and, 206
  lactic acid and, 61
  mineral water and, 209
anti-inflammatory responses, promoting
  explained, 38
  importance of, 33
apparel, functional, 26, 41, 279–81, 286
average career lengths, NFL, 34

B

back
  low back, 89
  paraspinal muscles, 90
  in between shoulder blades, 92–93
back of the thigh, partner pliability and, 114
balance and moderation
  explained, 37
  importance of, 33
Belichick, Bill, 14, 16, 29, 272
bioceramics, 26, 41, 279–80
Bledsoe, Drew, 16
blood flow
  See oxygen-rich blood flow, promoting
blood pressure, 37, 220, 223
BMI, 37
body fat, 37, 51–52
bottom of foot
  diagram, 79
  explained, 70
  inflammation of, 68
  partner pliability, 111
  self-assisted pliability, 83
  self-pliability, 81
brain
  brain exercises
    divided attention, 276
    double decision, 276
    explained, 41
    freeze frame, 276
    importance of, 35
    mixed signals, 275
    proper hydration and, 41
    target tracker, 275
  brain rest, recentering, recovery
    explained, 41
    importance of, 33
  training, rest, and recovery
    brain exercises, 274–76
    centering yourself, 272–73
    keeping positive, 271–72
    overview, 270
    proper mind-set, 270–71
    sleep and, 276–80
    TB12 action steps, 281
    TB12 brain training and fitness program, 273–76
BrainHQ, 274–75
Buffalo Bills, 27

C

caffeine, 40, 207, 212, 225, 240, 276, 286
calf
  diagram, 79
  partner pliability, 112
  self-pliability, 82, 102–3
  See also gastrocnemius and soleus
carbohydrates
  complex, 220
  digestion of, 228
  protein powder and, 230
  refined, 223
carbonated water, 209
  See also proper hydration
cardio
  conditioning and, 15, 120
  resistance bands and, 125, 241
Carr, Jason, 8–9
Carr, Lloyd, 9–13
carrots, 226
cartilage, 207
Cartwright, Kit, 7, 9
centering yourself, 272–73, 281, 294
chest muscles, 91
cholesterol, 37
Clark, Dwight, 2
cleanliness, sleep and, 278
collagen, 57, 66–67
conditioning for endurance & vitality
  explained, 37
  importance of, 33

core stability exercises
    core angel, 158–59
    four-way overhead resisted foot
        fire, 174–75
    high to low/low to high rotation,
        172–73
    lateral resisted bird dog, 168–69
    overhead arm flutters, 162–63
    overhead core shuffle, 160–61
    overview, 153
    Pallof core shuffle, 156–57
    Pallof squat, 154–55
    plank with a row, 164–65
    resisted walking plank, 176–77
    single leg balance with halo,
        170–71
    x plank, 166–67
cytokines, 66

D

dairy, 223
Dallas Cowboys, 2
dehydration
    See proper hydration
digestion, 40, 207, 212–13, 223,
        225, 227–28, 230
Dreisbach, Scott, 8–11
durability, 26–28, 51, 62, 66, 122

E

ElAttrache, Neal, 23
electrolytes
    hydration and, 33, 206–8, 212,
        235, 241, 286
    importance of, 211
    supplementation and, 41, 228
    TB12 Electrolytes, 206, 209–10
    trace minerals and, 229
    See also proper hydration
Ellis, Shaun, 16

Elway, John, 11
exercises
    core stability
        core angel, 158–59
        four-way overhead resisted foot
            fire, 174–75
        high to low/low to high rotation,
            172–73
        lateral resisted bird dog,
            168–69
        overhead arm flutters, 162–63
        overhead core shuffle, 160–61
        overview, 153
        Pallof core shuffle, 156–57
        Pallof squat, 154–55
        plank with a row, 164–65
        resisted walking plank, 176–77
        single leg balance with halo,
            170–71
        x plank, 166–67
    lower-body
        band dead lift, 202–3
        forward lunge with high hold,
            186–87
        four-way band running in place,
            188–89
        glute medius side plank,
            184–85
        Heiden hop, 192–93
        hip thrusters, 200–201
        lateral resisted squat, 182–83
        overview, 179
        resisted shuffle, 190–91
        single-leg clock jumps, 194–95
        squat, 180–81
        squat jump, 196–97
        squat to press, 198–99
    upper-body
        alternating arm punches,
            132–33
        alternating rows, 134–35
        band core rotation, 142–43
        band front raise, 146–47
        band pull-aparts, 148–49
        band-resisted push-up, 144–45

        cross-body pull, 140–41
        cross-body step and press,
            138–39
        front-facing core angel, 150–51
        overview, 127
        single-arm chest press,
            128–29
        single-arm row, 130–31
        standing lateral extension,
            136–37

F

far infrared rays (FIRs), 279
fast food, 40, 223, 240, 267, 286
    See also processed foods
fats
    carbohydrates and, 223
    eating seasonally and, 220
    processed foods and, 224, 240
    saturated, 223
    supplements and, 234
fatty acids, 40, 220, 223, 230, 232,
        234
fiber, 40, 218, 220, 225, 234
flexibility and stretching
    pliability *vs.*, 73
forearms
    inside (flexors), 99, 106–7
    outer (extensors), 100, 108–9
    with assisted devices, 99–100
    unassisted, 106–9
form, importance of, 123, 125
fruits, 218–20, 222, 224, 227–29,
        236, 238
functional apparel and sleepwear,
        279–80

G

gastrocnemius and soleus
    diagram, 79
    See also calf
Gittleson, Mike, 6
gluten, 235, 237–38, 240
glutes and piriformis
    diagram, 79
    exercises
        alternating rows, 134–35
        band front raise, 146–47
        chest press and, 128–29
        cross-body step and press,
            138–39
        four-way band running in place,
            188–89
        glute medius side plank,
            184–85
        lateral resisted bird dog,
            168–69
        overhead core shuffle, 160–61
        pallof core shuffle, 156–57
        resisted shuffle, 190–91
        single-arm row, 130–31
        single-leg clock jumps, 194–95
        squats, 180–81
        standing lateral extension and,
            136–37
        x plank, 166–67
    self-pliability, 88, 101
Griese, Brian, 8–11
Guerrero, Alex
    author's introduction to, 18, 61
    background, 18
    on brain training, 65
    development of pliability ap-
        proach, 22–26, 55
    on electrolytes, 211
    initial treatments by, 18–19
    injury treatment, 70, 72
    pliability treatments, 61, 63, 70,
        101, 279
    TB12 Method and, 26, 284
    on training speed, 122

H

hamstrings
    diagram, 79
    injury to, 51
    partner pliability, 114
    self-pliability, 86, 101
Harden, Greg, 9
Harris, Bill, 7
heart rate
    conditioning and, 15, 48, 240
    resistance bands and, 125, 241
    weight training and, 120
Henson, Drew, 11–13
holistic and integrative training
    explained, 37, 39
    importance of, 35
Howard, Desmond, 9–10
hydration
    explained, 42
    importance of, 35
    See also proper hydration

I

inner thigh/groin, 78, 79, 85
IT band and TFL, 87, 101

J

Johnson, DiAllo, 8
Junipero Serra High School, 4, 6, 271

K

Kansas City Chiefs, 23
Kapsner, Jason, 10–11
keeping positive, 271–72
Krystofiak, Kevin, 6–7

L

leptin, 218
Lewis, Mo, 16
Little League baseball, 3
load, 33, 38, 45–46, 65, 121
    See also no-load strength training
local foods, 219
lower body
    adductors, 85
    bottom of foot, 81
    calf, 82
    exercises
        band dead lift, 202–3
        forward lunge with high hold,
            186–87
        four-way band running in place,
            188–89
        glute medius side plank,
            184–85
        Heiden hop, 192–93
        hip thrusters, 200–201
        lateral resisted squat, 182–83
        overview, 179
        resisted shuffle, 190–91
        single-leg clock jumps, 194–95
        squat, 180–81
        squat jump, 196–97
        squat to press, 198–99
    front of leg, 83
    front thigh muscles, 84
    hamstrings, 86
    IT band and TFL, 87
    See also calf; hamstrings;
        quadriceps
lymphatic system, 57

M

mattress and bedding, 278
    See also sleep
McGinest, Willie, 18
MCL injuries, 23, 25, 288
McNabb, Donovan, 12

mineral water, 209
    See also proper hydration
moderation
    alcohol and, 225
    explained, 37
    importance of, 33
Moeller, Gary, 7
Montana, Joe, 2–3
Montreal Expos, 7
muscle groups, 78–79
muscle pliability
    See pliability
muscle pump function, 25, 33, 40,
        48, 55–57, 61, 72, 110

N

neurons
    muscles and, 84–85, 122
    neural pathways, 55, 57, 62–65
    neural priming, 34, 55, 127, 273
    neurostimulation, 77
    pliability and, 84–85, 295
    neuroplasticity, 33, 41, 276
    See also brain
New York Giants, 23
New York Yankees, 11–12
nightshades, 224–25
no-load strength training
    explained, 38
    importance of, 33
    noise, sleep and, 278
nutrition
    alkaline *vs.* acidic foods, 225–26
    combining foods, 228
    eating local foods, 219
    eating seasonally, 220
    effects of poor nutrition, 69,
        206–7
    essential fatty acids, 220
    explained, 40
    fitness and nutrition myths,
        240–41
    food industry, 224

general guidelines, 218–25
    don'ts, 223–25
    dos, 218–23
    high fiber, 220
    importance of, 33
    inflammation and, 69
    organic foods, 218
    overview, 216–17
    portion sizes, 227
    reading labels, 232–33
    recipes, 243–67
        avocado ice cream, 267
        Brady Bowl, 261
        chicken burgers with radishes,
            253
        fresh veggie lasagna, 249
        green juice, 262
        green risotto with lemon cream,
            250
        pasta with creamy sauce, 258
        potato and broccoli frittata,
            246
        roast chicken with pumpkin and
            brussels sprouts, 254
        salmon burger with avocado
            and salad, 257
        seasonal salad with savory vin-
            aigrette, 245
        smoothies, 264–65
    snacking, 227
    vegetables, 218

O

organic foods, 218
oxygen-rich blood flow, promoting
    explained, 42
    importance of, 35

P

Pallof core shuffle, 156–57
Pallof squat, 154–55
paraspinal muscles, 90
partner pliability
    back of shoulder, 116
    back of thigh, 114
    basics, 110
    bottom of foot, 111
    calf, 112
    forearms, 115
    front of leg, 113
    See also pliability; self-pliability
plantar fascia
    diagram, 79
    See also bottom of foot
plantar fasciitis, 70
pliability
    age and, 17–18, 67–68
    anti-inflammatory responses and,
        33, 38
    balance and, 37
    basics, 66
    body imbalances and, 58, 61
    collagen and, 66
    common sports injuries and, 70
    conditioning and, 17–18, 22–23,
        25–26
    diagram, 47
    explained, 36–37, 44, 55–57
    flexibility and stretching *vs.*, 73
    holistic training and, 35
    how a brain learns, 57
    importance of, 33
    inflammation and, 69
    injury and, 15–16
    lactic acid, 61
    lymphatic system, 57
    muscle groups and, 78–79
    muscle memory, 62
    negative *vs.* positive trauma,
        63–64
    no-load strength training and, 38
    nutrition and, 40

overview, 45–53
oxygen-rich blood flow and, 40
partner pliability, 110–16
performance training and, 34–35
pressure and, 55, 106–7, 109,
    115, 287, 293
proper hydration and, 26, 33, 40,
    72
Q&A, 72
rehabilitation and, 44
self-pliability
    with assisted devices, 80–100
    unassisted, 101–9
TB12 Method and, 26–27, 35,
    37–38, 40
training the brain, 64–65
See also partner pliability;
    self-pliability
portion sizes, 227
posterior, 88
See also glutes and piriformis
pressure
    exercise and, 180
    on IT band and TFL, 87
    negative *vs.* positive trauma and,
        63
    pliability and, 55, 106–7, 109,
        115, 287, 293
probiotics, 41, 228, 230
processed foods, 40, 217–18, 236,
    238, 240, 267, 286
See also fast food
productivity, 26–27, 34, 276
proper hydration
    alcohol consumption and, 225
    anti-inflammatory responses and,
        33, 38, 241
    brain exercises and, 41
    carbonated water, 209
    developing a water routine, 212
    distilled or filtered water, 208
    electrolytes and, 211
    explained, 40
    importance of, 33, 213
    mineral water, 209
    overhydrating, 211

overview, 206–7
pliability and, 26, 33, 40, 72
purified water, 209
signs of dehydration, 209
spring water, 208
tap water, 208
TB12 Method and, 270, 280, 286,
    293–95
water basics, 207–9
protein
    acidic foods and, 226
    collagen, 66
    combining foods, 228
    cytokines, 66
    dairy and, 223
    diet and, 218, 220, 223, 226
    inflammation and, 69
    leptin, 218
    protein powder, 230–31, 286
    supplements and, 41, 218
purified water, 209
See also proper hydration

Q

quadratus lumborum, 79, 89
quadriceps
    body imbalances and, 58
    core stability and, 153
    diagram, 78–79
    pliability and, 55–56, 101
    quadriceps femoris, 84
    See also front thigh muscles

R

recipes, 243–67
    avocado ice cream, 267
    Brady Bowl, 261
    chicken burgers with radishes,
        253
    fresh veggie lasagna, 249
    green juice, 262

green risotto with lemon cream,
    250
pasta with creamy sauce, 258
potato and broccoli frittata, 246
roast chicken with pumpkin and
    brussels sprouts, 254
salmon burger with avocado and
    salad, 257
seasonal salad with savory vinai-
    grette, 245
smoothies, 264–265
recovery
    ACL recovery, 23, 25–26
    alkalinity and, 225–26
    anti-inflammatory responses and,
        33, 38
    blood flow and, 40
    body imbalances and, 61
    brain rest and, 33, 41, 57
    electrolytes and, 211
    inflammation and, 69
    nutrition and, 33, 216
    pliability and, 66, 77, 293
    post-injury, 13, 27, 52, 294
    rest and, 227, 276–80
    supplementation and, 41
    TB12 Method and, 23, 37–38,
        286, 294–95
Rehbein, Dick, 13
resistance bands
    core work, 36, 60
    exercises
        alternating arm punches,
            132–33
        alternating rows, 134–35
        band core rotation, 142–43
        band dead lift, 202–3
        band front raise, 146–47
        band pull-aparts, 148–49
        band-resisted push-up, 144–45
        core angel, 158–59
        core stability, 154–77
        cross-body pull, 140–41
        cross-body step and press,
            138–39

resistance bands: exercises (*cont.*)
   forward lunge with high hold, 186–87
   four-way band running in place, 188–89
   four-way overhead resisted foot fire, 174–75
   front-facing core angel, 150–51
   high to low/low to high rotation, 172–73
   hip thrusters, 200–201
   lateral resisted bird dog, 168–69
   lateral resisted squat, 182–83
   lower-body, 180–203
   overhead arm flutters, 162–63
   overhead core shuffle, 160–61
   Pallof core shuffle, 156–57
   Pallof squat, 154–55
   plank with a row, 164–65
   resisted shuffle, 190–91
   resisted walking plank, 176–77
   single leg balance with halo, 170–71
   single-arm chest press, 128–29
   single-arm row, 130–31
   squat to press, 198–99
   standing lateral extension, 136–37
   upper-body, 128–51
heart rate and, 125, 241
importance of using, 294
looped, 124
neural priming and, 65
no-load strength training, 38
pliability and, 56, 120
primer, 124
range of resistance, 124
sheathed, 124–25
shorter-looped, 124
training speed and, 122
weights *vs.*, 121, 241
rhomboids and levator scapulae
   diagram, 79
   See also shoulders

rotational athletes, 38
rotator cuff
   diagram, 79
   partner pliability, 116
   self-pliability, 96
   See also shoulders, back of shoulder

S

salt, 223–24
San Francisco 49ers, 2
seasonal foods, 220
self-pliability
   with assisted devices, 80–100
      back of shoulder, 96
      back of thigh, 86
      back shoulder muscles, 97
      between shoulder and neck, 98
      between shoulder blades, 92–93
      bottom of foot, 81
      calf, 82
      chest muscle, 91
      front of leg, 83
      front thigh muscles, 84
      inner thigh/groin, 84
      inside of forearm, 99
      IT band and TFL, 87
      low back, 89
      mid to upper back, 90
      outer forearm, 99
      posterior, 88
      shoulder muscle, 94–95
      vibrating foam rollers and spheres, 77, 80
   lower body, 81–87
   torso, 88–90
   unassisted
      calf, 102–3
      inside of forearm, 106–7
      outer forearm, 108–9
      overview, 101
      triceps, 104–5

upper body, 91–100
   See also partner pliability; pliability
shoulders
   back of shoulder (rotator cuff), 96
   back shoulder muscles, 97
   between shoulders and neck, 98
   between shoulder blades, 92–93
   front/middle/back muscles, 94–95
sleep
   cleanliness and, 278
   diet and, 276
   functional apparel and sleepwear, 279–80
   mattress and bedding, 278
   noise and, 278
   overview, 276
   sleep environment, 278
   temperature and, 278
   timing exercise right, 278
snacking, 227
sports drinks, 211, 241
St. Louis Rams, 17
strains, 46, 53, 70
sugar, 40, 207, 211, 218, 223–25, 227, 230, 234, 237–38, 240–41, 276
Super Bowl, 2, 6, 17–18, 23, 271–72
supplementation
   choosing, 232–33
   essential fatty acids, 230
   explained, 41
   how to take, 234
   importance of, 33, 270
   multivitamins, 229
   nutrition and, 228–30, 241, 267, 286, 294
   protein powder and twenty-minute rule, 231
   reading labels for, 232–33
   recovery and, 41

T

tap water, 208, 278
   See also proper hydration
TB12 grocery list, 236–38
   See also nutrition
TB12 Method, principles of
   balance and moderation, 37
   brain exercises, 41
   brain rest, recentering, and recovery, 41
   conditioning for endurance and vitality, 37
   healthy nutrition, 40
   holistic and integrative training, 35
   list, 33
   no-load strength training, 38
   overview, 32
   pliability, 34–35
   promote oxygen-rich blood flow, 40
   promoting anti-inflammatory responses in the body, 38
   proper hydration, 40
   supplementation, 41
temperature, sleep and, 278
tennis, 68, 70, 76, 291
tennis elbow, 70, 99
tibialis anterior, 83, 113
   diagram, 78
timing between eating and rest, 227
timing exercise right, 278
torso
   front thigh muscles, 84
   IT band and TFL, 87
   low back, 89
   mid to upper back, 90
   posterior, 88
training speed, 122
trapezius, 98
triceps
   exercises, 134
   self-pliability, 49, 71, 104–5

U

University of Michigan, 5–15, 206
upper body
   back of shoulder (rotator cuff), 96
   back shoulder muscles, 97
   chest muscle, 91
   inside of forearm, 99
   outer forearm, 100
   rhomboids and levator scapulae, 92–93
   shoulder muscle, 94–95
   upper trapezius, 98

V

variety in diet, 220, 223
vegetables, 218
   alkaline and, 225–26
   antioxidants and, 229
   combining foods, 228
   eating raw, 286
   fiber and, 220
   food industry and, 224
   importance of eating, 218, 235
   local foods and, 219
   nightshades, 224–25
   portion sizes, 227
   recipes
      fresh veggie lasagna, 249
      potato and broccoli frittata, 246
      seasonal salad with savory vinaigrette, 245
   seasonal, 220
   shopping for, 236–37
   steaming, 208
vibrating foam rollers
   neural stimulation, 295
   self-pliability and
      adductors, 85
      back shoulder muscles, 97
      bottom of foot, 81

      calf, 82
      chest muscle, 91
      front of leg, 83
      front thigh muscles, 84
      hamstrings, 86
      inside of forearm, 99
      IT band and TFL, 87
      low back, 89
      mid to upper back, 90
      outer forearm, 100
      posterior, 88
      rhomboids and levator scapulae, 92–93
      rotator cuff, 96
      shoulder muscle, 94
vibrating sphere
   choosing, 80
   self-pliability and
      between shoulders and neck, 98
      IT band and TFL, 87
      neural stimulation, 295
      posterior, 88
      shoulders, 94–95
Vinatieri, Adam, 17
vitamins
   essential fatty acids and, 220
   identifying on food labels, 232
   inflammation and, 69
   multivitamins, 229
   produce and, 219, 225
   supplements and, 41, 228–30
   trace minerals and, 229
   vitamin B complex, 229
   vitamin D, 69, 228–29

W

water
   See proper hydration
Wersching, Ray, 2
Woicik, Mike, 6, 14
Wooden, John, 6, 271

TOM BRADY is the quarterback and offensive captain of the New England Patriots, a team he has played for since 2000. During his time with the team, he has won five Super Bowls, and was named MVP in four of them (Super Bowls XXXVI, XXXVIII, XLIX, and LI). Additionally, he has won two league MVP awards (2007 and 2010), has been selected to twelve Pro Bowls, and has led the New England Patriots to more division titles (fourteen) than any other quarterback in NFL history. As of the end of the 2016 season, Brady is fourth all-time in career passing yards, fourth in career touchdown passes, and third in career passer rating. With a career postseason record of 25-9, he has won more playoff games than any other quarterback and has appeared in more playoff games than any player at any position. *The TB12 Method* is his first book.